"This engaging collection reveals the vital links between the humanities and the SDG framework. An integrative humanities perspective calls attention to the work of global artists, writers, and texts underrepresented in studies of environment, climate, and sustainability. Foregrounding the 2030 Agenda, the book centers on the themes of Planet, People, and Prosperity. Through an exploration of science fiction, photography, documentary film, and other genres, this highly accessible collection brings the global humanities into generative dialogue with education for sustainable development."

John C. Ryan, *Adjunct Associate Professor at Southern Cross University, Australia, and Adjunct Senior Research Fellow at the Nulungu Institute, Notre Dame University, Australia*

T0292828

A Global Humanities Approach to the United Nations' Sustainable Development Goals

This edited textbook explores the 17 UN SDGs through 12 works from the humanities, including films, novels, and photographic collections. It provides students with the knowledge and understanding of how the humanities engage in broader social, political, economic, and environmental dialogue, offering a global perspective that crosses national and continental borders.

The book takes students through the UN SDGs from a theoretical perspective through to practical applications, first through specific global humanities examples and then through students' own final projects and reflections. Centered around three major themes of planet, people, and prosperity, the textbook encourages students to explore and apply the Goals using a place-based, culturally rooted approach while simultaneously acknowledging and understanding their global importance. The text's examples range from documentary and feature film to photography and literature, including Wang Jiuliang's *Plastic China*, Kip Andersen and Keegan Kuhn's *Cowspiracy: The Sustainability Secret*, Barbara Dombrowski's *Tropic Ice: Dialog Between Places Affected by Climate Change*, and Aravind Adiga's *The White Tiger*, among others. Providing diverse geographic and cultural perspectives, the works take readers to Argentina, Australia, China, Costa Rica, Ecuador, France, Greenland, Haiti, India, Japan, Peru, Rwanda, Senegal, and the United States.

This broad textbook can be used by students and instructors at undergraduate and postgraduate levels from any subject background, particularly, but not exclusively, those in the humanities. With added discussion questions, research assignments, writing prompts, and creative project ideas, students will gain a nuanced understanding of the interconnectivity between social, cultural, ethical, political, economic, and environmental factors.

Kelly Comfort is Professor in the School of Modern Languages at the Georgia Institute of Technology, USA.

A Global Humanities Approach to the United Nations' Sustainable Development Goals

Understanding Planet, People, and Prosperity

Edited by
Kelly Comfort

Routledge
Taylor & Francis Group
LONDON AND NEW YORK

earthscan
from Routledge

Designed cover image: © Getty Images

First published 2024
by Routledge
4 Park Square, Milton Park, Abingdon, Oxon OX14 4RN

and by Routledge
605 Third Avenue, New York, NY 10158

Routledge is an imprint of the Taylor & Francis Group, an informa business

Funded by Georgia Institute of Technology.

British Library Cataloguing-in-Publication Data
A catalogue record for this book is available from the British Library

Library of Congress Cataloging-in-Publication Data
Names: Comfort, Kelly.
Title: A global humanities approach to the United Nations' sustainable development goals : understanding planet, people, and prosperity / edited by Kelly Comfort.
Description: Abingdon, Oxon ; New York, NY : Routledge, 2024. | Includes bibliographical references and index.
Identifiers: LCCN 2023025792 (print) | LCCN 2023025793 (ebook) | ISBN 9781032484020 (hardback) | ISBN 9781032484013 (paperback) | ISBN 9781003388869 (ebook)
Subjects: LCSH: Corporate governance—Social aspects. | Corporate governance—Environmental aspects. | Social responsibility of business. | Sustainability.
Classification: LCC HD2741 .G57 2024 (print) | LCC HD2741 (ebook) | DDC 658.4—dc23/eng/20230721
LC record available at https://lccn.loc.gov/2023025792
LC ebook record available at https://lccn.loc.gov/2023025793

ISBN: 978-1-032-48402-0 (hbk)
ISBN: 978-1-032-48401-3 (pbk)
ISBN: 978-1-003-38886-9 (ebk)

DOI: 10.4324/9781003388869

Typeset in Times New Roman
by codeMantra

Contents

Figures

Contributors

Stéphanie Boulard is Professor of French in the School of Modern Languages at Georgia Tech. Her research interests are in 19th to 21st-century French literature, with a focus on the novel and visual arts, including the relationship between word and image, and the aesthetic and political dimensions of literary and artistic thinking. Dr Boulard has authored and co-authored several books, including *Rouge Hugo* (Septentrion, 2014) and *Hugographies: Rêveries de Victor Hugo sur les lettres de l'alphabet* (Hermann, 2022), and has edited and co-edited several volumes such as *Ententes-A partir d'Hélène Cixous* (PSN, 2019). She has published in over 30 peer-reviewed publications in the United States, France, Canada, the UK, and Spain about creation and art, migration and exile, women in society, trauma, and revolutions. She is the winner of the 2021 French Voices Award for her translation with Tim Lavenz of *The Answer to Lord Chandos* by Pascal Quignard. In addition, she has won 24 institute-wide teaching awards and received the IAC 2023 Faculty Excellence in Research Award.

Miguel Rosas Buendía is Assistant Professor of Spanish and Latin American Studies at Georgia Tech. He specializes in intellectual and cultural Latin American history. His research interests include history of science, environmental studies, nationalism, and extractive industries, as well as the transatlantic exchange of ideas about Pre-Columbian material culture. His book manuscript, in progress, examines the circulation of new scientific and engineering paradigms and their role in the question of nation-building in nineteenth-century Peru through the intellectual trajectory, governmental work, and academic writings of the Peruvian scientist and archaeologist Mariano de Rivero (1798–1857). Trained in literary studies and cultural history, he has also published on poetry and travel writing and examined the intersections between natural sciences, mining, and aesthetics in a global context.

Seung-Eun Chang earned a PhD in Linguistics from the University of Texas at Austin, specializing in Phonetics and Phonology. Her work has been published in influential journals, including the *Journal of Acoustical Society of America*, the *International Journal of Bilingualism*, and *Language and Speech*. She has developed new courses that integrate media, culture, sustainability, and service learning into language teaching and published journal articles and a book chapter examining these topics. She is also the author of *Media, Culture, and Debate in Korean* (Routledge, 2022) and was honored with three grants for her media curation project. She received the Student Recognition of Excellence in Teaching: Class of 1934 CIOS Award and Honor Roll multiple times, as well as the Faces of Inclusive Excellence Award from the Institute of Diversity, Equity, and Inclusion.

Kelly Comfort is Professor in the School of Modern Languages at the Georgia Institute of Technology. A specialist in transatlantic modernisms, she is the author of *European Aestheticism and Spanish American Modernismo* (Palgrave, 2011) and editor of the volume *Art and Life in Aestheticism* (Palgrave, 2008). Her textbook and anthology, *Cien años de identidad: Introducción a la literatura latinoamerican del siglo XX* (Georgetown University Press) received the 2019 Most Promising New Textbook Award from the Textbook & Academic Authors Association. Her impactful contributions to the fields of urban studies and *flânerie* studies include two co-edited volumes—*Twenty-First Century Flânerie: From Social Distance to Social Justice* (*South Atlantic Review*, 2022) and *New Directions in Flânerie: Global Perspectives for the Twenty-First Century* (Routledge, 2021) as well as numerous articles and book chapters. Comfort has received 15 teaching awards, including the USG Board of Regents Teaching Excellence Award. She serves as Director of Undergraduate Studies and a member of the Undergraduate Sustainability Education Committee and the Global Student Experience and Partnerships Committee at Georgia Tech.

Smita Daftardar received her MS in Chemical Engineering from The Indian Institute of Technology, Mumbai and MA in Hindi-Urdu Pedagogy from Kean University, NJ. She has worked extensively in developing curriculum aligned with the World-Readiness Standards for Learning Languages, for heritage and foreign language learners. She has developed and taught new online and in-person Hindi courses at Georgia Tech that adopt the communicative approach to teaching Heritage/Foreign languages and strive to teach intercultural competence by integrating culture, history, and sustainable development goals into the curriculum. She has incorporated technology as a tool for language teaching and learning and developed online content for heritage and foreign language learners of Hindi, a less commonly taught language that uses a non-Roman script. Her research interests are Heritage Language Acquisition and Heritage Language Pedagogy with a special focus on heritage language learners of Hindi and other Indian languages.

Vicki Galloway is Professor Emerita of Spanish at Georgia Tech. She has authored eight textbooks, including *Saldo a favor, Spanish for International Business*; has published extensively in nationally prominent journals and professional volumes on second-language acquisition and intercultural learning; and has been Editor of three volumes of intercultural pedagogy and of the journal *Foreign Language Annals*. She is a recipient of the American Council on the Teaching of Foreign Language's Nelson Brooks Award for the Teaching of Culture in recognition of her writings in the field of intercultural pedagogy, Georgia Tech's E. Rowe Stamps Award for Excellence in Teaching, and the Ivan Allen College Faculty Legacy Award for leadership. Before coming to Georgia Tech, she served as Project Director for the American Council on the Teaching of Foreign Languages (NY) and as South Carolina's State Supervisor for Foreign Language and International Education. Dr Galloway also has extensive experience in study abroad program design and has taught a wide variety of courses in language, literature, business, film, and culture studies, focusing on themes of sustainable development, immigration, indigenous issues and perspectives, and intercultural communication.

Mirla González received her PhD from the University of Kansas in Spanish Literature. She specializes in 19th- to 21st-century Peninsular literature and film, particularly the intersection between science, technology, ethics, and literature. Interested in the portrayal of sex and gender in science fiction, her work is part of the edited volume *A Laboratory of Her Own: Women and Science in Spanish Culture*. An advocate of Open Educational Resources, she is the Development Editor of OER *Acceso*, an open-access digital platform that supports the development of transcultural competence among language learners. She oversaw the new edition of the curriculum as part of a four-year federally funded project through the Open Language Resource Center at KU during the 2018–2022 cycle. Dr González also serves as the Assistant Director of Undergraduate Studies, Online and Professional Education at Georgia Tech.

Jennifer Hirsch is the inaugural Director of the Center for Serve-Learn-Sustain at the Georgia Institute of Technology, which facilitates collaborations among students, faculty, and community partners to address the world's most pressing sustainability challenges in their own backyard, the Southeastern United States. Hirsch is also Adjunct Associate Professor in the School of City and Regional Planning at Georgia Tech. An applied cultural anthropologist, Hirsch is known internationally for facilitating broad-based collaborations bringing together grassroots organizations and large institutions to advance sustainability and climate action. Hirsch is co-founder and lead coordinator of the regional sustainability education network RCE Greater Atlanta, officially acknowledged by the United Nations University in 2017; served on the Board of Directors of the Association for the Advancement of Sustainability in Higher Education (AASHE) from 2018 to 2023 (and as President in 2023); and serves as an affiliate of The Asset-Based Community Development Institute hosted by DePaul University. She received her PhD in Cultural Anthropology from Duke University and her BA in American Culture from Northwestern University.

Britta Kallin serves as Associate Professor of German Studies and Associate Chair in the School of Modern Languages at the Georgia Institute of Technology in Atlanta, GA. She has published articles on German and Austrian authors Franz Kafka, Christa Wolf, Günter Grass, Elfriede Jelinek, Marlene Streeruwitz, Cornelia Funke, and others. Her monograph *The Presentation of Racism in Contemporary German and Austrian Plays* (2007) examines gender roles, racism, and nationalism in plays by German and Austrian female authors after 1990. Dr. Kallin has worked closely with the Center for Serve-Learn-Sustain at Georgia Tech and directed the German Language for Business and Technology (LBAT) summer study abroad program for many years. She has taught a wide variety of courses on literature, film, language, and culture studies, addressing themes of sustainable development, climate change, immigration, and intercultural communication.

Natalie Khazaal is Associate Professor in the School of Modern Languages at Georgia Tech. She studies links between disenfranchisement, media, and language, and is recipient of multiple research and teaching awards. Her work on speciesism in the media has received international recognition. Her co-edited volume on borders and the displacement of human refugees and nonhuman animals, *Like an Animal: Critical Animal Studies Perspectives on Borders, Displacement, and Othering* (Brill, 2021) and edited journal issue *Media, Racism, Speciesism* (FiC, 2024) are of interest to scholars, journalists, and a range of (non-)governmental organizations. An American Council of Learned Societies (ACLS) fellow for her work on Arab atheists, she has contributed to the topic with publications on the use of pseudonyms by Arab atheists and the embedded atheism in Mohamed Choukri's literary oeuvre. Her book, *Pretty Liar: Television, Language, and Gender in Wartime Lebanon* (Syracuse University Press, 2018), explores the role of audiences in the development of media legitimacy during violent crises, with a focus on Lebanon. She's also a contributor to *Global Media and Strategic Narratives of Contested Democracy* (Routledge, 2019).

Jin Liu is Associate Professor of Chinese Media, Culture, and Linguistics at Georgia Tech. She is the author of *Signifying the Local: Media Productions Rendered in Local Languages in Mainland China in the New Millennium* (2013), and the co-editor of the book *Chinese Under Globalization: Emerging Trends in Language Use in China* (2012). She has widely published articles on Chinese independent films, eco-cinema, rap music, Internet culture, youth culture, sociolinguistics, pedagogy, and digital humanities in top peer-reviewed journals including *Digital Scholarship in the Humanities, positions: Asia Critique, East Asian Journal of Popular Culture, Journal of Chinese Cinema*, and *Modern Chinese Literature and Culture*. Liu has won six Institute-wide teaching awards, including the Georgia Tech CETL/BP Junior Faculty Teaching Excellence in 2012. She is a founding member of Georgia Tech's Global Media Festival: Sustainability Across Languages and Cultures and has invited Mr Wang Jiuliang and other awarded filmmakers and artists to the Global Media Fest events.

Lu Liu is Assistant Professor of Chinese at Georgia Tech. A scholar of modern Chinese literature and media, her research broadly examines the interplay of science and technology, visual cultures, and subject formation. Her published and forthcoming articles examine the politicization of bacteria, viruses, and pests in modern China's revolution and nation-building, the history of virology and phage therapy, and the making of China's space father, Qian Xuesen.

Amanda Weiss is Associate Professor of Japanese at the Georgia Institute of Technology, where she teaches courses on Japanese media and society. She is editor and founder of *Hivemind: Global Speculative Fiction*, a science fiction and fantasy magazine with a focus on language and culture. She also leads a VIP or Vertically Integrated Project in East Asian Media. VIP student projects have included archival work, translation, photography, and media analysis. Her forthcoming book, *Han Heroes and Yamato Warriors: Competing Masculinities in Chinese and Japanese War Cinema* (Hong Kong University Press, 2023), explores contemporary East Asian remembrance of WWII.

Acknowledgments

This book would not have been possible without the mentorship of Vicki Galloway, Professor Emerita of Spanish at Georgia Tech, who first introduced me to the concept of Education for Sustainable Development (ESD) and taught me so much about the importance of place-based and culturally rooted approaches to global sustainability challenges.

I am also grateful to Jennifer Hirsch, the inaugural Director of Georgia Tech's Center for Serve-Learn-Sustain and founding leader of RCE Greater Atlanta, for championing the importance of creating sustainable communities in partnerships with community, nonprofit, business, and academic stakeholders. Her collaborative spirit and insightful feedback have been invaluable in shaping this book. I also greatly enjoyed co-writing the concluding chapter with her.

This textbook is largely the result of a collaborative effort with 11 of my colleagues from the School of Modern Languages who contributed as chapter authors. As linguistic, cultural, and regional experts in the global humanities, they adopt a nuanced approach to the UN SDGs and to ESD. I thank each contributor for their insightful contributions and collaborative spirit throughout this process.

My home department has a long history of integrating ESD into humanities disciplines generally and foreign language and culture curriculum specifically. A key factor that influenced the direction and approach of this textbook has been the Global Media Festival (GMF), the School of Modern Languages' annual film and discussion series focusing on sustainability across languages and cultures. Established in 2017 and directed by Juan Carlos Rodríguez (2017–2020), Amanda Weiss (2020–2021), and Paul Alonso (2022–2023), the GMF aims to foster awareness of the different cultural frameworks that inform and impact sustainability issues around the world. Many of this book's chapter authors have contributed to this festival, and several of the works treated in this textbook have been showcased. In addition to this book's contributors, I wish to thank Juan Carlos Rodríguez and Jan Uelzmann, whose work on promoting the UN SDGs in the School of Modern Languages has been truly inspirational.

I also attribute the origins of this textbook to Georgia Tech's decades-long commitment to sustainability. The Institute's "The Next 10 Years: 2020–2030" Strategic Plan includes the "Connect Globally" focus area, which aims to "strengthen our role as a convener of worldwide collaboration" and "build a global learning network to expand our reach and amplify our impact" through these four action items:

- "*Prepare all Georgia Tech students to be cross-culturally competent, globally minded leaders.*"
- "Be a leader in study abroad participation among leading public research universities."
- "Be a *hub of a global learning and an innovation network through global partnerships*, alumni engagement, lifelong learning, and research collaborations."

- "*Lead and contribute to global collaborative efforts that advance the U.N. Sustainable Development Goals through our education, research, and service*" (Connect Globally," emphasis added).

Owing to Georgia Tech's commitment to cross-cultural education, global citizenship, and the advancement of the UN SDGs, I have been fortunate to have received generous funding in support of this textbook. I wish to thank the School of Modern Languages, the Atlanta Global Studies Center, the Ivan Allen College of Liberal Arts, Global Student Experiences, the Office of International Education, and Sustainability Next for their financial support of this project.

Finally, I wish to thank my family and friends for their interest and encouragement in this endeavor. I am especially grateful to Diego, Adrian, and Alicia!

Kelly Comfort

Works Cited

"Connect Globally." *Georgia Tech Strategic Plan: Progress and Service for All*. https://strategicplan.gatech.edu/focus/global. Accessed 1 May 2023.

Introduction

A Global Humanities Approach to the United Nations' Sustainable Development Goals (SDGs) and Education for Sustainable Development (ESD)

Kelly Comfort

This introductory chapter first establishes the theoretical foundations of *A Global Humanities Approach to the United Nations' Sustainable Development Goals: Understanding Planet, People, and Prosperity* by outlining the origin, evolution, and current state of three fields: the United Nations' Sustainable Development Goals (SDGs), Education for Sustainable Development (ESD), and the Global Humanities. The Introduction then goes on to explain the methodological approach and organizational structure employed throughout the textbook. Next, it summarizes the 12 global humanities texts featured in Chapters 1–12 and includes details on the intersection of each text with the SDG framework. Finally, the opening chapter concludes with detailed guidelines for instructors on how to best use this textbook. Sections I, II, and III of this "Introduction" are intended for both instructors and students, while Section IV is written for teachers who plan to adopt this textbook as the primary material in a college-level course.

I   Theoretical Foundations

This textbook sits at the crossroads between three theoretical foundations—the UN SDGs, ESD, and the growing field of the Global Humanities; the origin and evolution of each field is outlined in this opening section.

1   The United Nations' Sustainable Development Goals

In "The 17 Goals," the United Nations' Department of Economic and Social Affairs explains the decades-long history behind the emergence of the UN SDGs by outlining five major events leading up to the 2015 adoption of the *2030 Agenda for Sustainable Development* and the 17 SDGs. First, in 1992 at the Earth Summit in Rio de Janeiro, Brazil, 178 countries adopted *Agenda 21*, which was "a comprehensive plan of action to build a global partnership for sustainable development to improve human lives and protect the environment" ("The 17 Goals"). The next milestone came in 2000 during the Millennium Summit in New York, when UN Member States adopted the Millennium Declaration that led to the creation of these eight Millennium Development Goals (MDGs):

1   eradicate extreme poverty and hunger;
2   achieve universal primary education;
3   promote gender equality and empower women;
4   reduce child mortality;
5   improve maternal health;
6   combat HIV/AIDS, malaria, and other diseases;

DOI: 10.4324/9781003388869-1

7   ensure environmental sustainability;
8   develop a global partnership for development

("We Can End Poverty")

Then, in 2002, at the World Summit on Sustainable Development in Johannesburg, South Africa, the "Johannesburg Declaration on Sustainable Development and the Plan of Implementation" was adopted, which reaffirmed the commitment of the global community to not only poverty eradication, but so too the environment. In 2012, at the UN Conference on Sustainable Development in Rio de Janeiro, Brazil, the UN Member States adopted *The Future We Want* document "to launch the process to develop a set of SDGs to build upon the MDGs and to establish the UN High Level Political Forum on Sustainable Development" ("The 17 Goals"). The following year, the UN General Assembly created an Open Working Group with 30 members to develop a proposal for the SDGs ("The 17 Goals").

Following these initial steps, in January 2015 the UN General Assembly began to negotiate the post-2015 development agenda, which "culminated in the subsequent adoption of the *2030 Agenda for Sustainable Development*" at the UN Sustainable Development Summit in New York in September 2015 ("The 17 Goals"). This is when all UN Member States adopted the following 17 SDGs (Figure 0.1) together with 169 targets and 231 indicators to monitor progress.

These goals, which serve as "an urgent call for action by all countries—developed and developing—in a global partnership," are the basis for "a shared blueprint for peace and prosperity for people and the planet, now and into the future" ("The 17 Goals"). UN Secretary-General Ban Ki-moon calls the SDGs "our shared vision of humanity and a social contract between the world's leaders and the people" ("We Can End Poverty"). He also designates them "a to-do list for the people and planet" ("We Can End Poverty").

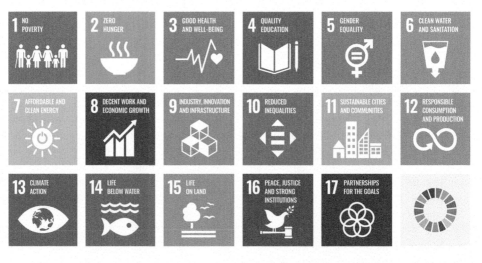

Figure 0.1 The United Nations sustainable development goals, https://www.un.org/sustainabledevelopment/. Reprinted with permission. The content of this publication has not been approved by the United Nations and does not reflect the views of the United Nations or its officials or Member States.

According to *Transforming Our World: The 2030 Agenda for Sustainable Development*, the SDGs and their targets would come into effect on January 1, 2016 and "guide the decisions we take over the next fifteen years." During this period, the annual High-level Political Forum on Sustainable Development would serve as the central UN platform for "the follow-up and review of the SDGs," while the Division for Sustainable Development Goals (DSDGs) in the UN Department of Economic and Social Affairs (UNDESA) would provide "substantive support and capacity-building for the SDGs and their related thematic issues" and play a key role in "the evaluation of UN systemwide implementation" and also "on advocacy and outreach activities relating to the SDGs" ("The 17 Goals"). Finally, the UN Secretary General publishes an annual SDG Progress Report in cooperation with the UN System that is based on "the global indicator framework and data produced by national statistical systems and information collected at the regional level" ("The 17 Goals").

When compared to the MDGs that they replaced, the UN SDGs are "wider in scale and in ambition" and are also more "universal—covering every country in the world—and no longer applicable only to developing countries" ("What Are the Sustainable Development Goals?"). In a 2015 Briefing Sheet published by the ICLEI Local Governments for Sustainability titled "From MDGs to SDGs: What Are the Sustainable Development Goals?" Michael Woodbridge outlines what makes the SDGs different from the MDGs. He notes three key distinctions. First, the SDGs "are uniformly applicable to all countries of the world," a change that removes "the 'developing' versus 'developed' dichotomy that left the MDGs open to criticism" (Woodbridge 2). Second, the SDGs have "significantly expanded on the scale and content of the MDGs" (Woodbridge 2). The overall expansion of content stems from the fact that the SDGs are focused on "a global development with-and-for sustainability" insofar as they "demonstrate the understanding that the environment is not an add-on or in opposition to sustainable development, but rather the base that underpins all other goals" (Woodbridge 2). The overall expansion of scope has to do with the notion that the SDGs differ from the MDGs' "narrow focus on poverty reduction" by including "new themes which reflect an approach that sees the environment, economy, and society as embedded systems rather than separate competing 'pillars'" (Woodbridge 2). Third, whereas with the MDGs "countries of the Global South" had "collectively played a minimum role in their design" to the extent that the MDGs were criticized as having been "imposed on the developing countries by the more developed," the SDGs have been created through "an unparalleled participatory process" that has allowed developing countries "to provide significant input into the content" and has also included local and subnational governments as well as civil society and the private sector as "prominent actors" in the design and implementation process (Woodbridge 2).

The SDG framework thus merges "economic, social or environmental aspects of development questions" to "put inequality at the heart of the agenda," which is evidenced by the "guiding principle that global development should 'leave no-one behind'" ("What Are the Sustainable Development Goals?"). In short, the adoption of the UN SDGs recognizes "that ending poverty and other deprivations must go hand-in-hand with strategies that improve health and education, reduce inequality, and spur economic growth—all while tackling climate change and working to preserve our oceans and forests" ("The 17 Goals"). Moreover, the UN SDGs are deemed "global in nature and universally applicable," while at the same time "taking into account different national realities, capacities and levels of development" and "respecting national policies and priorities" (*Transforming Our World*). In this way, the SDG framework rests on a firm acknowledgment of the importance of "the natural and cultural diversity of the world" as well as the need for "inter-cultural understanding, tolerance, mutual respect and an ethic of global citizenship and shared responsibility" (*Transforming Our World*). *A Global Humanities Approach to the United Nations' Sustainable Development Goals: Understanding Planet, People, and Prosperity* reinforces this emphasis on place-based, locally rooted, and culturally anchored approaches to sustainability challenges, while also calling for a global vision in the implementation of the SDGs that is inclusive of all cultures and civilizations.

2   *Education for Sustainable Development*

Education for Sustainable Development (ESD) was officially introduced on an international scale in 1992 with the publication of Chapter 36 ("Promoting Education, Public Awareness and Training") of *Agenda 21*, the official document of the 1992 Earth Summit. The table below outlines the three ESD program areas and related objectives set forth in *Agenda 21*:

Program Area	Objectives
a Reorienting education toward sustainable development	"Education is critical for promoting sustainable development and improving the capacity of the people to address environment and development issues" and should "promote integration of environment and development concepts."
b Increasing public awareness	"There is a need to increase public sensitivity to environment and development problems and involvement in their solutions and foster a sense of personal environmental responsibility and greater motivation and commitment towards sustainable development."
c Promoting training	"Training is one of the most important tools to develop human resources and facilitate the transition to a more sustainable world. It should have a job-specific focus, aimed at filling the gaps in knowledge and skill that would help individuals find employment and be involved in environmental and development work."

The next major step in solidifying ESD came in 2005, when the United Nations Educational, Scientific, and Cultural Organization (UNESCO) launched *The United Nations Decade of Education for Sustainable Development* (DESD). Spanning the period 2005–2014, DESD aimed to "reorient education towards sustainability," "integrate the principles, values and practices of sustainable development into all aspects of education and learning," and "mobilize the educational resources of the world to help create a more sustainable future" ("UN Decade of ESD"). More specifically, DESD promoted educational efforts that "encouraged changes in behaviour that created a more sustainable future in terms of environmental integrity, economic viability and a just society for present and future generations" ("UN Decade of ESD"). This integration of environmental, economic, and social factors was a key step in shaping the future of ESD. The overarching belief underpinning DESD can be summed up as follows: "Education alone cannot achieve a more sustainable future; however, without education and learning for sustainable development, we will not be able to reach that goal" ("UN Decade of ESD"). This additional emphasis on the key role of education in shaping the values that support sustainable development and sustainable societies marks a key moment in the genealogy of ESD.

In 2012, the importance of ESD was reiterated in the section on "Education" of *The Future We Want*. This section includes seven numbered paragraphs; the main points of each paragraph are outlined in the table below:

Paragraph	Summary of main points
229	• Reaffirm commitments "to the right to education," including "universal access to primary education," "full access to quality education at all levels," and "equal access to education." • Underscore that education is "an essential condition for achieving sustainable development."
230	• Recognize that "the younger generations are the custodians of the future" and highlight the "need for better quality and access to education beyond the primary level." • Resolve to "improve the capacity of our education systems to prepare people to pursue sustainable development." • Promote "enhanced cooperation among schools, communities and authorities in efforts to promote access to quality education at all levels."
231	• Promote "Sustainable Development awareness among youth" in accordance with the DESD goals.
232	• Emphasize "the importance of greater international cooperation to improve access to education" through increased education infrastructure, investment, and partnerships.
233	• Promote ESD and integrate sustainable development more actively into education beyond the 2005–2014 DESD period.
234	• Encourage "educational institutions to consider adopting good practises in sustainability management on their campuses and in their communities."
235	• Support "educational institutions" to carry out "research and innovation for sustainable development" (The Future We Want).

At UNESCO's "Global Education for All Meeting" in 2014, the publication of what is known as "The Muscat Agreement" placed education "at the top of the global development agenda for the period 2015–2030" (Zhang and Wang 479). In the section titled "Vision, Principles and Scope of the Post-2015 Education Agenda," "The Muscat Agreement" insists that education "is a fundamental human right for every person" and "an essential condition for human fulfilment, peace, sustainable development, economic growth, decent work, gender equality, and responsible global citizenship" that contributes to "the reduction of inequalities and the eradication of poverty." This agreement argues that "education must be placed at the heart of the global development agenda" and that "the post-2015 educational agenda" should "be an integral part of the broader international development framework" ("The Muscat Agreement").

Also in 2014, UNESCO launched its "Global Action Programme on ESD" (GAP) at the World Conference on ESD in Japan. The stated objective of the GAP is "generating and scaling up ESD action at all levels and in all areas of education, and in all sustainable development sectors" ("The Global Action Programme"). The GAP reaffirms ESD "as a vital means of implementation for sustainable development" in areas including climate change, biodiversity, disaster risk reduction, sustainable consumption and production, and children's rights ("The Global Action Programme"). The GAP insists that ESD is both "an opportunity and a responsibility" that "should engage both developed and developing countries" and "fully take into consideration local, national, regional, and global contexts, as well as the contribution of culture to sustainable development" ("The Global Action Programme"). This new appreciation for "cultural diversity" as well as "local and traditional knowledge and indigenous wisdom and practices" is a noteworthy addition to ESD's ongoing interest in "universal principals such as human rights, gender equality, democracy, and social justice" ("The Global Action Programme"). This textbook's approach is similar insofar as it underscores the importance of deep cultural knowledge to both the global humanities and the UN SDGs.

With the adoption of the *2030 Agenda for Sustainable Development* in September 2015, SDG 4 on Quality Education underscored the importance of education in general and ESD in particular for achieving a sustainable world. Target 4.7 on "Education for Sustainable Development and Global Citizenship" relates directly to ESD with the following objective:

> By 2030, ensure that all learners acquire the knowledge and skills needed to promote sustainable development, including, among others, through education for sustainable development and sustainable lifestyles, human rights, gender equality, promotion of a culture of peace and non-violence, global citizenship and appreciation of cultural diversity and of culture's contribution to sustainable development. ("The Global Goals: 4")

Target 4.7, in mentioning education for both "sustainable development" and "global citizenship," adds a new layer to ESD. The aim of Global Citizen Education (GCED), according to the UN, is "nurturing respect for all, building a sense of belonging to a common humanity and helping learners become responsible and active global citizens" ("Global Citizen Education"). GCED strives to help "young people develop the core competencies which allow them to actively engage with the world, and help to make it a more just and sustainable place" ("Global Citizen Education"). Education for global citizenship is thus a form of "civic learning" that involves "students' active participation in projects that address global issues of a social, political, economic, or environmental nature" ("Global Citizen Education"). It is important to recognize the connection between ESD and GCED insofar as

> both prioritize the relevance and content of education in order ensure that education helps build a peaceful and sustainable world and both emphasize the need to foster knowledge, skills, values, attitudes and behaviours that allow individuals to take informed decisions and assume active roles locally, nationally, and globally. ("Global Citizen Education")

This textbook aims to promote both ESD and GCED at colleges and universities across the world. It is part of a growing effort in higher education to prepare and engage students to enact sustainable development, which requires education "for" sustainable development, and not just "about" sustainable development. This textbook strives to reinforce the message of Target 4.7 by promoting an "appreciation of cultural diversity and of culture's contribution to sustainable development" ("The Global Goals: 4").

Finally, the "ESD for 2030 Roadmap" identifies five priority action areas aimed at increasing the contributions of education "to building a more just and sustainable world": (1) "advancing policy"; (2) "transforming learning environments"; (3) "building capacities of educators"; (4) "empowering and mobilizing youth"; and (5) "accelerating local level actions" ("Education for Sustainable Development for 2030 Toolbox"). This book overlaps with action areas 2, 3, and 4. It transforms learning environments through its transdisciplinary approach to both the UN SDGs and the global humanities. It builds the capacities of educators by providing all of the tools needed (contextualization and background information; discussion questions and assignments; and final projects and presentations) for instructors to teach this important subject matter to their students. It empowers and mobilizes youth by introducing them to inspiring and provocative global humanities texts and guiding them through various practical applications and activities that connect the global to the local.

3   ***The Global Humanities***

The remainder of this section traces the origin and evolution of the recent field of global humanities and notes the intersection of the global humanities with the UN SDGs and ESD. The global
humanities as a discipline should be seen as stemming from two separate disciplines, namely,
the humanities and global studies.[1] Let us begin with a brief history of the humanities. The origin
of the humanities is often traced back to Ancient Greece, although in recent years there has been
increased consideration and awareness of the ways in which the field emerged in other cultures
and civilizations across the world as well as earlier in human history. Defined as a field of study
that investigates "the expressions of the human mind," humanities disciplines have traditionally
included: "archaeology, art history, history, linguistics, literature studies, musicology, philology,
philosophy, and religious studies" (Amirell). Most disciplines in the humanities "were forged
during the nineteenth century, when they were institutionalised under the influence of the German academic model formulated and promoted by, among others, Wilhelm von Humboldt" as
standing in contrast to the more practical natural sciences. At this time in history, they became
intimately linked to the concept of the nation-state and were "delimited by national borders,
whether these were geographical, historical, cultural, or linguistic" (Amirell). The humanities,
particularly the study of language, history, literature, and culture, frequently focused "on European or Western history and culture" with "the study of the rest of humanity often [. . .] relegated
to a few specialised and relatively minor disciplines such as Oriental studies, religious studies,
and certain sections of philology" (Amirell). This trend continued well into the 20th century,
until the humanities, particularly in the period after 1945, became "more critical of the nation-
states and of nationalism" (Amirell). By the end of the 20th century, as a result of the influence
of globalization and increasing criticism against "Eurocentric, colonial, and other exclusionary
biases in academia," this "national paradigm" was further challenged in more fundamental ways
(Amirell). In the 2000s, the humanities experienced "a global turn" that aimed "to include all of
humankind in the humanities," which marked an effort to "transcend Eurocentric and colonial
worldviews" and to become "more globally inclusive, critical, and transdisciplinary" (Amirell).
This is when it became possible to conceive of the global humanities.

Yet before global humanities emerged as a discipline, global studies, which can be traced
back to the mid-1990s, became established as a field of study in its own right. Amirell outlines
the "rapid rise and institutionalization" of global studies from around 1995 as well as the "spectacular expansion" of the field around 2010 with the emergence of "several journals dedicated
to global studies, scholarly associations, regular conferences, numerous research centres, and
schools of global studies around the world, as well as hundreds of study programs in global
studies at all levels." Often defined as "a broad interdisciplinary field spanning many disciplines in the humanities and social sciences," global studies has been highly dominated by the
social sciences and has had a narrower scope than that of the humanities (Amirell). "Despite
the global turn in many humanities disciplines in recent years," Amirell explains, "history is
the only major humanities discipline that has a prominent place in global studies," particularly
when "historical scholarship" is narrowly focused on "the history of globalisation" rather than
broadly conceived as "global history as a whole." Amirell documents two ways in which global
studies marginalizes the humanities: first, through the "heavy bias toward the social sciences"
in both education and research; second, through the "appropriation of the traditional fields of
research of the humanities" by various social sciences disciplines that "have increasingly come
to claim culture as 'their field.'" To overcome such marginalization, the global humanities has
"the potential to flourish as a field of study separate from that of global studies," which "can
be achieved by embracing global perspectives but not confining them to the study of modern
globalisation" (Amirell).

The global humanities, Amirell explains further, is typically defined in one of three ways: (1) as a field that "enhance[s] international collaboration and mobility within the humanities"; (2) as a field marked by "the study of non-Western cultures and languages"; (3) as a field that "seems akin to global studies" but "has a slightly larger representation of humanities disciplines." Amirell advocates for the importance of the global humanities in terms of its ability to produce and promote "global, inclusive, and transdisciplinary frameworks of analysis," "globally useful knowledge," and "mutual understanding and communication across national, regional, cultural, and linguistic borders." He insists further that the "global humanities should aim to develop frameworks of analysis that can be used to study all cultural expressions of humankind and to foster intercultural dialogue and understanding" (Amirell). By taking on

> the study of cultural and historical processes without geographic or chronological limitations and unfettered from the bonds of Eurocentrism and methodological nationalism, which often are associated with the traditional humanities disciplines as they have developed in the West,

the global humanities as an emerging discipline should be seen, Amirell insists, as "one of the most promising attempts in recent years to break free from the discourse of crisis" in the humanities more generally. Other scholars of the global humanities agree. For example, Wiebke Denecke in her 2021 article "Comparative Global Humanities Now," proposes "to energize the mission of the humanities by radically globalizing their subject matter and methods, taking inspiration from the world's monumental archive of humanistic creativity over 5,000 years of recorded experience" (479). According to Denecke, the global humanities, which she calls the "Comparative Global Humanities," should aim "to be inclusively global in terms of subject matter and participants, conceptually comparative, and based on rigorous historical and philological research" (482). Michael Patrick Rutter and Steven Mintz, in their October 12, 2022 blog post "Internationalizing the Humanities" on *Inside Higher Ed*, ask the question: "Can the humanities' future be global and comparative?" They mention "a growing concern with internationalizing our conception of the humanities" and consider it "imperative" that the humanities become "truly inclusive" by taking on "more explicitly international and cross-cultural" subject matter (Rutter and Mintz). Rutter and Mintz mention the work of Denecke, who they see as aiming "to re-energize the humanities by internationalizing its subject matter and championing methods that involve systematic comparisons and contrasts." Calling Denecke's "vision" "extraordinarily exciting and inspiring," that also ask whether it is "realistic and realizable" given the "limits" of "language skills" and "historical knowledge." Rutter and Mintz thus point out some of the challenges to "globalizing the humanities." The greatest challenge they see is that most humanities scholars are "[t]rained in specific national and linguistic traditions" and therefore are not "prepared to offer truly global, comparative perspectives" that "require deep knowledge about specific contexts and language skills that most [. . .] lack." Another obstacle stems from the fact the comparatists must work hard "to avoid implicit assumptions about cultural hierarchies" such as "Eurocentric standards or assumptions," so as to instead "make comparisons and contrasts explicit" and account for "cultural difference" (Rutter and Mintz).

Much of the discussion of the global humanities by Amirell, Denecke, and Rutter and Mintz centers around the challenge of ensuring deep cultural, linguistic, and regional knowledge and expertise, on the one hand, and internationalizing the discipline to be more inclusive, open, and cross-cultural, on the other hand. Interestingly enough, similar discussions have taken place regarding the role of culture and of the arts and humanities in relation to the UN SDGs and ESD. While certainly not an exhaustive list, these four efforts to establish the importance of the humanities—broadly conceived—in advancing the global sustainable development goals are worth noting: "The Hangzhou Declaration" (2013); The World Humanities Conference (2017); the British Council's "The Missing Pillar: Culture's Contribution to the UN Sustainable Development Goals" publication (2020); and the University College London's Institute of Advanced Studies' "The UN Sustainable Development Goals (SDGs): Contributions from the Humanities, A Research Report" (2021). Each of these efforts is briefly explained below.

"The Hangzhou Declaration: Placing Culture at the Heart of Sustainable Development Policies," a UNESCO publication adopted on May 17, 2013, locates "an urgent need for new approaches" to "mounting challenges" that "should fully acknowledge the role of culture as a system of values and a resource and framework to build truly sustainable development." This new cultural approach is grounded in "the recognition of culture as part of the global and local commons as well as a wellspring of creativity and renewal" ("The Hangzhou Declaration"). Reaffirming culture as "a fundamental enabler of" and "a driver for" sustainability, the "Hangzhou Declaration" calls for "a people-centred and place-based approach" to development and peace-building initiatives ("The Hangzhou Declaration"). By placing culture "at the heart of future policies for sustainable development," cultural studies experts from a variety of global humanities disciplines have the potential to play a key role in the advancement of the 17 global goals.

The World Humanities Conference, jointly organized by UNESCO and the International Council for Philosophy and Human Sciences (CIPSH) and held between August 6 and 11, 2017 in Liège, Belgium, aimed "to establish a new agenda for the humanities of the 21st century" and to "redefine the foundations, role and responsibilities of the humanities in contemporary society" ("A New Humanities Agenda"). Specifically, the conference sought to identify ways in which the competencies and specific approaches of the humanities—understood as including literature and language, philosophy, history, and the arts—could actively contribute to the *2030 Agenda*. According to John Crowley, Chief of Research, Policy and Foresight in the UNESCO Sector for Social and Human Science, the conference's main objective involved setting an "ambitions" new "global agenda" for the humanities (qtd. in McKenzie). In particular, "A New Humanities Agenda for the 21st Century: Outcome Document" celebrates the ability of the humanities to foster diversity and freedom of thought, to promote transparency, to engage in "epistemological decolonization," and to take "a critical approach" to the concept of universal values.

Another important contribution, the British Council's 2020 publication "The Missing Pillar: Culture's Contribution to the UN Sustainable Development Goals" outlines nine recommendations for "incorporating the SDGs into arts and culture programmes and measuring culture's contribution to the SDGs" (8). While seemingly similar in language to "The Hangzhou Declaration," "The Missing Pillar" differs insofar as it focuses on arts and culture as a sector and as a creative process. For example, its recommendations include: developing training programs that "highlight the role of arts and culture in the SDGs"; working with community partners "in developing, delivering and evaluating cultural initiatives"; and advocating "for specific outcomes that respond to individual SDGs through arts and culture" ("The Missing Pillar" 8). Noting that there is no specific SDG on culture in *Agenda 30*, "The Missing Pillar" initiative questions why "Culture," described as "the glue that binds humanity together," "is not formally recognized alongside the three pillars of development—social, economic and environmental" (Lewis). Overall, "The Missing Pillar" marks a pivotal moment in the thinking on how arts and culture—two key areas for the global humanities—can address global challenges and make the SDGs more accessible and impactful.

Finally, in 2021, University College London's Institute of Advanced Studies conducted a research project in conjunction with the consultancy firm SHM "to investigate the reasons" for the perceived "gap between the potential and actual contribution of the Humanities" to ongoing work to promote and achieve the UN SDGs ("The UN Sustainable Development Goals (SDGs): Contributions from the Humanities"). The aims of this project were "to identify ways of applying Humanities insights to work on SDGS and to make proposals for policies to help ensure that the Humanities are fully integrated into the debates from now on" ("The UN Sustainable Development Goals (SDGs): Contributions from the Humanities"). The study's final publication, titled "The UN Sustainable Development Goals (SDGs): Contributions from the Humanities, A Research Report," laments that the UN Reports on the SDGs, which tend to "advocate technocratic, resource-management solutions," refer "to human behaviour only insofar as it impedes policy implementation" and pay "[l]ittle attention [. . .] to the human factors—social, political and ethical—essential to any prospect of lasting success in transforming what people can or will do." The report also complains that "policy-makers rarely draw upon the vast reservoir of cultural expertise that is the Humanities" ("The UN Sustainable Development Goals (SDGs): Contributions from the Humanities"). Hoping to rectify these shortcomings, the authors insist on the value that the humanities offer in terms of "a set of concepts, theories and methods for understanding human behaviour, individual and collective" ("The UN Sustainable Development Goals (SDGs): Contributions from the Humanities"). This project proposes many clear ways in which the humanities might contribute to improving the UN SDG framework—by offering "critical scrutiny" to any claims to "universal knowledge" or to any assumptions that knowledge can be transferred intact from one context or culture to another; by introducing "greater translatability" to the SDGs that allow for "the best, tailored solutions" for each country based on their specific cultural values and local realities; by critiquing "anthropocentric perspectives" that present humans as "unique and entitled to exploit the natural world"; by promoting "critical thinking" and "an evaluative approach" based on "a multiplicity of perspectives" that contextualizes knowledge and questions engrained assumptions and values as well as reductive ways of thinking; by being inclusive of "the diversity of epistemological approaches taken by the various stakeholders," including by Indigenous peoples ("The UN Sustainable Development Goals (SDGs): Contributions from the Humanities"). This textbook aims to further the work of University College London's Institute of Advanced Studies by offering a new contribution from the humanities to the UN SDGs.

II   Methodological Approach

This textbook—as the title suggests—takes a "global humanities approach" to the UN SDGs. This occurs in two distinct yet overlapping ways. First, the textbook presents 12 global humanities texts in Chapters 1–12: five documentary films (Aya Hanabusa's *Holy Island*, Kip Andersen and Keegan Kuhn's *Cowspiracy*, Agnès Varda's *The Gleaners and I*, Kief Davidson and Pedro Kos's *Bending the Arc*, and Wang Jiuliang's *Plastic China*), one feature film (Ivan Sanjinés, Nicolás Ipamo and Alejandro Noza's *Cry of the Forest*), two photographic collections (Barbara Dombrowski's *Tropic Ice: Dialog between Places Affected by Climate Change* and Fabrice Monteiro's *The Prophecy*), three novels (Fernando Contreras Castro's *Única Looking at the Sea*, Agustina Bazterrica's *Tender is the Flesh*, and Aravind Adiga's *The White Tiger*), and one short story (Hao Jingfang's "Folding Beijing"). A global humanities text is here defined broadly as any creative work (regardless of length, genre, language of production, place of geographical origin, etc.) that conveys a set of meanings and is embedded in a particular culture and context. The photographers, authors, and directors examined are "practitioners" or "artists" of the global humanities. They hail from Argentina, Belgium, Benin, Bolivia, Brazil, Costa

Rica, China, France, Germany, India, Japan, and the United States, while their works take us to many of these homelands and to additional nations such as Australia, Ecuador, Greenland, Haiti, Kiribati, Mongolia, Peru, Rwanda, Senegal, and Tanzania. Overall, the chosen texts are humanistic creations that reflect on the relationship between humans and their local and global environments.

Second, the individual chapter authors are themselves scholars of the global humanities with a wide range of disciplinary expertise as outlined below:

Chapter author:	Disciplinary specialization:
Kelly Comfort Introduction, Chapter 3, Conclusion	Comparative Literature, Latin American Studies, Global Modernisms, Critical Theory, *Flânerie* Studies, Sustainability Studies
Amanda Weiss Chapter 1	East Asian Studies, Media Studies, Cultural Studies, Gender Studies
Britta Kallin Chapter 2	German and Austrian Literature and Culture, Gender Studies, Critical Race Studies, Postcolonial Studies, Sustainability Studies
Natalie Khazaal Chapter 4	Arabic Media and Language, Minority Disenfranchisement, Critical Animal and Media Studies
Miguel Rosas Buendía Chapter 5	Latin American Studies, History of Science, Environmental Humanities, Indigenous Studies
Stéphanie Boulard Chapter 6	French Literature, Visual Arts, Film and Media Studies, Word and Image Studies, Environmental Humanities
Mirla González Chapter 7	Peninsular Literature and Film, Science Fiction Studies, Women, Science, and Technology Studies, Online Instructional Design
Seung-Eun Chang Chapter 8	Linguistics, Phonology and Phonetics, Heritage Language Acquisition, Content-Based Language Teaching, Korean Language Teaching
Smita Daftardar Chapter 9	Hindi-Urdu Pedagogy, Heritage, and Foreign Language Acquisition
Vicki Galloway Chapter 10	Latin American Studies and Literature, Intercultural Education, Indigenous Studies, Language Pedagogy
Lu Liu Chapter 11	Asian Studies, Visual Culture Studies, Media Studies, the History of Science and Technology
Jin Liu Chapter 12	East Asian Languages and Cultures, Media Studies, Eco-cinema, Cultural Studies of Language
Jennifer Hirsch Conclusion	Cultural and Environmental Anthropology, Sustainability Studies, Equity and Social Justice Studies

Trained in the analysis and critique of a variety of texts—from literature to film; from visual and performative arts to digital media—the chapter contributors aim to model deep humanistic inquiry and analysis through the questions and assignments they propose. It is essential to recognize that this textbook is multi-authored on purpose, since no single scholar would have the expertise to cover all of the featured geographic, linguistic, and cultural traditions. By using regional and cultural experts as the individual chapter authors, *A Global Humanities Approach to the United Nations' Sustainable Development Goals* merges local insight and expertise with global scope and awareness.

A Global Humanities Approach to the United Nations' Sustainable Development Goals: Understanding Planet, People, and Prosperity is designed as a college-level textbook for courses in a wide range of disciplines. By using 12 global humanities texts from a variety of genres, this textbook has two main objectives. First, it strives to train students with a disciplinary background in the humanities to understand, apply, and evaluate the UN SDGs and the concept of sustainable development. Second, it aims to teach students with a disciplinary background outside of the humanities to understand, analyze, and evaluate global humanities texts and their specific contributions—artistic, cultural, linguistic, etc.—to understanding and attaining a sustainable world. Overall, the book's approach intentionally sets out to break down disciplinary boundaries and to combine humanistic, artistic, ethical, social, cultural, political, scientific, technological, environmental, and economic discourses.

This textbook was written (2022–2023) and first published (2024) at approximately the midway point between the initial adoption of the UN SDGs in 2015 and the target year for their "full implementation" in 2030 (*Transforming Our World*). Of the 12 global humanities texts featured in Chapters 1–12, seven were published before the adoption of the UN SDGs in 2015: Fernando Contreras Castro's *Única Looking at the Sea* (1993[2]), Angés Varda's *The Gleaners and I* (2000), Aravind Adiga's *The White Tiger* (2008), Ivan Sanjinés, Nicolás Ipamo and Alejandro Noza's *Cry of the Forest* (2008), Aya Hanabusa's *Holy Island* (2010), Hao Jingfang's "Folding Beijing" (2012), and Kip Andersen and Keegan Kuhn's *Cowspiracy: The Sustainability Secret* (2014). Two works—Barbara Dombrowski's *Tropic Ice: Dialog between Places Affected by Climate Change* (2010–2022) and Fabrice Monteiro's *The Prophecy* series (2013 to present)—began before 2015 and continued into the present decade. Three texts were published after the adoption of the UN SDGs: Wang Jiuliang's *Plastic China* (2016), Agustina Bazterrica's *Tender is the Flesh* (2017), and Kief Davidson and Pedro Kos's *Bending the Arc* (2017). The artists, authors, and directors of each featured global humanities text are historically positioned to reflect on the need for and successes and failures of these SDGs. They too bear witness to the state of "[o]ur world today" with its "immense challenges to sustainable development" in which "[b]illions of our citizens continue to live in poverty and are denied a life of dignity," in which we face "rising inequalities within and among countries" and "enormous disparities of opportunity, wealth and power," and in which we suffer from "[g]lobal health threats," "[n]atural resource depletion," and "environmental degradation" (*Transforming Our World*). They too must gauge whether this is also "a time of immense opportunity" in which "[s]ignificant progress has been made in meeting many development challenges" (*Transforming Our World*). Those using *A Global Humanities Approach to the United Nations' Sustainable Development Goals: Understanding Planet, People, and Prosperity* will continue these reflections on the need for and the successes and failures of the UN SDGs in meeting the world's sustainability challenges as we advance toward the target year of 2030 and beyond.

The textbook is divided into three parts. Each part treats four global humanities texts (one per chapter) and five or six of the SDGs as shown in Figure 0.2.

Within each chapter, there is a twofold approach: (1) use the featured text as the lens through which to explore the selected UN SDGs; (2) use the selected UN SDGs as a lens through which to explore the featured text. Despite the use of Parts to organize this textbook, the editor wishes to underscore the notion that the UN SDGs and their targets are—and should be—considered "integrated and indivisible" (*Transforming Our World*).

The textbook closes with a practical conclusion, "Think Global, Act Local: Partnerships and Projects (SDG 17)," which asks students to re-examine the 12 global humanities texts in relation to SDG 17 (Partnerships for the Goals). Students will identify examples from the texts of successful partnerships and also analyze the need for new or better partnerships. Additionally, this chapter offers a variety of final course projects that guide students in applying the Global Goals to local contexts. The final chapter also facilitates end-of-semester reflection and dialogue.

As explained above, *A Global Humanities Approach to the United Nations' Sustainable Development Goals: Understanding Planet, People, and Prosperity* addresses the Planet SDGs in Part 1, the People SDGs in Part 2, the Prosperity SDGs in Part 3, and SDG 17 on Partnerships in the Conclusion. This textbook's structure overlaps in clear ways with the notion of the "5 Ps" of People, Planet, Prosperity, Peace, and Partnership set forth in the *2030 Agenda*.

Part 1 - Planet: Relating Global Humanities Texts to UN SDGs 6, 7, 12, 13, 14, and 15

Part 2 - People: Relating Global Humanities Texts to UN SDGs 1, 2, 3, 4, and 5

Part 3 - Prosperity: Relating Global Humanities Texts to UN SDGs 8, 9, 10, 11, and 16

Figure 0.2 Textbook organization with United Nations sustainable development goals, https://www.un.org/sustainabledevelopment/. Icons reprinted with permission. The content of this publication has not been approved by the United Nations and does not reflect the views of the United Nations or its officials or Member States.

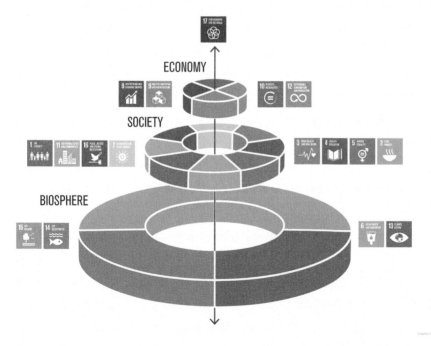

Figure 0.3 Grouping of UN SDGs into four categories: (1) Biosphere and Planet; (2) Society and People; (3) Economy and Prosperity; (4) Partnerships. Image by Azote, reprinted with permission from the Stockholm Resilience Centre.

This textbook focuses on three of the "five Ps" in the main three units: (1) Planet, (2) People, and (3) Prosperity, while Peace is treated as part of the unit on Prosperity, and Partnership is incorporated into the Conclusion. The textbook's organizational structure also partially coincides with the grouping model shown in Figure 0.2, often referred to as the "Wedding Cake" model for the SDGs.

The grouping of the SDGs in this textbook differs slightly insofar as it places SDG 7 (Affordable and Clean Energy) and SDG 12 (Responsible Consumption and Production) in the section on Planet and SDG 11 (Sustainable Cities and Communities) and SDG 16 (Peace Justice and Strong Institutions) in the section on Prosperity. The model in Figure 0.3 places SDG 17 (Partnership) in its own grouping as an area that cross-cuts the entire framework, which this textbook also does by incorporating SDG 17 into the textbook's concluding chapter. This textbook also follows the same order in that it starts with planet and then goes on to examine people, prosperity, and partnerships.

III Global Humanities Texts and Chapter Summaries

Within each part on Planet, People, and Prosperity, chapters are arranged chronologically according to the publication date of the featured global humanities text. This section includes brief summaries of the 12 global humanities works treated in the textbook's chapters and provides details on the intersection of each text with the SDG framework. "Part 1: Planet and UN SDGs 6, 7, 12, 13, 14, and 15" includes two documentary films and two photographic collections in Chapters 1–4. "Part 2: People and UN SDGs 1, 2, 3, 4, and 5" includes two novels and two documentary films in Chapters 5–8. "Part 3: Prosperity and UN SDGs 8, 9, 10, 11, and 16" includes one novel, one short story, one feature film, and one documentary film in Chapters 9–12.

In "Chapter 1: Aya Hanabusa's *Holy Island*: Nuclear Power and Political Resistance in Iwaishima, Japan," Amanda Weiss examines the 2010 documentary film *Holy Island* and its treatment of nuclear resistance on Iwaishima (Iwai Island) in Western Japan. For decades, Iwaishima residents have resisted Chugoku Electric's Kaminoseki Nuclear Power Plant Project. As an island community of farmers and fishers deeply connected to the land and sea, the people are highly concerned about the potential ecological impact on Iwaishima and its surrounding waters. The film documents the daily lives and political resistance of the island's 500 residents, who not only face political challenges but also the pressures of an aging and declining population. The chapter first summarizes the historical context framing these protests, establishing how nuclear power and nuclear weapons are intertwining issues within Japanese discourse. Then, through a series of activities centered on a variety of SDGs, it explores both resident concerns over environmental impact (especially SDGs 6, 12, 14, and 15) as well as arguments in favor of the nuclear power plant (SDG 7).

In "Chapter 2: Barbara Dombrowski's *Tropic Ice: Dialog Between Places Affected by Climate Change* – Photographs and Art Installations of People and Landscapes," Britta Kallin explores four portraits, three art installations, and one landscape photograph from the period 2010–2022 that create a visual exchange between people living in different climate zones whose portraits act as ambassadors for their culture and geographic area. Dombrowski chose these locations because the indigenous people in these areas are the ones who will be affected by climate change first, even though they have hardly contributed to carbon dioxide emissions. They still live in harmony with nature, hunt only what they can eat, and do not follow a Western lifestyle. This chapter offers student-centered activities that explore *Tropic Ice* in terms of Clean Water and Life below Water (SDGs 6 and 14) as well as Affordable and Clean Energy, Responsible Consumption and Production, Climate Action, and Life on Land (SDGs 7, 12, 13, and 15).

In "Chapter 3: Fabrice Monteiro's *The Prophecy*: Trash Art Photography Protests Trashing the Planet," Kelly Comfort analyzes the work of Fabrice Monteiro, a Belgian-Beninese photographer working out of Senegal. Monteiro's *The Prophecy* collection began in 2013 with plans to take 9 photographs in Senegal, although the collection currently includes 15 photographs taken in 7 countries. Monteiro, in collaboration with Senegalese fashion designer Jah Gal, uses upcycled waste to create the costumes of the featured djinn in each image, thus employing a unique trash aesthetic to promote his environmental message. This chapter examines six of these photographs in terms of the six Planet-related UN SDGs treated in Part 1. SDG 6 (Clean Water and Sanitation) and SDG 14 (Life below Water) are the focus of three images: "Untitled #2" portrays the problem of oil spills for marine and coastal ecosystems; "Untitled #3" depicts untreated waste running directly into the Atlantic Ocean; "Untitled #10" exposes coral bleaching and marine biodiversity loss in Australia's Great Barrier Reef. SDG 12 (Responsible Consumption and Production) and SDG 13 (Climate Action) are targeted in "Untitled #1," which calls attention to unsustainable production, overconsumption, and failed waste management, and in "Untitled #9," which shows the problem of charcoal and wood consumption and points to the need for SDG 7 (Affordable and Clean Energy). Four images ("Untitled #1," "Untitled #3," "Untitled #5," and "Untitled #9") address SDG 15 (Life on Land) as they protest land and air pollution, soil erosion, deforestation, and desertification.

In "Chapter 4: Kip Andersen and Keegan Kuhn's *Cowspiracy*: Animal Agriculture and the 'Sustainability Secret,'" Natalie Khazaal analyzes this provocative yet humourous documentary (2014–2015) about the animal agriculture industry and its negative consequences in terms of greenhouse gas production, species extinction, deforestation, polluted water supplies, weakened biodiversity, increased air pollution, Amazon rainforest destruction, and augmented waste pollution. Although these consequences make animal agriculture a leading cause of environmental destruction, the filmmakers discovered that most environmental organizations never address this issue. In the film, they try to understand the depths and reasons for this failure, inspired by the words of Martin Luther King, Jr.: "In the end, we will remember not the words of our enemies, but the silence of our friends." This chapter examines the film's artistic and scientific aspects and how they engage with SDG 6 (Clean Water and Sanitation), SDG 7 (Affordable and Clean Energy), SDG 12 (Responsible Consumption and Production), SDG 13 (Climate Action), SDG 14 (Life below Water), and SDG 15 (Life on Land).

In "Chapter 5: Fernando Contreras Castro's Única Looking at the Sea: Marginalization, Community, and Politics from a Garbage Dump," Miguel Rosas Buendía examines a Costa Rican novel published in 1993, whose first English translation appeared in 2017. Única Looking at the Sea tells the story of a marginalized community that inhabits a garbage dump next to Río Azul (Blue River), a fictional suburb near the Costa Rican capital, San José. The narration follows scavengers' daily lives as they become a gateway to reflect on the issue of garbage production and, more importantly, on the extent to which a sense of community can be built within this precarious setting. This chapter covers five UN SDGs through the novel. The dump as an impoverished location and its inhabitants as marginalized individuals allow us to explore SDG 1 (No Poverty), SDG 2 (Zero Hunger), and SDG 3 (Good Health and Well-Being). This narration suggests that the persistence of these profound social problems is intrinsically related to systems of production and consumption. The main character, Única, is a woman who acts as a leader within the dump and against the dump's closing. Her noticeable personality speaks about the crucial role of women in imagining powerful forms of leadership (SDG 5, Gender Equality). Finally, education as a human right (SDG 4, Quality Education) is addressed in the novel through both Única as former schoolteacher and a male character, Mondolfo, as former worker at the National Library.

In "Chapter 6: Agnès Varda's *The Gleaners and I*: From Waste to Wonder—A Cinematic Odyssey on Food Loss and Gleaning," Stéphanie Boulard explores a documentary film from 2000 that delves into issues such as food poverty, hunger, food wastage, ecology, art, and autobiography. The film investigates the concept of gleaning in France and its various forms, including human trash-picking and art built on recycled materials, revealing the vast amounts of food wasted in France and its impact on food poverty. While this chapter highlights the value of gleaning in reducing food loss and waste and ensuring food security, it also analyzes the film's socio-environmental commentary on postmodern consumerism and explores themes of compassion, fragility, and marginalization. The film challenges traditional beauty standards by showcasing subjects that are typically excluded from mainstream media, such as elderly individuals, homeless people, and those who do not conform to societal norms of beauty. Additionally, Varda's film not only provokes reflection on the portrayal of women in history (SDG 5) but also offers insights on the interconnectedness of social and environmental justice (SDG 16). *The Gleaners and I* aligns with several UN SDGs, including No Poverty (SDG 1), Zero Hunger (SDG 2), Responsible Consumption and Production (SDG 12), and Quality Education (SDG 4), emphasizing the need for greater social and economic equality and environmental sustainability. The chapter also emphasizes the importance of individual action in promoting positive change and fostering a more equitable and sustainable world.

In "Chapter 7: Agustina Bazterrica's *Tender is the Flesh*: Devouring Each Other in Consumerist Society," Mirla Gonzalez examines the science fiction novel *Tender is the Flesh* (2017) by Argentinian author, Agustina Bazterrica. The novel portrays an oppressive society in which a virus has contaminated all animal meat, which paves the way for government-legalized cannibalism and the creation of a society in which animals and certain groups of human beings, particularly women, endure the same levels of cruelty and savagery. This chapter analyzes gender-based violence, as well as the marginalization of other vulnerable populations such as immigrants in the context of a consumerist and capitalist society obsessed with meat consumption that has undergone an environmental catastrophe. This environmental challenge, in the form of a viral outbreak, provides the groundwork for a discussion on SDG 3 (Good Health and Well-Being). Economic inequality, one of the many consequences of the outbreak that has created this dystopian cannibalistic society, allows for an analysis of SDG 1 (No Poverty) and SDG 2 (Zero Hunger). Lastly, through the female protagonist, the novel brings attention to SDG 4 (Quality Education) and SDG 5 (Gender Equality), drawing parallels to gender (in)equality and femicide in contemporary society.

In "Chapter 8: Kief Davidson and Pedro Kos's *Bending the Arc*: Public Health Pioneers Fight for Universal Health Equity and Global Justice," Seung-Eun Chang analyzes a 2017 award-winning documentary film. *Bending the Arc* depicts the inspiring battle beginning 30 years ago to save lives in a rural Haitian village through relevant photos, historic world news videos, and the narratives of Dr. Paul Farmer, Dr. Jim Yong Kim, Ophelia Dahl, and other extraordinary doctors and patients who participated in this endeavor. The film highlights their brave and persistent fight against insurmountable obstacles to bring medical care to the poorest people in some of the most neglected regions around the world and ultimately for the right to health for all. The text is not only directly related to the health issue (SDG 3) in Haiti but also connects to poverty (SDG 1), hunger (SDG 2), education (SDG 4), gender equality (SDG 5), and justice (SDG 16) in any community in the world. This chapter examines ways to create sustainable communities and societies through the topics of SDGs 1–5 and explores the role of non-profit organizations such as Partners in Health in this endeavor.

In "Chapter 9: Aravind Adiga's *The White Tiger*: Stagnation or Social Mobility in Modern India," Smita Daftardar analyzes this award-winning Indian novel published in 2008. *The White*

Tiger tells the story of Balram, a young man who has grown up in poverty and ultimately takes to a life of crime to escape the hopelessness of servitude. The novel begins by pointing out the need for SDG 4 (Quality Education) and SDG 1 (No Poverty), since the protagonist's lack of education and overall destitution set the story in motion. As Balram grows older and leaves his village to seek out work and opportunity in the city, the story focuses on the Prosperity-related SDGs, especially SDG 8 (Decent Work and Economic Growth), SDG 9 (Industry, Innovation, and Infrastructure), SDG 10 (Reduced Inequalities), SDG 11 (Sustainable Cities and Communities) and SDG 16 (Peace, Justice and Strong Institutions). By depicting the opposite of these SDGs, *The White Tiger* highlights the vicious cycle of poverty, the lack of opportunity for economic advancement and social mobility, and the exclusionary practices inherent in a large power-distance society.

In "Chapter 10: Ivan Sanjinés, Nicolás Ipamo and Alejandro Noza's *Cry of the Forest*: Sustainable Development and the Indigenous Communities of Bolivia," Vicki Galloway examines a Bolivian feature film from 2008 that is a collective production funded by indigenous community organizations and educational centers and led by indigenous filmmakers. *Cry of the Forest* demonstrates the interconnectedness of all four dimensions of sustainability—economic, environmental, social, and cultural—and the impacts of decision making based on immediate economic gain. The film also reveals the complex relation that indigenous communities have historically had with a logging industry that has marginalized them as menial workers on their own lands and whose concepts of "territory" as ownership and "nature" as a consumable commodity are in conflict with their cultural values. While the film readily lends itself to examination of sustainable practices in forest management and sourcing in wood-product manufacturing (SDGs 8, 9, and 12), it also provokes reflection in both story and production process on the power of community dignity, solidarity, and activism in achieving voice and creating change and equity (SDGs 10 and 11). Importantly, *Cry of the Forest* takes us inside the indigenous community to hear and witness the cultural dialogue of everyday life whose values and practices may differ from our own, such as decision-making and power structures and the meaning of gender "equality" (SDG 5) and concepts of health, medicine, and well-being (SDG 3) that are directly tied to the cry of the forest.

In "Chapter 11: Hao Jingfang's 'Folding Beijing': Unequal Time and Space in a Dystopian City," Lu Liu examines a 2012 science-fiction short story from a Hugo award-winning Chinese writer. Set in a futuristic Beijing that is divided into three segregated zones, "Folding Beijing" follows the journey of a waste worker named Lao Dao, from the lowest Third Space to the elite First Space. From Lao Dao's perspective, the story reveals the irony of technologized development that selectively renders human labor invisible and reinforces structural inequality. This chapter examines how the story's realistic and speculative style dramatizes and elicits actions to tackle challenges of sustainability in terms of decent work (SDG 8), infrastructure design and construction (SDG 9), access to resources (SDG 10), urban planning and community building (SDG 11), and non-discriminatory policy-making (SDG 16). Additionally, contextualizing the story in China's social reality, the questions and assignments designed in this chapter serve as a starting point to interrogate how the abject condition of urban working classes is often overshadowed by explosive economic growth and stigmatized as low-end.

In "Chapter 12: Wang Jiuliang's *Plastic China*: Unveiling the Façade of Prosperity," Jin Liu explores how this 2016 Chinese documentary follows the members of two families who spend their lives sorting and recycling plastic waste from the United States, Europe, and Asia. Yi-Jie, an 11-year-old girl, works alongside her parents in a recycling facility while dreaming of attending school. Kun, the facility's ambitious boss, dreams of buying a new car and a better life. Through the experience of these two families, this poignant film explores key issues on sustainability. As Kun transforms from an agricultural peasant to an industrial worker and Yijie's family migrates from the rural villages to coastal cities for job opportunities, the text is closely related to SDG 8 (Decent Work and Economic Growth), SDG 9 (Industry, Innovation, and Infrastructure), and SDG 10 (Reduced Inequalities). Moreover, the imported trash has degraded the natural landscape, ruined the local community, and made Kun's hometown inhabitable and unsustainable, thus relating to SDG 11 (Sustainable Cities and Communities) and SDG 3 (Good Health and Well-Being). In addition, a major narrative theme is the migrant girl's desire to go to school, so this text is closely related to SDG 4 (Quality Education) and SDG 5 (Gender Equality).

IV   A Guide to Instructors on How to Use This Textbook

This final section offers guidelines to instructors on how best to use this textbook and outlines best practices for course design and lesson planning.

1   *Course Design*

The best way to use this textbook is to progress in order through the parts and their respective chapters. A sample week-by-week syllabus for a semester-long class would thus be as follows:

Week 1—Overview of ESD and the UN SDGs (Introduction)
Week 2—Planet SDGs - Chapter 1
Week 3—Planet SDGs - Chapter 2
Week 4—Planet SDGs - Chapter 3
Week 5—Planet SDGs - Chapter 4
Week 6—People SDGs - Chapter 5
Week 7—People SDGs - Chapter 6
Week 8—People SDGs - Chapter 7
Week 9—People SDGs - Chapter 8
Week 10—Prosperity SDGs - Chapter 9
Week 11—Prosperity SDGs - Chapter 10
Week 12—Prosperity SDGs - Chapter 11
Week 13—Prosperity SDGs - Chapter 12
Week 14—Partnerships SDG and Final Projects
Week 15—Partnerships SDG and Final Projects

This approach makes the UN SDGs and the focus on planet, people, prosperity, and partnerships the main organizing framework for the course. Instructors teaching during a shorter time frame (quarter system or accelerated summer term) may want to teach only nine of the twelve texts by eliminating one chapter from each of the three parts.

Alternatively, an instructor might choose to employ a thematic grouping of texts around issues of: waste (Chapters 3, 5, 6, and 12); food and health (Chapters 4, 7, and 8); environmental challenges (Chapters 1, 2, and 10); and economic challenges (Chapters 9 and 11). While not the intended structure, this thematic approach could work particularly well for a team-taught course that brings together disciplinary experts from a variety of fields such as engineering, healthcare, environmental studies, business, and economics.

Finally, the course could be designed around geographical areas as follows: North America (Chapters 4 and 8); Latin America (Chapters 5, 7, and 10); Europe (Chapters 2 and 6); Asia

(Chapters 1, 9, 11, and 12); and Africa (Chapter 13). This structure, which adopts a place-based and culturally rooted approach to the 12 humanities texts, would work best for courses that are team-taught by cultural and regional experts from these chosen areas. Additionally, this grouping of texts would be appropriate for courses offered as part of the curriculum in cultural, global, or area studies. The challenge with this grouping, however, is that many chapters include authors and/or texts that cross national and regional borders. For instance, Chapter 8 traces the work of a US-based organization (Partners in Health) doing work abroad in Haiti, Peru, and Rwanda, while Chapter 3 examines a photographic series by a Belgian-Beninese artist whose selected work includes images taken in Senegal and Australia, and Chapter 2 treats a German photographer whose art installations combine images from various places around the globe that are most threatened by climate change. This approach also reveals inadequate treatment of Africa as a region, even though the textbook intentionally includes a variety of texts from the Global South. Instructors may thus wish to incorporate additional texts from Africa if using this geographical structure.

2   *Lesson Planning*

Each chapter (1–12) follows the same structure and is divided into seven sections:

- In Section I, "Text," the chapter's author provides basic information about the title and genre of the selected text as well as the author, artist, or director of the work and its publication date and country of origin. This section also anthologizes the two photographic collections in Chapters 2 and 3 and provides details on how instructors and students can access each of the additional 10 texts.
- Section II, "Context," gives relevant and detailed background information—social, cultural, historical, etc.—on the work to help instructors and students better understand the text.
- Section III, "Interpretation," includes a total of ten questions aimed at literary, filmic, or photographic analysis of the featured text. This section aims to build skills in textual analysis and humanities-centered interpretation.
- Section IV, titled "Planet-Focused Applications to SDGs 6, 7, 12, 13, 14, and 15" for the chapters in Part 1, "People-Focused Applications to SDGs 1, 2, 3, 4, and 5" for the chapters in Part 2, and "Prosperity-Focused Applications to SDGs 8, 9, 10, 11, and 16" for the chapters in Part 3, includes 15 specific questions about how the chapter's text intersects and engages with the specific SDGs. Within Section V, questions integrate the related SDGs in numerical order and culminate in a penultimate question involving a class debate on the application of the selected SDGs to the featured text and a final question asking how the global humanities text in the chapter not only reinforces or illuminates the principles underpinning the UN SDGs and the concept of sustainable development, but so too questions any inherent presuppositions, biases, shortcomings, flaws, or gaps in the UN SDG framework or in the notion of sustainable development.
- Section V, alternatively titled "Beyond Planet – Connections to SDGs on People, Prosperity, and Partnerships" for the chapters in Part 1, "Beyond People – Connections to SDGs on Planet, Prosperity, and Partnerships" for the chapters in Part 2, and "Beyond Prosperity – Connections to SDGs on Planet, People, and Partnerships" for the chapters in Part 3, facilitates connections by asking students to complete and discuss a chart that applies the chapter text to the other SDGs. For example, in a chapter from Part 1, instructors and students consider the relationship between the text and the "non-Planet" SDGs, which are 1, 2, 3, 4, 5, 8, 9, 10, 11, 16, and 17.
- Section VI, "From Global to Local: On a Personal Level," poses three questions that ask students to consider how the text relates to them on a personal level, relates to their local

environment, and elicits a response in them by changing their point of view and/or by moving them to action.

- Finally, Section VII, "Assignments," includes prompts for two research assignments, two writing assignments, and two creative assignments that relate to both the global humanities text and the most relevant SDGs.

Instructors and students are advised to progress through these seven sections in order.

It is important to recognize that this textbook has far more questions and activities than it is possible to complete in a given university-level course. Although the book is designed for a semester-long course of roughly 15 weeks, neither all chapter questions can be posed nor can all assignments be given. Instructors will need to pick and choose the most relevant and interesting questions and prompts for their course. Teachers from the humanities may wish to ask more questions from Section III, for example, while those from other disciplines may wish to focus more on the questions in Sections IV and V. Instructors will also want to avoid repetition and redundancy to keep the course fresh and engaging, so they might skip certain questions in one chapter, but discuss them in another chapter, based on which questions they deem most relevant to each assigned text. Additionally, they may wish to assign some sections for homework (I and II), while leaving others for in-class discussion (III, IV, and V), and others for post-class follow-up activities and assignments (VI and VII). Although most questions will be discussed orally in class through a combination of small group and whole class discussion, some questions can be assigned as written work in the form of homework, quizzes, reflection assignments, or online discussion threads. Similarly, instructors may wish to divide the class into groups according to the textbook's three parts (planet, people, and prosperity) or its 12 chapters (1–12) and only give an assignment from Section VII to the students responsible for that particular part or chapter, so that not all students will do all assignments. Since each chapter includes six assignments in Section VII, instructors will need to decide which one(s) are most useful for their students and how many should be assigned per chapter, unit, or course. Some instructors may choose to assign only the "research" prompts, while others will assign the "write" prompts, and still others will assign the "create" prompts. Alternatively, instructors may choose to let students decide which option—research, write, or create—is most appealing.

Finally, instructors will also have to decide on the most suitable approach to the "Think Global, Act Local: Partnerships and Projects (SDG 17)" concluding chapter. It is recommended that instructors first lead the class in a consideration of SDG 17 using the information provided in Section I, titled "Summary of SDG 17: Partnerships for the Goals." Next, instructors should facilitate a discussion of question 1 and question 3 (Part A only) from Section II, titled "Partnerships and Projects: Global Humanities Texts." Lastly, instructors should choose one or two of the final projects from the eight options presented in Sections 2 and 3 to assign to students. Final project options include:

- Proposing a new organizational structure for this textbook using a different SDG grouping model and the same 12 global humanities texts;
- Designing a curricular development project using selected ESD themes;
- Developing a global partnership to address a selected issue of importance to two or more featured authors, artists, or directors;
- Analyzing published critiques of the UN SDGs;
- Writing a new textbook chapter based on a selected local humanities text;
- Exploring a local sustainability challenge and creating a new humanities text;

- Researching a local educational effort that advances the SDGs;
- Developing a course lesson about a local partnership that advances the SDGs.

Alternatively, instructors could allow students to choose the final project option(s). Final projects are designed to be completed in groups, although individual completion is possible. Instructors should allow for class time for final project presentations, as this contributes to students' overall learning and promotes end-of-course reflection and dialogue.

Notes

1 In the 2023 article "From Global Studies to Global Humanities," Stefan Amirell maps out the history of the humanities, global studies, and the global humanities. This section of the "Introduction" is greatly indebted to his illuminating article.
2 Fernando Contreras Castro's novel *Única Looking at the Sea* is the only text included in this book that was not published in the 2000s. The decision to include this novel is based on the fact that the first English translation appeared in 2017, making the book only recently accessible to an English-speaking audience. All other global humanities texts are from the current millennium.

Works Cited

Agenda 21: Programme of Action for Sustainable Development. United Nations Sustainable Development, https://sustainabledevelopment.un.org/content/documents/Agenda21.pdf. Accessed May 1, 2023.

Amirell, Stefan. "From Global Studies to Global Humanities." *Humanities*, vol. 12.2, no. 27, 2023, pp. 1–14.

"A New Humanities Agenda for the 21st Century: Outcome Document of the 2017 World Humanities Conference." *The International Council for Philosophy and Human Sciences*, http://www.cipsh.net/web/channel-112.htm. Accessed May 1, 2023.

Denecke, Wiebke. "Comparative Global Humanities Now." *Journal of World Literature*, vol. 6, no. 4, 2021, pp. 479–508.

"Education for Sustainable Development for 2030 Toolbox." UNESCO Sustainable Development, https://en.unesco.org/themes/education-sustainable-development/toolbox. Accessed May 1, 2023.

"Global Citizenship Education." United Nations: Academic Impact, https://www.un.org/en/academic-impact/page/global-citizenship-education. Accessed May 1, 2023.

Lewis, Rosanna. "The Missing Pillar—Culture's Contribution to the UN Sustainable Development Goals." *British Council, Our Stories*, https://www.britishcouncil.org/arts/culture-development/our-stories/the-missing-pillar-sdgs. Accessed May 1, 2023.

McKenzie, A. D. "Humanities to the Rescue of Sustainability." *SDGs for All*, https://www.sdgsforall.net/index.php/goal-16/389-humanities-to-the-rescue-of-sustainability. Accessed May 1, 2023.

Rutter, Michael Patrick and Steven Mintz. "Internationalizing the Humanities: Can the Humanities' Future Be Global and Comparative." *Inside Higher Ed Opinions: Blogs*, 12 Oct. 2022, https://www.insidehighered.com/blogs/higher-ed-gamma/internationalizing-humanities. Accessed May 1, 2023.

The Future We Want. United Nations, https://www.un.org/disabilities/documents/rio20_outcome_document_complete.pdf. Accessed May 1, 2023."The 17 Goals." *United Nations Department of Economic and Social Affairs: Sustainable Development*, https://sdgs.un.org/goals. Accessed May 1, 2023.

"The Global Action Programme on ESD." *UNESCO Global Action Programme on Education for Sustainable Development: Information Folder*, May 2018, https://unesdoc.unesco.org/ark:/48223/pf0000246270. Accessed May 1, 2023.

"The Global Goals: 4." *The Global Goals*, https://www.globalgoals.org/goals/4-quality-education/. Accessed May 1, 2023.

"The Hangzhou Declaration: Placing Culture at the Heart of Sustainable Development Policies." *International Congress "Culture: Key to Sustainable Development,"* 2013, https://unesdoc.unesco.org/ark:/48223/pf0000221238. Accessed May 1, 2023.

"The Missing Pillar: Culture's Contribution to the UN Sustainable Development Goals." *British Council*, https://www.britishcouncil.org/arts/culture-development/our-stories/the-missing-pillar-sdgs. Accessed May 1, 2023.

"The Muscat Agreement." *UNESCO Global Education for All Meeting, 2014 GEM Final Statement*, https://unesdoc.unesco.org/ark:/48223/pf0000228122. Accessed May 1, 2023.

"The UN Sustainable Development Goals (SDGs): Contributions from the Humanities, A Research Report." *University College London Institute of Advanced Studies*, https://www.ucl.ac.uk/institute-of-advanced-studies/sites/institute_of_advanced_studies/files/the_un_sustainable_development_goals_220207.pdf. Accessed May 1, 2023.

Transforming Our World: The 2030 Agenda for Sustainable Development. United Nations Department of Economic and Social Affairs: Sustainable Development, https://sdgs.un.org/2030agenda. Accessed May 1, 2023.

"UN Decade of ESD." *UNESCO: Education for Sustainable Development*, https://en.unesco.org/themes/education-sustainable-development/what-is-esd/un-decade-of-esd. Accessed May 1, 2023.

"We Can End Poverty: Millennium Development Goals and Beyond 2015." *United Nations*, https://www.un.org/millenniumgoals/. Accessed May 1, 2023.

"What Are the Sustainable Development Goals?" *Focus 2030: Data, Innovation, Development*, 2 Sept. 2019, https://focus2030.org/What-are-the-Sustainable-Development-Goals#:~:text=The%20UN%20Sustainable%20Development%20Goals,development%20actors%20around%20the%20world. Accessed May 1, 2023.

Woodbridge, Michael. "From MDGs to SDGs: What Are the Sustainable Development Goals?" *ICLEI Briefing Sheet, Urban Issues*, no. 1, 2015, pp. 1–4.

Zhang, YuYing and Peng Wang. "Detecting the Historical Roots of Education for Sustainable Development (ESD): A Bibliometric Analysis." *International Journal of Sustainability in Higher Education*, vol. 23, no. 3, 2022, pp. 478–502.

Part I

Planet

Relating Global Humanities Texts to
UN SDGs 6, 7, 12, 13, 14, and 15

1 Aya Hanabusa's *Holy Island*

Nuclear Power and Political Resistance in Iwaishima, Japan

Amanda Weiss

I Text

Title	*Holy Island*
Genre	Documentary
Director	Director Aya Hanabusa was born in 1974 in Tokyo, Japan. A graduate of Jiyu Gakuen, a historic Christian academy famed for its Frank Lloyd Wright-designed "House of Tomorrow," Hanabusa worked at documentary production company Pole Pole Times before becoming a freelance filmmaker. Her first film, *Holy Island* (Hōri no shima, 2010), documents Iwaishima residents' decades-long resistance to the Kaminoseki Nuclear Power Plant Project. The film won Best Documentary at the 2012 Sicily Environmental Film Festival (SiciliaAmbiente). Hanabusa's work bears witness to the struggles of people at the margins of society: the elderly, the vulnerable, and the unseen.
Year	2010
Country	Japan

Holy Island (Hōri no shima, 2010) is a Japanese documentary about nuclear resistance on Iwaishima (Iwai Island) in Western Japan. For decades, Iwaishima residents have resisted Chugoku Electric's Kaminoseki Nuclear Power Plant Project, which aims to build a nuclear power plant about 2 miles from the island. The film documents the daily lives and political resistance of Iwaishima's 500 residents, who not only face political challenges but also the pressures of an aging and declining population whose political stance and relationship to the land is undermined by the trend toward a materialistic capitalist and urban society. This chapter explores both the specific Iwaishima case and the wider social and historical issues framing this battle. Note: the film introduces subjects using the Japanese name order of family name followed by given name, e.g. "Hanabusa Aya" instead of "Aya Hanabusa." This text follows the same naming conventions used in the film.

To watch the documentary film *Holy Island*, please purchase from Zakka Films at https://www.zakkafilms.com/product/holy-island/.

II Context

Iwaishima Island is located in the westernmost part of the Seto Inland Sea on a body of water referred to as the Suo Nada. Historically, this island stood at the center of many important maritime travel and trade routes, particularly between southern Honshu and northern Kyushu, two of Japan's major islands. The island appeared earliest in the famous 8th-century Classical Japanese poetry collection, the Man'yōshū, and was known as a site for kami (divine spirits) who prayed

DOI: 10.4324/9781003388869-3

for the safety of ships. As portrayed in the film, a vessel from Imi (Kyushu) was shipwrecked on Iwaishima and rescued by the islanders. The Imi people gave the islanders barley seeds and a kami named Kōjin, who is an agricultural deity. Every four years, they commemorate this event in a famous Shintō ritual called the Kanmai (god dance).

While Iwaishima reached a peak population of 5,000 people in the immediate postwar period, it currently has less than 500 residents, the majority of whom are 65 and older. This demographic change reflects a widespread trend toward rural population loss and an aging society affecting many regions in Japan. The coastline of Iwaishima is very steep, so the majority of homes are on a more gradual slope on the eastern side. Mount Nagami stands at 357 meters tall at the center of the island. The island's main industry is fishing, with residents relying on sea bream, snapper, horse mackerel, kingfish, squid, and yellowtail. Agriculture is also important to the residents, who grow oranges, loquats, biwa, and rice, among other crops.

In 1982, Chugoku Electric, or CEPCO, announced the building of a nuclear power plant in nearby Kaminoseki. While the project was strongly supported by Kaminoseki mayor Katayama Hideyuki, subsequent mayors, the majority of local people and politicians, and national policy, it was vigorously opposed by over 90% of the villagers on Iwaishima Island. Their main concerns were the land filling of Tanoura Bay and the discharge of chloride into the water, not to mention the potential danger of catastrophic nuclear accidents. While the municipal government of Kaminoseki has received billions of yen from the Japanese government for welcoming nuclear plants—in addition to billions of yen in "gifts" from CEPCO—Iwaishima fishermen have rejected these payments (Ankei). Since 1982, Iwaishima residents have conducted over 1,000 protests, which include both Monday night protests on the island and special protests in response to CEPCO and Kaminoseki governmental actions. These were documented in two films in 2010: Aya Hanabusa's *Holy Island* and Hitomi Kamanaka's *Ashes to Honey: A Search for Energy Independence in Sweden and Japan*.

Hanabusa's film documents the struggles and daily lives of the Iwaishima residents as a fly on the wall with occasional expository explanations from the narrator. She documents the villagers as they fish, harvest, and plant on the island, highlighting their daily interaction with the land and sea. She also follows them as they engage in special protests against votes in Kaminoseki, block construction with their boats, and participate in special events on the island like a school entrance ceremony and a nightly get-together of elderly island residents.

The film also highlights the particular issues facing Japanese society when it comes to the question of nuclear power. Nuclear energy is controversial in Japan, despite being viewed by some experts as a form of clean and sustainable energy. This is in part because nuclear power is tied to nuclear weapons in Japanese discourse, with both associated with radiation, contamination, and catastrophic destruction. Japan's singular experience of Hiroshima and Nagasaki has shaped this perception, as Japan is the only country in the world to experience firsthand the environmental, physical, and social devastation of the atomic bomb. The effects of radiation experienced by hibakusha (victims of the bombings), who suffered from protracted consequences that included leukemia, cataracts, burns, keloid scars, and social effects like discrimination and ostracism, have left a deep and lingering social trauma in Japanese society. Moreover, further nuclear disasters like the Castle Bravo test that poisoned the crew of the Lucky Dragon 5 in 1954, the Three Mile Island Accident, and Chernobyl further raised concerns about the safety of nuclear energy, with the islanders forming the No Nukes Yamaguchi Network in 1987 one year after the Chernobyl accident. Islander resistance to nuclear power is also informed by their personal experiences working within nuclear power plants, such as carpenter Hashimoto Hisao's recollections of safety issues at the Fukui Power Plant on Honshu (01:18:35). Notably, the film was released right before the March 2011 Tohoku earthquake and tsunami that triggered 14-meter-tall waves that damaged the plant and caused a level seven International Nuclear Event Scale (the same as Chernobyl).

The majority of the islanders came of age during Japan's tumultuous postwar era, a highly dynamic time socially, economically, and politically. As one islander highlights, "[t]hose born before and during the war have strong convictions. We lived through hard times, so we're grateful for what we have" (01:28:19). The Iwaishima generation grew up in the aftermath of World War II, a period of deprivation and suffering focused on economic reconstruction and political change. They entered adulthood in the 1960s and 1970s, an era that saw strong political resistance to war and imperialism, such as widespread protests against the US-Japan Security Treaty and the Vietnam War. This era also saw the birth of the environmental movement, as unbridled economic development wrought unexpected environmental destruction. People who grew up during that era are thus more resistant to "national policy" like nuclear power, because they have seen unquestioned "national policy" lead to environmental destruction and war.

Culturally, while Japan has been portrayed as a world "in harmony with nature," an image often conflated with images of cherry blossoms, bonsai, and the films of Studio Ghibli, the reality is more complex (Saito 239). On the one hand, indigenous beliefs and Shintō emphasize the connection between man and nature, such as the emphasis on kami (sacred spirits) being present in the natural world. The connection between Japanese aesthetics and appreciation of nature has also long been emphasized, such as how the brief flowering of the cherry blossom is the epitome of the concept of mono no aware, or the pathos of things (Prusinski 27–28). This image was cemented in the animations of Miyazaki, whose films *My Neighbor Totoro* (1988) and *Princess Mononoke* (1997) are seen as quintessential depictions of the Japanese perception of kami and of nature. Yet, even as Japanese society has a long history of emphasizing nature through religion, poetry, design, architecture, and food, the desire for rapid economic growth means that there has been rampant deforestation since preindustrial times (Totman).

As mentioned above, in the postwar era, industrial pollution of the water, land, and air led to the Four Big Pollution Diseases, which citizens tried and failed to address for decades (Stolz). This has also contributed to some of the resistance of Iwaishima residents, who are aware of this history and the implications: that the government and corporations are not always on the side of local people or the environment. Due to these struggles, as well as the strengthening of the American environmentalist movement in the 1960s in response to the release of Rachel Carson's *Silent Spring*, the Japanese environmentalist movement emerged alongside the struggles of the Minamata movement and during the general struggles of the Vietnam War (Avenell).

Contemporary Japanese and international conservation movements have adopted concepts from preindustrial Japan like "satoyama" to encourage a more harmonious relationship between man and nature, arguing that borderland regions that feature the interaction of man and flora/fauna in productive ways can ultimately serve as a path forward (Takeuchi). "Satoyama" is described as a traditional landscape in Japanese society, a space between overbearing human development and unbridled nature. Traditionally "satoyama" referred to the "forests near the villages" (Indrawan et al.), a space where man and nature interact in mutually beneficial ways. These days, it is characterized as a harmonious approach to nature, wherein "traditional ecological knowledge" is integrated and where balance is a crucial part of the human intervention. In recent years, the concept of "satoumi" (land next to the sea) has also emerged as crucial to managing coastal biodiversity as well (Berque and Matsuda).

Holy Island is most directly connected to UN SDG 6 (Clean Water and Sanitation), as the residents of Iwaishima are concerned about the potential pollution of Japan's Inland Sea. As they declare in the film, "Iwaishima is an island, so we can only work in the sea and the hills . . . That's all the more reason we can't allow the sea to be polluted. The sea is really a treasure to us" (01:31:59). This chapter also connects to Life Below Water (SDG 14), as the people of Iwaishima fear the nuclear project's potentially devastating impact on the ocean surrounding their home. The families on Iwaishima largely rely on fishing, and any impact on the sea life could prove disastrous to both their livelihood and their health. SDG 14 is also central to their identity: Iwaishima is known for a nearly millennia-old ceremonial fishing dance, which was recently revived to unite the island in their resistance to the nuclear plant project. Third, this unit connects to Life on Land (SDG 15), as the proposed nuclear project site directly threatens the biodiversity of the Seto Inland Sea, described by some experts as the region's "biodiversity hotspot" (Ankei). The people of the island further rely on organic produce grown on the island, such as rice, loquat, mandarin oranges, sweet potatoes, daikon, and kokko (a type of kiwi).

Hanabusa's film is connected to bias toward action, as *Holy Island* documents the determined political action of the citizens of Iwaishima. Through their decades of resistance, they have strived to protect the island and the sea for future generations.

III   Interpretation

1   Iwaishima is usually written in Japanese as "祝島" with the kanji "祝" pronounced as "Iwai" and meaning to praise, celebrate, or pray. In the title page of the documentary (see Figure 1.1), the director has marked the pronunciation as "hōri" (which means "Shinto priest," but which also sounds like the English term "holy") and added the general modifier "no." This indicates that "iwai" is now to be read "hōri," transforming the reading of Iwaishima from "Celebration Island" to either "Shinto Priest's Island" or "Holy Island."

Figure 1.1 Film still of the title page of the documentary film *Holy Island*, Hōri no shima (00:07:39).

Why might this wording change be significant? Consider the following definitions of the term holy: (1) "declared sacred by religious use or authority," (2) "having a spiritually pure quality," or (3) "entitled to worship or veneration" ("Holy"). Discuss the differences between the two possible translations of Iwaishima as "Celebration Island" or "Holy Island." Which do you prefer? Why? Which is more accurate of the place depicted in the documentary?

2 *Holy Island* begins with the following quotation from Takagi Jinzaburo (1938–2000), former associate professor of nuclear chemistry at Tokyo Metropolitan University and co-founder of the Citizens' Nuclear Information Center: "Civilization was created by living things over an eternity of 3.5 billion years. Humans are exceedingly late arrivals. The development of nuclear reactors and other creations of a barbarous culture, ill-suited to the natural world, is a manifestation of this late arrival" (00:00:14). What do you think about this citation? Do you agree or disagree with Takagi? Why do you think the filmmaker chose to start the film with this quotation? Was this an effective choice?

3 Why are the islanders of Iwaishima so strongly opposed to the nuclear power plant? How does their relationship to the land and sea contribute to their resistance? Consider Figures 1.2 and 1.3.

Figure 1.2 Film still of Iwaishima residents protesting the building of the Kaminoseki nuclear power plant (00:02:20). The signs read "Don't destroy peaceful sea and nature" and "Live in harmony with nature and be self-reliant."

Now examine Figure 1.4. Compare and contrast the Iwaishima residents and the Chugoku Electric employees in terms of generation, perspective, and approach.

What do the Chugoku Electric people want? What do the Iwaishima people want? Who is most effective in making their voice heard?

4 The filmmaker does not depict the pro-nuclear power camp in detail. Why do you think she makes this choice? Was this an effective filmmaking choice? Who do you think would be in favor of the nuclear power plant, and why?

5 There are many different approaches to documentary filmmaking styles. Consider the following approaches as defined by Nichols below (22–23):

- Poetic—focus on "tonal qualities," visual and aural elements, evocative description
- Observational—filmmaker observes but does not interact with subjects, emphasis on the everyday experiences of the subjects
- Participatory—emphasis on the participation of filmmaker and interaction between filmmaker and subjects
- Reflexive—reflects on the process of documentary filmmaking itself

- Expository—story presents an argument or takes a position, narrative structured as problem/solution, filmmaker uses film/editing to provide evidence

What mode or modes does Director Hanabusa employ in *Holy Island*? Was this an effective choice? If you were to explore this topic, would you use the same mode of documentary film-making? Why or why not?

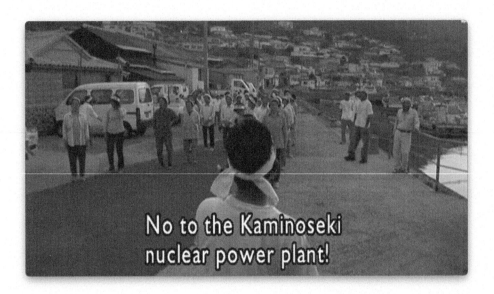

Figure 1.3 Film still of the islanders participating in their weekly Monday night protest on the island (00:42:09).

Figure 1.4 Film still of the Iwaishima residents blocking construction and giving speeches on their boats as the Chugoku Electric employees give their speeches from their boats (01:12:21).

The film is narrated by actor Saito Tomoko rather than director Hanabusa. In addition, the director's voice is rarely heard asking questions in the film, though we often hear the subjects responding to questions. How do these choices shape the role of the narrator in the film? What does this suggest to you about the Hanabusa's intent? What mode of documentary film-making is she employing by making these choices?

Can a documentary capture "truth"? Is a documentary "truer" than a narrative film? Does Hanabusa's film feel "true" to you?

6   Hanabusa focuses on a few specific villagers, following them for several scenes and return-ing to them periodically. For example, one of her main subjects is Shomoto-san, who fishes with a single line and has done it for many years. Why do you think she chose to follow this particular fisherman? What does this method and philosophy suggest to you about the relationship of the islanders to the sea and island? In addition to Shomoto-san, Taira-san, and Takebayashi-san, pick two more subjects such as Shomoto Emiko, Shimizu Toshiyasu, Hashimoto Hisao, Hashimoto Noriko, Ebesu Satoshi, Ito Fumiko, etc. and fill out the chart below. Who does Hanabusa follow and why? Also, why does she switch back and forth between subjects rather than following one villager at a time? What does her approach sug-gest about the relationships of the subjects?

Subject	Why does Hanabusa follow this subject?	Was this effective? Why or why not?
1 Shomoto Eiichi		
2 Taira Manji		
3 Takebayashi Tamiko		
4 Your choice		
5 Your choice		

7   What does the film still below (see Figure 1.5) suggest about Iwaishima community members? Why does Hanabusa devote two scenes to depicting this group of friends? Do you think this is a regular occurrence in contemporary Japanese society? What other scenes does she feature of the islanders' community, and why do you think she makes this choice? What is she trying to show the audience about Iwaishima? Is she making a larger point about Japan's aging society?

Figure 1.5 Film still of a nightly meeting of friends on Iwaishima, ongoing for decades, in which they sit in a traditional tatami room with their legs under a kotatsu (heated table) (01:36:41).

8 At the end of the film, rice farmer Taira Manji says: "Paddies return to nature in the course of time" (01:29:23). What does this reveal about Taira-san's perception of nature, and how does this contrast to Western concepts such as man as a "steward" of nature? What does this suggest about how the villagers see their relationship to nature in terms of time? Look at Figures 1.6 and 1.7. Why is Taira-san carving this saying—"Once more today/Clearing the fallen snow/I dig with joy/For my offspring"—on the stone (01:41:16)? What does this suggest about the perspective of Iwaishima residents in terms of their relationship to the land and their duty to future generations? What does this lesson mean to you?

9 How does the film touch on the following themes: (1) modernization versus traditional ways of life; (2) urbanization and its impact on rural areas; and (3) consumption versus sustainability? What is the film's attitude toward or stance on these topics? Examine the following list of citations from the film and discuss how they relate to these three themes:

- "Just because it's legal doesn't make it right" (01:14:24).
- "The most basic thing for humans to defend is nature. It's not money, right?" (01:17:09).
- "For 28 years, they have refused to accept compensation for their fishing rights" (00:01:20).
- Interviewer: "What does sea mean to you?" Tamiko-san: "It's our life. Living here, it's allowed us to thrive. We couldn't live here without the sea. With the sea and the hills, we can produce all we need to feed ourselves. We have to defend the beautiful sea and hills for our kids and grandkids. It's still beautiful because it's been defended for generations. Our heartfelt desire is to leave it to future generations" (01:24:07).

10 The film was released in 2010, one year before the March 2011 Fukushima Daiichi Nuclear Power Plant Disaster. The Fukushima accident released iodine-131 and caesium-137 into the atmosphere, the majority of which ended up in the Pacific Ocean. The coastal areas of Fukushima are most at risk due to the surface water carrying pollutants from contaminated

Figure 1.6 Film still of a close-up of Taira-san carving into a rock (00:50:28).

Figure 1.7 Film still of Taira-san's rock carving on Iwaishima (01:41:16).

soil and due to the sensitivity of organisms to caesium pollution. In many ways, Fukushima brought to light the most catastrophic concerns of the Iwaishima residents, reviving Iwaishima resistance to the Kaminoseki Power Plant. What do you think happened to public opinion after the disaster? How might this have changed in the years since?

IV   Planet-Focused Applications to SDGs 6, 7, 12, 13, 14, and 15

1   SDG 6 focuses on Clean Water and Sanitation. How are the islanders particularly focused on Target 6.3 (reduce pollution) and 6.6 ("protect and restore water-related ecosystems") ("Goal 6")? Are there other targets that they are promoting?

2   Postwar Japan saw several highly publicized water pollution cases. With your partner, look up the Four Big Pollution Diseases of Japan: Yokkaichi Asthma, Itai-Itai Disease, Minamata Disease, and Niigata Minamata Disease. When did these happen, what were the symptoms of each disease, what was the cause, which company caused it, and when did the company stop polluting? How many of these diseases were caused by water pollution (SDG 6)?

3   SDG 7 focuses on "Affordable and Clean Energy," with an emphasis on sustainable energy and energy efficiency ("Goal 7"). How might proponents of nuclear energy argue that the Kaminoseki Plant in fact promotes SDG 7? How might the people of Iwaishima respond?

4   How do the residents of Iwaishima attempt to promote SDG 12 ("Ensure sustainable consumption and production patterns") in their daily lives ("Goal 12")? For example, how might we read the following folk wisdom as emblematic of SDG 12:

- "The princess in the undersea palace decides how much we catch every day" (00:10:14)
- "If you have rice, you will always get by" (00:19:18)
- "I was fed and raised, thanks to the paddies Grandfather built. Then they fed and raised my children and grandchildren. We've never bought rice at the store" (01:27:10)?

Are there other scenes, quotations, traditions, or behaviors from the islanders that support SDG 12?

5   Compare and contrast your consumption patterns to those of the islanders by completing the SDG 12 Targets and Indicators chart below ("Goal 12"). After completing this chart, discuss your answers with your partner. Where are you similar, and where are you different? Do you think you could live like the islanders? Why or why not?

SDG 12 targets and indicators		
SGD 12 targets	*Iwaishima residents*	*You*
Sustainably manage and efficiently use natural resources (12.2)		
Avoid or reduce food waste and food loss (12.3)		
Reduce the release of waste into the air, water, and soil (12.4)		
Reduce waste generation through prevention, reduction, recycling, and reuse (12.5)		
Promote lifestyles in harmony with nature (12.8)		

6   Many UN experts argue that objectives to curb emissions and global warming will fail without the adoption of nuclear power. Therefore, the use of nuclear power in many ways promotes SDG 13 ("Take urgent action to combat climate change and its impacts") ("Sustainable Development Goal 13"). Do the efforts of the villagers and their lifestyle combat climate change, and if so, how?

7   If you were a representative of Chugoku Electric, how would you prove that nuclear energy is sustainable and supports SDG 13? What kinds of data would you cite to support this counterargument? How might the islanders, drawing from their cultural and historical perspective, respond? What about the islander who had previously worked as a carpenter in a nuclear power plant? In groups, complete the table below.

Chugoku electric	*Iwaishima resident*
Example: Nuclear energy is a low-carbon energy source that does not contribute to global warming.	*Response:* While nuclear energy does not produce carbon dioxide, it produces other forms of waste (warm chlorine water) that are detrimental to biodiversity.
Point 1:	Response:
Point 2:	Response:
Point 3:	Response:

8 The islanders are also deeply concerned by SDG 14 ("Conserve and sustainably use the oceans, seas and marine resources for sustainable development") ("Goal 14"). How does the prolonged focus on Shomoto Eiichi-san, who fishes with a single line, relate to SDG 14 (see Figure 1.8)?

Figure 1.8 Film still of Shomoto-san reflecting on seas and sustainability on his boat (01:30:49).

Look at the selected targets for SDG 14 listed in the chart below ("Goal 14"). For each row, choose one scene that best represents the target. Briefly note the scene's timecode and then describe how it connects to each target.

9 SDG 15 focuses on sustainable terrestrial ecosystems and biodiversity. How is this a central concern for the villagers? How do they promote biodiversity in their interaction with the island itself? In general, islands and inland seas tend to be central hubs for endemic

(limited to a specific geographic region) and vulnerable biodiversity. Due to the efforts of the Iwaishima residents, the sea in their region of the Suo-nada Sea (the western part of the Seto Inland Sea) has remained well-conserved, with the area right near the proposed Kaminoseki Nuclear Power Plant "the best-conserved shallow water maritime biodiversity in Japan" (Ankei). What do these efforts suggest about the success of their stewardship? With your partner, make a list of ways we can protect biodiversity as community members and as individuals. Feel free to use the internet to research other potential ideas. Afterward, discuss: what are the most effective ways to protect biodiversity?

Target	Timecode	How does this scene connect to this target or indicator?
Prevent and reduce marine pollution (14.1)		
Sustainably manage and protect marine and coastal ecosystems (14.2)		
Regulate destructive fishing practices (14.4)		
Provide access for small-scale artisanal fishers to marine resources and markets (14.b)		

Ways to protect biodiversity
1 Resist construction efforts that introduce wastewater into the environment.
2
3
4
5
6
7
8
9
10

10 Japanese culture values the concepts of "satoyama" (the space between human settlement and land where nature and human co-exist) and "satoumi" (the space between human settlement and ocean where nature and human co-exist). Please refer to the Context section for more details on these two terms. Examine Figures 1.9 and 1.10, film stills from *Holy Island*.
   How are these film stills emblematic of the concepts of "satoyama" and "satoumi"? What does the documentary suggest about the need for coexistence between humans and nature as well as the desired or ideal interrelation between land and ocean? Are there other scenes from the documentary that also represent these two concepts?

11 The English translation in the subtitles for Holy Island frequently uses the word "nuke" to translate the terms "genpatsu" (nuclear power) and "genshiryoku' (atomic energy"). Why do you think the filmmaker makes this choice in translating these words this way? Is it a rhetorical strategy? Does this suggest that the islanders/villagers see the power plant as a form or means of destruction?

Figure 1.9 Film still depicting Taira Manji working on a rice paddy, an area that might be referred to as the "satoyama" (01:06:15).

Figure 1.10 Film still depicting Tamiko-san, the island's only female fisherperson, searching for sea urchins in the coastal waters, an area that might be referred to as the "satoumi" (00:44:18).

12 Looking at SDGs 6, 7, 12, 13, 14, and 15, with which of these SDGs are the residents of Iwaishima most concerned? What actions are they taking to address that SDG? Which SDG are you most concerned with? What actions are you taking to address this SDG? If none, what actions can you take to address that SDG?

Iwaishima residents	*You*
Most Important SDG to the Iwaishima Residents:	Most Important SDG to you:
Action 1:	Action 1:
Action 2:	Action 2:
Action 3:	Action 3:

13 Shinto, the indigenous religion of Japan, includes a set of beliefs and practices that emphasizes man's relationship to divine nature. Some important concepts from Shinto include the veneration of nature as a force more powerful than man (man as the child of nature); "kami," or the belief in supernatural spirits or deities who are often connected to or emblematic of natural sites; and "musubi," the ties of the universe that bind us all together and foster creation. Did you note any scenes within *Holy Island* that reveal a Shinto relationship with nature? If so, explain. How might Shinto concepts of nature (kami, musubi, man as part of nature) contribute to the promotion of the SDGs? Which SDGs would it promote, and why?

14 Divide the class into six groups and assign one of the SDGs from Unit 1 (6, 7, 12, 13, 14, or 15) to each group. Each group will then prepare arguments for a debate in which they maintain that their assigned SDG is the most relevant or central to Aya Hanabusa's *Holy Island*. (The instructor of the course will decide on the format and length of the debate and facilitate a follow-up discussion with the class upon conclusion of the debate.)

15 Does Hanabusa's *Holy Island* documentary only reinforce and illuminate the principles underpinning the UN SDGs and the concept of sustainable development, or does it question any inherent presuppositions, biases, shortcomings, flaws, or gaps in the UN SDG framework or in the notion of sustainable development? Explain with details from the film. Does the film suggest that the term "sustainable development" is ultimately an oxymoron? How does this film question the economic and development goals of the SDGs?

V   Beyond the Planet—Connections to SDGs on People, Prosperity, and Partnerships

Beyond SDGs 6, 7, 12, 13, 14, and 15, what additional SDGs are addressed by Aya Hanabusa in *Holy Island*? Complete the table below with your ideas. Then compare and contrast your ideas with a classmate.

SDGs:	*Does Hanabusa's* Holy Island *connect with additional SDGs? If so, which ones and how?*

SDG 1 No Poverty

SDG 2 Zero Hunger

SDG 3 Good Health and Well Being

SDG 4 Quality Education

SDG 5 Gender Equality

SDG 8 Decent Work and Economic Growth

SDG 9 Industry, Innovation, and Infrastructure

SDG 10 Reduced Inequalities

SDG 11 Sustainable Cities and Communities

SDG 16 Peace, Justice, and Strong Institutions

SDG 17 Partnerships for the Goals

VI   From Global to Local: On a Personal Level

1 How do you relate personally to Hanabusa's *Holy Island*? Explain in detail how your own life experiences or personal beliefs intersect with the main ideas and themes of the featured work in this chapter.
2 How does Hanabusa's documentary relate to your local environment? Explain the global-local connection between *Holy Island* and your home or current residence. What place-based considerations permit or prevent the application of the text to your geographical location?
3 What type of response did Hanabusa's *Holy Island* elicit in you? Are you moved to action? Have your viewpoints or attitudes changed? Explain.

VII   Assignments

1   Research

1 Individually or in groups, research these nuclear issues in Japan:

- 1945 atomic bombing of Hiroshima
- 1945 atomic bombing of Nagasaki
- 1954 Lucky Dragon incident
- Sadako Sasaki (atomic bomb survivor)
- *Godzilla* (1954 film)
- 2011 Fukushima Daiichi nuclear disaster
- Barefoot Gen (character from a manga/anime)
- hibakusha
- black rain

Be sure to answer the following questions for each assigned issue:
- What is the historical context of the event/person/work?
- What was its aftermath or wider implication, especially in terms of its impact on Japanese society?
- How might this event/person/work have informed current Japanese attitudes toward and perceptions of nuclear power?

(The instructor of the course will determine the mode of presentation and delivery—oral presentation, written report, etc.—for this research assignment.)

2 The island's fields might be what we call the "satoyama" and its bays the "satoumi," or land and coastal regions where humans have interacted with and shaped ecosystems. These two concepts emphasize the human–nature interaction rather than humans acting over or owning nature. Since the 1980s and 1990s, the satoyama conservation movement emerged as a new perspective focused on fostering a harmonious human-nature relationship. Individually or in groups, watch the NHK/National Geographic documentary *Satoyama: Japan's Secret Water Garden* (Alternatively, find any video introducing the concept of "satoyama"). How does this documentary define "satoyama"? Did you see a location that was like satoyama in *Holy Island*? What was the role of the human in the "satoyama" of the documentary? Based on what you know about "satoyama," what is "satoumi," and what does "satoumi" look like in *Holy Island*? (The instructor of the course will determine the mode of presentation and delivery—oral presentation, written report, and photo essay—for this research assignment.)

2 *Write*

1 Letter to/from the Mayor. For this activity, the class will be divided into two perspectives. Write a letter based on one of the following prompts:

a Imagine you are a fisherman from Iwaishima writing a letter to the mayor, a politician famous for supporting the nuclear power plant project for over 20 years. State your case, highlighting the importance of SDGs 6, 7, and 12–15.

b Imagine you are the mayor of Kaminoseki. Write a letter to the Iwaishima residents, highlighting the importance of the plant. Cite any SDGs that you feel the plant supports and try to assuage their concerns.

(The instructor of the course will determine the appropriate length for this writing assignment.)

2 Studio Ghibli is famous for exploring the relationship between man and nature through sensitive films that feature kami, forests, animism, and Shintoism, among other natural themes. In recent years, emerging directors like Hosoda Mamoru and Shinkai Makoto have also developed a reputation for making films about the natural world. Select one animated film from the list below and analyze how it connects to the SDGs and/or to Japanese perceptions of nature. For instance, how does the figure of Totoro represent the Shinto relationship between man and animal (or man and environment) in *My Neighbor Totoro*? What kind of argument does the film *Ponyo* make about SDG 6, and how do the aesthetics of the film help to make that argument? Film List:

My Neighbor Totoro (1988, dir. Miyazaki Hayao)
Pom Poko (1994, dir. Takahata Isao)
Spirited Away (2001, dir. Miyazaki Hayao)
Ponyo (2008, dir. Miyazaki Hayao)
Wolf Children (2012, dir. Hosoda Mamoru)
The Garden of Words (2013, dir. Shinkai Makoto)

The Boy and the Beast (2015, dir. Hosoda Mamoru)
Weathering with You (2019, dir. Hosoda Mamoru)

(The instructor of the course will determine the appropriate length for this writing assignment.)

3   Create

1   Individually or in groups, take a picture of an area you would call "satoyama" or "satoumi." Introduce the image to the class and explain the following:

- the context of the image, such as where you took it and when;
- how you defined "satoyama" or "satoumi";
- why do you feel this image exemplifies either "satoyama" or "satoumi";
- how the area you depicted supports SDG 6, 14, and/or 15.

(The instructor of the course will determine the mode of presentation and delivery for this creative assignment.)

2   Working together in teams, make a brief documentary showing the side that Hanabusa does not depict—the islanders in favor of the nuclear power plant, the employees of Chugoku Electric, the mayor of Kaminoseki, et al. Try to make this documentary as persuasive as possible using whichever documentary mode (expository, poetic, reflexive, etc.) you prefer. Along with the film, submit an artist statement. Your statement should describe: the documentary mode you selected and why; the perspectives you presented and why; and whether or not you think this was ultimately as persuasive as Hanabusa's film and why or why not. How might they appeal to the SDGs to support their claim?

(The instructor of the course will determine the length of the documentary and the artist statement.)

Works Cited

Ankei, Yuji. "Nuclear Power Plants and Biocultural Renaissance: A Case Study of Iwaishima Island in the Seto Inland Sea of Japan." *Journal of Marine and Island Cultures*, vol. 1, no. 2, 2012, pp. 126–130. Science Direct, https://doi.org/10.1016/j.imic.2012.12.001.

Avenell, Simon. *Transnational Japan in the Global Environmental Movement*. U of Hawai'i P, 2017.

Berque, Joannes, and Osamu Matsuda. "Coastal Biodiversity Management in Japanese Satoumi." *Marine Policy*, vol. 39, 2013, pp. 191–200. Science Direct, https://doi.org/10.1016/j.marpol.2012.10.013.

"Goal 6: Ensure Availability and Sustainable Management of Water and Sanitation for All." United Nations Department of Economic and Social Affairs, https://sdgs.un.org/goals/goal6. Accessed January 16, 2023.

"Goal 7: Ensure Access to Affordable, Reliable, Sustainable, and Modern Energy for All." United Nations Department of Economic and Social Affairs, https://sdgs.un.org/goals/goal7. Accessed January 16, 2023.

"Goal 12: Ensure Sustainable Consumption and Production Patterns." United Nations Department of Economic and Social Affairs, https://sdgs.un.org/goals/goal12. Accessed January 16, 2023.

"Goal 14: Conserve and Sustainably Use the Oceans, Seas and Marine Resources for Sustainable Development." United Nations Department of Economic and Social Affairs, https://sdgs.un.org/goals/goal14. Accessed January 16, 2023.

"Holy." Dictionary.com, https://www.dictionary.com/browse/holy. Accessed January 16, 2023.

Holy Island [Hōri no shima]. Directed by Aya Hanabusa, Polepole Times, 2010.

Indrawan, Mochamad, Mitsuyasu Yabe, Hisako Nomura, and Rhett Harrison. "Deconstructing\Satoyama: The Socio-ecological Landscape in Japan." *Ecological Engineering*, vol. 64, 2014, pp. 77–84. Science Direct, doi: https://doi.org/10.1016/j.ecoleng.2013.12.038.

Nichols, Bill. *Introduction to Documentary, Third Edition*. Indiana U Press, 2017.

Prusinski, Lauren. "Wabi-sabi, Mono No Aware, and Ma: Tracing Traditional Japanese Aesthetics Through Japanese History." *Studies on Asia*, vol. 4, no. 2, 2012, pp. 25–49.

Saito, Yuriko. "The Japanese Appreciation of Nature." *The British Journal of Aesthetics*, vol. 25, no.3, 1985, pp. 239–251.

Stolz, Robert. "Money and Mercury: Environmental Pollution and the Limits of Japanese Postwar Democracy." *Positions Asia Critique*, vol. 26, no. 2, 2018, pp. 243–264.

"Sustainable Development Goal 13: Climate Action," International Atomic Energy Agency, https://www.iaea.org/about/overview/sustainable-development-goals/goal-13-climate-action. Accessed January 16, 2023.

Takeuchi, Kazuhiko. "Rebuilding the Relationship between People and Nature: The Satoyama Initiative." *Ecological Research*, vol. 25, no. 5, 2010, pp. 891–897.

Totman, Conrad D. *The Green Archipelago: Forestry in Preindustrial Japan*. U of California P, 1989.

2 Barbara Dombrowski's *Tropic Ice: Dialog Between Places Affected by Climate Change*

Photographs and Art Installations of People and Landscapes

Britta Kallin

I   Text

Title	*Tropic Ice: Dialog Between Places Affected by Climate Change*
Genre	Photography
Photographer	Barbara Dombrowski was born and raised in the greater Stuttgart area in Germany. After gaining some work experience in an advertising agency, she studied visual communication at the Dortmund University of Applied Sciences. She received a scholarship from the Franco-German Youth Office and worked for four years in Paris, France, for well-known German and French magazines and agencies, before moving to Hamburg, Germany, where she has been living since 1996. She is currently a member of the Cologne-based, award-winning laif agency, a co-op that protects the rights of 400 photographers worldwide and that is known for its documentary style, author photography, and reportages. Dombrowski teaches documentary photography at a private school for photography in Hamburg. In addition to commissioned work for well-known magazines, aid organizations, and direct customers, she has received several grants and prizes for her work. Dombrowski frequently works as a juror and curator in photo competitions. With her art exhibition *Tropic Ice: Dialog Between Places Affected by Climate Change*, Dombrowski traveled around the world and participated as a speaker in national and international congresses, joint exhibitions, and lectures. She served as an official partner of the UN at COP23 in Bonn with her work "Tropic Ice." Since 2022 Barbara Dombrowski is an appointed member of the DGPh (German Society for Photography).
Year	2010–2022
Country	Dombrowski lived with the Inuit in Tinetiqilaaq and Sermiligaaq in East Greenland and the Achuar in Sharamentsa and the Shuar in Yuvientsa in the Amazon rainforest in Ecuador. In both places, the Amazon rain forest and East Greenland, she hung the portraits of people of the different indigenous communities together in the forest and on icebergs off and on the shore of Greenland. The photo series *Tropic Ice: Dialog Between Places Affected by Climate Change* includes dozens of photographs and portraits taken in East Greenland and in Ecuador. Dombrowski's work aims to demonstrate the ways climate change threatens both places and people. Since that first exchange, she has visited people in climate-relevant places on five continents and portrayed them and the landscapes surrounding them, making them ambassadors for their continents and climate zones. In her art installation in the Hambacher Forest, *Tropic Ice: Five Continents* (2019), Dombrowski juxtaposes portraits of people in the form of a circle and links them with haunting, large-format photographs. As a result of *Tropic Ice: Dialog Between Places Affected by Climate Change*, Dombrowski has been able to bring her expertise into the global discussion about the visualization of and advocacy for climate change.

DOI: 10.4324/9781003388869-4

Figure 2.1 José in the Forest in front of Ceibo (José im Wald vor Ceibo), 2010, Barbara Dombrowski/laif agency.[1]

Figure 2.2 The Drum Dancer Anda Kuitse from Kulusuk (Der Trommeltänzer Anda Kuitse aus Kulusuk), 2012, Barbara Dombrowski/laif agency.

Figure 2.3 Young Shuar with Parrot (Junger Shuar mit Papagei), 2010, Barbara Dombrowski/laif agency.

Figure 2.4 Woman from Greenland with Seal Jacket (Grönländerin mit Robbenjacke), 2011, Barbara Dombrowski/ laif agency.

Figure 2.5 Installation at the Iceberg - Inuit, Achuar and Shuar together (*Installation am Eisberg*), 2013, Barbara Dombrowski/laif agency.

Figure 2.6 Installation of Young Achuar on the Dry Rack in Greenland (*Installation junger Achuar am Trockengerüst in Grönland*), 2013, Barbara Dombrowski/laif agency.

Figure 2.7 Installation of Iceberg in the Amazon Rainforest (Installation Eisberg im Amazonas Regenwald),
2013, Barbara Dombrowski/laif agency.

Figure 2.8 Ice_03, Tropic Ice/Greenland, 2012, Barbara Dombrowski/laif agency (the original title is in
English).

II   Context

Barbara Dombrowski worked on her *Tropic Ice: Dialog Between Places Affected by Climate Change* project between 2010 and 2020. She explains that her goal is to "give a face to climate change" (Dombrowski, "Tropisches Eis"). She recalls how initially there was little attention for her ideas from magazines and other media outlets: "In 2010, when I started my work on this, there was little interest in visualizing climate change, since it was not tangible for most people; as a result, most of my partners, many of whom were magazine editors, could not imagine how I wanted to tell the story" (Dombrowski, "Für die Kunst"). So, she had to set out on her own and pay for the trips with her own money. Later, however, Dombrowski received some stipends, while supporters financed parts of her work. Dombrowski wanted to depict people and landscapes from five continents so as to bring them into a photographic dialogue with each other. She represents those who are the first to be directly affected by climate change. Dombrowski decided not to create photographs that depict catastrophic events, namely, because she asserts that people are emotionally sated with photos showing destruction through droughts, fires, floods, and hurricanes in the media. "I try to create empathy," she explains, "so people will show an interest in other people" (Dombrowski, "Engagement"). By hanging portraits of indigenous people in climate-affected regions of the world, Dombrowski "tried to use [her] work to connect indigenous people with each other, those who are situated differently and those who are affected differently from us in the global North" (Dombrowski, "Für die Kunst"). She produces her photographs on thin TECCO textile banners and hangs them up in nature. At the time when Dombrowski started, the material was not biodegradable and got destroyed after being out in nature by the weather, but that is also her intention, to show what happens when the natural process of weathering destroys something unnatural made by men versus humankind destroying something as beautiful as nature on planet Earth.

Dombrowski's photographic installations create a visual exchange between people living in different climate zones whose portraits act as ambassadors for their culture and geographic area. The photographer describes her pictures and art installations as follows: "The beautiful pictures are representative of what we do: we destroy our own habitat. That's what I want to show and tell" (Dombrowski, "Für die Kunst"). The artist shows indigenous tribes and their dependence on clean water and sanitation for their culture's survival and for safe hunting and food consumption. For her art installation, *Tropic Ice: Dialog Between Places Affected by Climate Change*, Dombrowski took pictures in the following areas: Greenland, Kiribati (an atoll island in the South Pacific), the Amazon rainforest, the Gobi Desert, and savanna near Mt. Kilimanjaro. She maintains: "In order to give people a face, I have visited so-called tipping points, climate-relevant places all over the world" (Dombrowski, "Art and Climate Justice" 20:16–20:24). The images advocate for reduced inequalities between wealthier, protected countries and more vulnerable island nations that are threatened to drown from sea level rise in the coming years. Dombrowski's work has led to many meaningful collaborations, lectures, and publications.

Four photographs feature portraits of members of indigenous communities. *José in the Forest in front of Ceibo Tree* (Figure 2.1) shows a young man from the Achuar community in the midst of the Amazon rainforest. He has beads of sweat on his face and wears a colorful headband made of small glass beads. In its first 30 years of life, the bark of a Ceibo is covered with spines that protect the tree. The trunk later loses the thorns and turns smooth. This prevents one from climbing it without tools. These large trees can grow up to 40 meters high and three meters wide. Legend has it that the Ceibo tree is the tree of life. The featured man in *The Drum Dancer Anda Kuitse from Kulusuk* (Figure 2.2) smiles directly at the camera and holds a traditional, handmade instrument that he uses to make music to accompany his dance. His grey hair, beard, and wrinkles indicate his status as an elderly community member who serves his indigenous group through his music. *Young Shuar with Parrot* (Figure 2.3) shows a boy from the Shuar tribe in Ecuador who seems to live in harmony with nature. The green parrot sits calmly on his shoulder; the animal and the human trust and support each other. The boy's simple blue jacket and the blurred, brown hut in the background indicate a simple way of life in this rainforest community. *Woman from Greenland with Seal Jacket* (Figure 2.4) underscores the beauty of customs and wisdom of traditional ways of living, where people use the skin of dead animals for their warmth and protection. Yet, the jacket has a modern-looking zipper. The green silhouette of a house and the white background indicate that the woman lives in Greenland. She smiles directly at the camera; the viewer can look directly into her eyes. Dombrowski tried to capture the essence and spirit of the woman and offers an idea of closeness to her subject. We see through these four portrait photographs evidence of Dombrowski's belief in the need to find a way for the Global North to see the reciprocity between the human and the natural, something that has gotten lost during the centuries of industrialization.

Dombrowski takes her portraits of indigenous people and places them in distant locations in the art installations featured in Figures 2.5 and 2.6. *Installation at the Iceberg* (Figure 2.5) displays photographs taken of the Inuit in Greenland and the Shuar and Achuar in the Amazon rainforest on an iceberg off the waters in Greenland (Kumfert, Schloemer). The artist pinned six portraits to the iceberg. The faces alternate between indigenous people from Greenland and those from Ecuador. There are four men and two women. Three men are younger or middle-aged, while the two women are older. The faces of the portraits are reflected in the water in front of the iceberg. There are two pieces of a melting iceberg in the water in front of the iceberg, and behind the iceberg the viewer can see rock formations no longer covered in ice. Dombrowski claims that "presenting my pictures of one culture to the other, by pinning them together, onto an iceberg in Greenland and a tropical tree, I am combining their common problems, an in this way I was able to build a bridge between both worlds" (Dombrowski, "Art and Climate Justice" 10:02–11:17). The Inuit explained to Dombrowski that the increased warmth of the seasons has led to a faster speed of ice melting away, which affects their lifestyle in terms of the food they can catch and the dangers posed by ice that breaks under their feet more frequently. The men on the left and the two women carry a smile on their face, while the other three men look at the camera with a neutral expression. The green tree leaves in one photo and the bare-chested man in another contrast with the background of the iceberg. In *Installation Young Achuar on the Dry Rack in Greenland* (Figure 2.6), we see a photograph of a young, bare-chested indigenous Achuar taken in Ecuador placed on a triangular drying rack in Greenland where seal skins and other furs and pelts are typically hung to dry. This juxtaposition of ice and the bare-chested young man leaves a haunting impression. The floating image of the portrait shows the effects of the wind and its harsh force on the thin and fragile textile banner. On the right side of the image, a small rowboat rests on the rocks. However, the oars of the boat are missing which may symbolize a lack of control or mobility. In the background, the viewer can see dark waters that run through the rocks and some ice-capped hills in the distance. In these two installations, Dombrowski comments on the similarities and differences between the two indigenous groups and the threat to their livelihoods through climate change. She explains that by "[p]lacing them into the spectacular landscape of either country," she wanted them to get "worldwide recognition of their problems" ("Art and Climate," "New Photo Exhibition").

In *Ice_03, Tropic Ice/Greenland* (Figure 2.7), Dombrowski shows an iceberg in the waters off the coast of Greenland. Dombrowski's nature photograph shows the beauty and fragility of the landscape in the arctic cold. The smooth surface in the front of the iceberg reminds the viewer of a whale with its smooth skin, while the back of the iceberg shows dents and looks as if someone has scraped and scratched off pieces of the iceberg. The dark grey clouds look almost painted onto the sky rather than their natural color. The black waters around the iceberg show the threat of water that is too warm and that melts the iceberg into non-existence (Dombrowski, "Meeresmenschen"; Dombrowski, "Wie bist du"). The disappearance of this beautiful iceberg is just months away from the view that is caught on camera. The sky and ocean that melt into one another seem to be endless, but the endlessness is only a visual illusion that simultaneously shows the limits of this mass of ice. *Installation Iceberg in the Amazon Rainforest* (Figure 2.8) shows a photograph of an iceberg from Greenland that is placed under the foliage in the middle of a green rainforest environment in Ecuador. The white and grey iceberg with its dark grey background and the black water surrounding it seems out of place as it contrasts with the green, lush plants that frame the photographic installation ("Klima-Kunst Installation"). The juxtaposition of the cold, dark colors of the iceberg and the hot climate of the rainforest creates an impression of two very different landscapes from two continents that seem to want to interact with each other. In the background of the photograph, the viewer can see a pond that lies behind the image of the iceberg that is strung up between the trees with thin plastic twine.

III   Interpretation

1   How does the artist work with different photographic techniques such as camera angle, focus, zoom as well as stillness and motion? How does she include contrasts both in color and black and white as well as centering and decentering people and objects in the images? How would you describe the different textures, patterns, and shapes in the photos? Consider how Dombrowski uses foregrounding and backgrounding techniques and how she positions and frames the central figure in each photograph. Comment on her use of texture as well. What do you notice about the four portraits? Can you describe the role of the human figure in relation to the leaves that appear in front of the face (2.1)? What is the relationship between the drummer and the drum (2.2)? What is the connection between the young person and the parrot (2.3)? Can you describe the visualization of the woman's facial expression and the fur coat (2.4)? What do these photographs have in common? What visual and thematic elements are repeated? How do the photographs differ? What are the distinctive features of each?
2   Describe the people featured in these photographs. Note that the people in these images are generally alone and their faces are foregrounded as the focal point. They are looking directly into the camera or their faces are angled toward the camera. What is the effect of portraying a solitary face in each photograph? What facial expressions (smile, grin, frown, neutral look, etc.) does the viewer see? How do the facial expression and gaze used in each photo relate to the theme and setting of the image? What specifically keeps these faces in the viewers' minds?
3   What is the effect of using members from indigenous communities for all of the portraits in the *Tropic Ice: Dialog Between Places Affected by Climate Change* collection and for these four portraits (Figures 2.1–2.4) in particular? What kind of commentary does Dombrowski make through the juxtaposition of or dialogue between different indigenous cultures? What commentary does Dombrowski make about endangered (indigenous) communities and their coexistence?
4   Most of the images in the *Tropic Ice: Dialog Between Places Affected by Climate Change* collection show a central face or photograph in a landscape. What commentary does Dombrowski make through the portrayal of both faces and landscapes, both people and planet? How might such portrayal be tied to the person's (implied) race, ethnicity, gender, age, class, geographic location, or postcolonial status?

5   What commentary does Dombrowski make about nations threatened by climate change who still smile at the intended audience of the Global North? What does Dombrowski suggest about our roles as spectators?

6   What elements are alive and what elements are dead in each photograph? What elements are natural and what elements are unnatural? What elements are in motion or in flux and what elements are static or stagnant? Comment on the effects of these potential juxtapositions in Dombrowski's *Tropic Ice: Dialog Between Places Affected by Climate Change.*

7   Dombrowski describes in an interview that she did not want to depict the people she photographed as victims:

>   I lived in the Amazonas rainforest and Greenland repeatedly, over several years, and I have spent much time with the people who live there. We knew each other well. I tried to explain to them that my goal is to give them a face, because they are the ones who are most affected by climate change already. They do not create any pollution that has led to climate change, but rather, they are only those who suffer. (Dombrowski, "Für die Kunst")

How does Dombrowski's photographic project relate to the effects of postcolonialism, the regional challenges for the Global South, and the global challenges to the entire planet? Why do you think Dombrowski selected the Amazon and Greenland as the sites for her first two photo shoots of *Tropic Ice: Dialog Between Places Affected by Climate Change* and for the featured *Tropic Ice: Dialog Between Places Affected by Climate Change* installations?

8   What are the additional effects of the three installations? How are they different than the individual photographs? What does the installation add?

9   Why do you think Dombrowski refrains from creating photographs of destroyed nature or suffering people in *Tropic Ice: Dialog Between Places Affected by Climate Change*? Is her approach more effective for her stated aims? Why or why not?

10 What do the titles say about the individual photographs or the photographic installations? Do you agree with the choice of titles by the artist? Why or why not? If not, what titles would you suggest for these eight photographs? The title of her collection *Tropic Ice: Dialog Between Places Affected by Climate Change* refers to a contrast between the hot tropics and the cold arctic. What else does Dombrowski evoke with the title *Tropic Ice: Dialog Between Places Affected by Climate Change*? How does Dombrowski's title or her overall project intersect with the unit themes of this book: planet, people, prosperity, and partnerships?

IV   Planet-Focused Applications to SDGs 6, 12, 13, 14, and 15

1   SDG 6 aims to "ensure availability and sustainable management of water and sanitation for all" and target 6.1 for this SDG is: "By 2030, achieve universal and equitable access to safe and affordable drinking water for all" ("SDG 6"). Does Dombrowski engage with SDG 6 (Clean Water and Sanitation) in these featured photographs from her *Tropic Ice: Dialog Between Places Affected by Climate Change* collection? If so, how and in what ways?

2   SDG 7 aims to "ensure access to affordable, reliable, sustainable and modern energy for all" and target 7.2 for this SDG is: "By 2030, increase substantially the share of renewable energy in the global energy mix" ("SDG 7"). Does Dombrowski engage with SDG 7 (Affordable and Clean Energy) in these featured photographs from her *Tropic Ice: Dialog Between Places Affected by Climate Change* collection? If so, how and in what ways?

3   SDG 12 aims to "ensure sustainable consumption and production patterns" and one of the targets for SDG 12 is: "By 2030, achieve the sustainable management and efficient use of

natural resources" ("SDG 12"). How does the artist directly or indirectly engage with SDG 12 (Responsible Production and Consumption)?

4   SDG 13, which aims to "take urgent action to combat climate change and its impacts," has three targets: (1) to "[s]trengthen resilience and adaptive capacity to climate-related disasters"; (2) to "[i]ntegrate climate change measures into national policies, strategies, and planning," and (3) to "[b]uild knowledge and capacity to meet climate change ("SDG 13"). How do these eight photographs from Dombrowski's *Tropic Ice: Dialog Between Places Affected by Climate Change* series relate to SDG 13 and its targets? How do they highlight the need for climate action? What solutions do they propose? Complete the table below with your ideas. Then, compare and contrast your completed table with that of a classmate.

	How climate change affects the planet:	How climate change affects indigenous communities differently or uniquely:
Installation at the Iceberg *Installation of Iceberg in the Amazon Rainforest* *Installation of Young Achuar on the Dry Rack in Greenland* *Ice_03, Tropic Ice/Greenland* *Young Shuar with Parrot* *Woman from Greenland with Seal Jacket* *Jose in the Forest in front of Ceibo Tree* *The Drum Dancer Anda Kuitse from Kulusuk*		

5   SDG 14 promotes the need "to conserve and sustainably use the oceans, seas, and marine resources" ("SDG 14"). How does Dombrowski engage with "Life below Water" in *Installation at the Iceberg, Installation Iceberg in the Amazon* Rainforest, *Installation Young Achuar on the Dry Rack in Greenland*, and *Ice_03, Tropic Ice/Greenland*? Which specific sustainability challenges to icebergs, ocean water, the Amazon rain forest, and other natural resources does Dombrowski depict?

6   SDG 15 aims to "protect, restore and promote sustainable use of terrestrial ecosystems, sustainable manage forests, combat desertification, and halt and reverse land degradation and halt biodiversity loss" ("SDG 15"). How does *Tropic Ice: Dialog Between Places Affected by Climate Change* engage with SDG 15? How do the portraits and the installations depict forests and the loss of biodiversity, including the loss of indigenous communities?

7   As a viewer, do you find any beauty in Dombrowski's photographs? If so, please explain. How and why does she depict natural and/or human beauty? What is the connection between beauty and the human and between beauty and the natural in *Tropic Ice: Dialog Between Places Affected by Climate Change*? How would you define Dombrowski's aesthetic approach or message? What commentary does she make regarding the fragility of these beautiful places and faces?

8   When asked what she learned while living with indigenous communities, Dombrowski explains:

I have learned quite a lot, and I have intentionally decided to work with indigenous communities on all five continents, and all these indigenous cultures are or have been animist cultures. The animist cultures are closely connected to nature: they believe in the circle of life so to speak; all life is connected in this circle, everything that is alive has a soul and it is equal to other living things. And this animist belief is very different from the ideas about the world and nature in our enlightened Western world, with all its problems that the Enlightenment and Christianity have created … these indigenous cultures can open our eyes to nature and its importance, something we must learn to see and to understand: nature as part of ourselves and us as part of nature so that we do not put ourselves above nature and do not consider nature as an environment we can exploit. (Dombrowski, "Für die Kunst")

How does Dombrowski capture these animist ideas in her work? How does she promote the idea of "nature as part of ourselves and us as part of nature?" Is this message clearer in her installations than in her individual photographs? If so, why?

9   Why do you think Dombrowski portrays those who suffer the consequences first (indigenous communities) from tropical and arctic regions, rather than the culprits (the wealthy industrial nations) from the Global North? What is the purpose of excluding representatives—both faces and places—from the Global North? What is the effect of this omission in the photographic works included here?

10 Consider the place-based nature of Dombrowski's art and the culturally rooted nature of her photographs. Examine also the uprooted, misplaced, and replanted nature of her installations and the effects of this "rearrangement" or "reconnection" of faces and places.

11 What is the relationship between the local and the global in Dombrowski's work? How does she portray this relationship? What is the ideal way to approach both local and global people and places? How does Dombrowski leave out the global North? Does that indicate that her art shows only those affected first (indigenous communities) but not the culprits (the wealthy industrial nations in the Global North)?

12 What is Dombrowski's research method and her approach? Read about the time and work she invests prior to taking photos. What linguistic and cultural skills did she acquire or need to complete her projects? How does her connection to people lead her to work toward protecting the planet?

13 Would Dombrowski's *Tropic Ice: Dialog Between Places Affected by Climate Change* project be better suited for Part 1 on Planet or Part 2 on People? Debate the best placement of her work in this textbook.

14 Divide the class into six groups and assign one of the SDGs from Part 1 (6, 12, 13, 14, or 15) to each group. Each group will then prepare arguments for a debate in which they maintain that their assigned SDG is the most relevant or central to Dombrowski's *Tropic Ice: Dialog Between Places Affected by Climate Change* series. (The instructor of the course will decide on the format and length of the debate and facilitate a follow-up discussion with the class upon conclusion of the debate.)

15 Does the featured text in this chapter only reinforce and illuminate the principles underpinning the UN SDGs and the concept of sustainable development, or does it question any inherent presuppositions, biases, shortcomings, flaws, or gaps in the UN SDG framework or the notion of sustainable development? Explain with details from the photographs featured in this chapter.

V   Beyond Planet—Connections to SDGs on People, Prosperity, and Partnerships

Beyond SDGs 6, 7, 12, 13, 14, and 15, what additional SDGs are addressed by Barbara Dombrowski in the *Tropic Ice: Dialog Between Places Affected by Climate Change* collection? Complete the table below with your ideas. Then compare and contrast your ideas with a classmate.

SDGs:	*Does Dombrowski's* Tropic Ice: Dialog Between Places Affected by Climate Change *series connect with additional SDGs? If so, which ones and how?*
SDG 1 No Poverty	
SDG 2 Zero Hunger	
SDG 3 Good Health and Well Being	
SDG 4 Quality Education	
SDG 5 Gender Equality	
SDG 8 Decent Work and Economic Growth	
SDG 9 Industry, Innovation, and Infrastructure	
SDG 10 Reduced Inequalities	
SDG 11 Sustainable Cities and Communities	
SDG 16 Peace, Justice, and Strong Institutions	
SDG 17 Partnerships for the Goals	

VI   From Global to Local: On a Personal Level

1   How do you relate personally to the featured text in Chapter 2? Explain in detail how your own life experiences or personal beliefs intersect with the main ideas and themes of Barbara Dombrowski's *Tropic Ice: Dialog Between Places Affected by Climate Change.*
2   How does the global humanities text featured in Chapter 2 relate to your local environment? Explain the global-local connection between Dombrowski's *Tropic Ice: Dialog Between Places Affected by Climate Change* and your home or current residence. What place-based considerations permit or prevent the application of the text to your geographical location?
3   What type of response did Dombrowski's *Tropic Ice: Dialog Between Places Affected by Climate Change* elicit in you? Are you moved to action? If so, explain. If not, why not? Have your viewpoints or attitudes changed? Explain.

VII   Assignments

1   Research

1   Individually or in groups, research two German movements that may have been inspirational or foundational to the *Tropic Ice: Dialog Between Places Affected by Climate Change* series: (1) the German Peace Movement and (2) the German Green Party.
The German Peace Movement. The anti-war movement in Germany first gained momentum in the late 1960s after many U.S. Americans demonstrated against the Vietnam War and the "Hippie Movement" advocated for worldwide peace. In Germany, the Easter marches against the threat of World War III in the 1960s paved the way for a peace movement that fought against the nuclear arms race between NATO and the Warsaw Pact. The NATO Double-Track Decision and the deployment and stationing of Pershing II missiles in West Germany were some of many factors strengthening the German peace movement. As the Cold War was at its height in the

1980s, West Germans did not want to experience another war on German soil as it was likely that war would culminate between West Germany and East Germany, two countries that were divided by the Iron Curtain. The German peace movement became closely linked with the anti-nuclear movement and the third feminist wave (Heinrich). The Chernobyl nuclear accident in 1986 also led to a strengthening of the anti-nuclear movement, which included protests about the storing of used Uranium from nuclear power plants in the German Harz mountains.

The German Green Party. The German Green Party can trace its origins to the student movements of the late 1960s. In the late 1970s, some Green representatives were elected at the local level, while in 1980, the party held a conference and became a federal party. Throughout the 1980s and 1990s, the Green Party stood for environmental protection and peace. After the fall of the Berlin Wall in 1989, the East German Greens and some grassroot organizations that called themselves the Alliance '90 joined forces with the West German Green Party. However, it took the unified party until 1998 to become a junior coalition member in the federal government. In September 2021, the party finally captured about 15% of federal election votes. The German Green Party now has about 118 seats in the federal government or *Bundestag* (Conradt). The German Green Party shares the government with the Social Democrats and the Free Democratic Party; this coalition has governed Germany since fall 2021.

Going beyond the brief descriptions provided above, explain in detail how the German Peace Movement and the development of the German Green Party relate both to the *Tropic Ice: Dialog Between Places Affected by Climate Change* collection and to SDGs 6, 12, 13, 14, and/or 15. (The instructor of the course will determine the mode of presentation and delivery—oral presentation, written report, annotated bibliography, and photo essay—for this research assignment.)

2   Since Dombrowski began the *Tropic Ice: Dialog Between Places Affected by Climate Change* series in 2010, Germany has taken many important steps to improve climate action and promote renewable energy. Individually or in groups, research policies and laws in

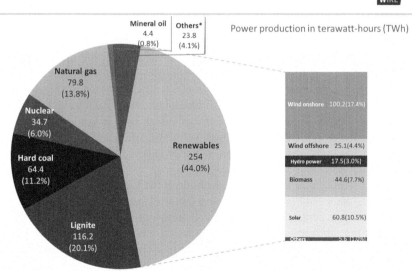

Share of energy sources in gross German power production in 2022.
Data: AGEB 2023.

*Includes power generation from pumped storage

Note: Government renewables targets are in relation to total power consumption (549.2 TWh in 2022), not production.
Renewables share in gross German power consumption 2022: 46.2%.   BY SA 4.0

Figure 2.9 German electricity sources in 2022 (Appunn, Haas, Wettengel).

Germany from 2010 to the present that relate to SDGs 6, 12, 13, 14, and 15 and to the specific planetary issues addressed by Dombrowski in the selected images from *Tropic Ice: Dialog Between Places Affected by Climate Change*. Figure 2.9 outlines some of the energy sources for electricity in Germany's "ambitious new green energy goals" and provides a good starting point for your research ("German Coalition"). (The instructor of the course will determine the mode of presentation and delivery—oral presentation, written report, short video documentary, digital timeline project, etc.—for this research assignment as well as the number of policies and laws to be included.)

2 Write

1 Write an essay in which you compare and contrast two of the images from Dombrowski's *Tropic Ice: Dialog Between Places Affected by Climate Change* collection in terms of: (1) the environmental issue depicted; (2) the climate action issues addressed; and (3) the life cycles of indigenous communities portrayed. In the concluding paragraph of your essay, discuss which of the two images best relates to SDG 13 and most successfully advocates for taking "urgent action to combat climate change and its impacts" ("SDG 13"). (The instructor of the course will determine the appropriate length for this writing assignment.)

2 Write an essay in which you examine the relevance of SDG 14 (Life below Water) and SDG 15 (Life on Land) in one or more of the installation images treated in this chapter: *Installation at the Iceberg* (Figure 5.1), *Installation Iceberg in the Amazon Rainforest* (Figure 2.2), and/or *Installation Young Achuar on the Dry Rack in Greenland* (Figure 2.3). How does Dombrowski highlight the interrelation between life on land and water through the selected installation(s)? In the concluding paragraph of your essay, discuss whether the chosen image(s) best relate(s) to SDG 14 or SDG 15, that is, to the conservation and sustainable use of marine or terrestrial ecosystems and resources. (The instructor of the course will determine the appropriate length for this writing assignment.)

3 Create

1 Individually or in groups, imagine that you were asked to choose the location(s) and topic(s) for the next photograph(s) in the *Tropic Ice: Dialog Between Places Affected by Climate Change* series. Where would you choose and why? Which indigenous community would you choose and how would you depict one or several of its members? How would your photograph(s) relate to SDGs 6, 12, 13, 14, and/or 15? How would you stage the scene? Where and how would you create an art installation using your photograph(s)? Describe the photographic image and the art installation as you envision it. (The instructor of the course will determine the mode of presentation and delivery—written proposal, sketch or mockup, oral presentation of the proposed image and location, etc.—for this creative assignment.)

2 In pairs, create a skit in which one student interviews Barbara Dombrowski about the *Tropic Ice: Dialog Between Places Affected by Climate Change* series and its contributions in the areas of climate action, sustainable development, and environmental justice. The performance of the interview should include questions and answers about the relevance of the *Tropic Ice: Dialog Between Places Affected by Climate Change* photographs and art installations to SDGs 6, 12, 13, 14, and 15 as well as other topics of interest to the group. For groups of more than two, students could be assigned the role of additional interviewer(s)

and/or members of the indigenous communities featured in the images. (The instructor of the course will determine the mode of presentation and delivery—role play, video project, and interview script—for this creative assignment.)

Note

1 All translations of titles of Dombrowski's photographs and installations are mine unless otherwise noted.

Works Cited

Appunn, Kerstine, Yannick Haas, and Julian Wettengel. "Germany's Energy Consumption and Power Mix in Charts." *Clean Energy Wire*. 18 April 2023. https://www.cleanenergywire.org/factsheets/germanys-energy-consumption-and-power-mix-charts. Accessed 18 April 2023.

Conradt, David P. "Green Party of Germany." *Encyclopedia Britannica*. 27 September 2021. https://www.britannica.com/topic/Green-Party-of-Germany. Accessed 25 October 2022.

Dombrowski, Barbara. "Art and Climate Justice Exhibition: Global Climate Action Symposium." Georgia Institute of Technology. 14 October 2020. https://www.youtube.com/watch?v=HM53RqVqeAE. Accessed 25 October 2022.

———. "Engagement für den Klimaschutz: Fotografin Dombrowski setzt auf die Kraft der Bilder" (Commitment to Climate Protection: Photographer Dombrowski Counts on the Power of Images). Interview with Marietta Schwarz. *Deutschlandfunk Kultur.* 25 September 2020. https://www.deutschlandfunkkultur.de/engagement-fuer-den-klimaschutz-fotografin-dombrowski-setzt-100.html. Accessed 25 October 2022.

———. "Für die Kunst 'setze ich mich auch ins Flugzeug'" (For Art I Also Travel by Plane). Interview with Pascal Fischer. *Deutschlandfunk.* 15 May 2021. https://www.deutschlandfunk.de/fotografin-ueber-klimawandel-fuer-die-kunst-setze-ich-mich-100.html. Accessed 25 October 2022.

———. "Meeresmenschen im Gespräch: *Tropic Ice* Fotografin Barbara Dombrowski" (Ocean People in Conversation: *Tropic Ice* Photographer Barbara Dombrowski). *Ocean Summit Kiel.* Interview with Katharina Troch. 6 August 2020. https://ocean-summit.de/meer-klima/meeresmenschen-im-gespraech-tropic-ice-fotografin-barbara-dombrowski/. Accessed 25 October 2022.

———. *Tropic Ice: Dialog Between Places Affected by Climate Change. Barbara Dombrowski Photography.* Professional Website. https://www.barbaradombrowski.com/tropicice. Accessed 25 October 2022.

———. *Tropic Ice: Dialog Between Places Affected by Climate Change.* Vimeo. 2013. https://vimeo.com/83806318. Accessed 25 October 2022.

———. *Tropic Ice: Dialog Between Places Affected by Climate Change.* Exhibit. 30 July 2021–24 April 2022. https://www.wuerth-haus-rorschach.ch/en/wuerth_management_ag_haus_rorschach/7_catering_1/ausstellungen_2/barbaradombrowski/barbaradombrowski.php. Accessed 25 October 2022.

———. "Tropisches Eis? Die Macht der Kunst im Kampf um 1.5 Grad" (Tropical Ice? The Power of Art in the Struggle for 1.5 Degrees). Interview with Alice Classen. 14 December 2021. *Bavarian Climate Research Network.* https://www.bayklif.de/klimadiskurse/. Accessed 25 October 2022.

———. "Wie bist du zum Meer gekommen?" (How Did You Get to the Ocean?). *Ocean Summit Talk mit Barbara Dombrowski. Europäische Wochen Passau – Pastorale Beethoven's 6th Symphony.* August 2020. https://vimeo.com/436370221. Accessed 25 October 2022.

German Coalition Plan Sets Bigger Green Targets." *BBC*, 15 October 2021, https://www.bbc.com/news/world-europe-58924480. Accessed 25 October 2022.

Heinrich, Daniel. "The Generations of Germans Aiming to Protect Peace." *Deutsche Welle.* 23 October 2018. https://www.dw.com/en/the-generations-of-germans-aiming-to-protect-peace/a-46009448. Accessed 25 October 2022.

"Klima-Kunst-Installation *Tropic Ice* am Braunkohlentagebau Hambach" (Climate Art Installation at the Brown Coal Mines in Hambach). *BUND-NRW.* September 2019. https://www.bund-nrw.de/themen/braunkohle/aktionen/klima-kunst-installation-tropic-ice/. Accessed 25 October 2022.

Kumfert, Cornelia. "Reise-Schönheit: Grönlands eisige Schönheit." *Reader's Digest*. n.d. https://readers-digest.de/ch/digitale-fotos/item/reise-fotos-groenlands-eisige-schoenheit. Accessed 25 October 2022.

"New Photo Exhibition at Hamburg Fair Halls: *Tropic Ice*." *Hamburg Messe*. May–October 2022. https://www.hamburg-messe.de/en/the-company/photo-exhibition-tropic-ice. Accessed 25 October 2022.

Schloemer, Katrin. "Art Connecting the Amazon Rainforest and Greenland's Glaciers." *Deutsche Welle*. 23 May 2019. https://www.dw.com/en/art-connecting-the-amazon-rainforest-and-greenlands-glaciers/a-48816479. Accessed 25 October 2022.

"SDG 6," United Nations: Department of Economic and Social Affairs. https://sdgs.un.org/goals/goal6 . Accessed 25 October 2022.

"SDG 7," United Nations: Department of Economic and Social Affairs. https://sdgs.un.org/goals/goal7. Accessed 25 October 2022.

"SDG 12," United Nations: Department of Economic and Social Affairs. https://sdgs.un.org/goals/goal12. Accessed 25 October 2022.

"SDG 13," United Nations: Department of Economic and Social Affairs. https://sdgs.un.org/goals/goal13. Accessed 25 October 2022.

"SDG 14," United Nations: Department of Economic and Social Affairs. https://sdgs.un.org/goals/goal14. Accessed 25 October 2022.

"SDG 15," United Nations: Department of Economic and Social Affairs. https://sdgs.un.org/goals/goal15. Accessed 25 October 2022.

3 Fabrice Monteiro's *The Prophecy*

Trash Art Photography Protests Trashing the Planet

Kelly Comfort

I   Text

Title	*The Prophecy*
Genre	Photography
Photographer	Fabrice Monteiro was born in 1972 in Belgium (his mother is Belgian), grew up in Benin (his father is Beninese), then returned to Belgium at the age of 17 to begin university studies in industrial engineering. Monteiro later became a professional fashion model for over a decade, before launching a career in photography. He moved to Dakar, Senegal in 2011, where he continues to reside and work as a professional photographer and visual artist. Monteiro collaborated with Senegalese fashion designer Jah Gal (a.k.a Doulsy) in creating the costumes and staging the scene for each photo shoot in the series.
Year	2013 to present
Country	Monteiro and Gal staged the first nine photographs in *The Prophecy* collection in or near Dakar, Senegal, where they both currently reside. They initially intended to create "9 images inspired by 9 ecological plagues in Senegal" (Juzga 00:03:24–00:03:32). At the time of publication, *The Prophecy* series includes 15 images. Five of the last six photographs were taken abroad in Australia ("Untitled #10"), Ghana ("Untitled #11"), Kenya ("Untitled #12"), Colombia ("Untitled #13"), and the United States ("Untitled #14") in what Monteiro now calls a "global prophecy" (Monteiro "Interview" 00:00:25–00:00:26).

This chapter treats six of the fifteen photographs in the collection (see Figures 3.1-3.6). To view additional photographs from *The Prophecy* series, visit Fabrice Monteiro's collection: https://fabricemonteiro.viewbook.com/.

II   Context

Monteiro explains that "[e]very single image" in *The Prophecy* collection "is about one specific issue, and that issue is global; it is not just in Senegal, it is not just in Africa, it is planetary" ("'We already live'"). Nonetheless, Monteiro's initial plan for *The Prophecy* series was to create a story that would be distributed to Senegalese schoolchildren. He explains the backstory for the originally conceived children's tale and the actual photographic collection as follows: "Gaia, the mother earth, exhausted by her incapacity to maintain the natural cycles of the planet in front of new modes of life and consumption, resolves to send her djinns, to let them appear to the humans and deliver a message of warning and empowerment" (Juzga 00:10:17–00:10:36). In

DOI: 10.4324/9781003388869-5

Figure 3.1 "Untitled #1," *The Prophecy* Series, 2013, Fabrice Monteiro/INSTITUTE.

Figure 3.2 "Untitled #2," *The Prophecy* Series, 2013, Fabrice Monteiro/INSTITUTE.

Figure 3.3 "Untitled #3," *The Prophecy* Series, 2014, Fabrice Monteiro/INSTITUTE.

Figure 3.4 "Untitled #5," *The Prophecy* Series, 2014, Fabrice Monteiro/INSTITUTE.

Figure 3.5 "Untitled #9," *The Prophecy* Series, 2015, Fabrice Monteiro/INSTITUTE.

Figure 3.6 "Untitled #10," *The Prophecy* Series, 2014, Fabrice Monteiro/INSTITUTE.

line with his own multicultural heritage, Monteiro thus mixes European and African traditions by incorporating both the Greek goddess Gaia, ancestral mother of the Earth, and West African djinns, supernatural beings of the animist tradition that also extend into Islam. Monteiro deems the "concept of animism" "essential" given that Africans were animists before they became Muslim or Catholic (Juzga 00:10:04–00:10:12). Gal expands on this notion of using djinns: "Here, it is our culture to believe in djinns. And we believe in it [. . .]. Every forbidden thing is protected by a djinn. But now, with progress and religions that come from abroad we forgot a little about those beliefs" (Juzga 00:09:36–00:09:43, 00:09:51–00:10:04). According to Gal, *The Prophecy* "is warning us about what is going to be the misfortune of everyone" (Juzga 00:03:09–00:03:13). Yet "[t]he djinns offer no solutions," Monteiro explains, and serve only to "make humankind confront its responsibilities" ("Of Djinn and Man").

"Untitled #1" was photographed in Mbeubeuss, an "unauthorized dump site" located approximately 16 miles northeast of Dakar, where "350 rubbish trucks dump an estimated 1,300 tons of household waste" per day ("Ecofund The Prophecy" 00:02:10–00:02:26). Turned from a green marsh district into Senegal's largest open landfill, Mbeubeuss sits on a drying lake and flood plain, polluting "the surrounding water, soil, and environment, jeopardizing economic activities like cattle breeding and agriculture" (Italia, 2019, p. 8). According to the "Ecofund The Prophecy" video, Mbeubeuss is "an ecological bomb: Since its creation in 1968, the dumpsite has been growing and increasingly gaining ground." (00:02:10–00:02:26). Dressed in a massive gown made predominantly of plastic waste, the female figure in this image highlights what Monteiro calls the "unbelievable system of plastic consumption" (Juzga 00:01:02–00:01:04).[5] Jah Gal explains further the image's message of unchecked consumption: "How much waste, how many of these materials can be re-used? But no, all we think about is consuming, consuming, consuming" (Juzga 00:02:22–00:02:30).

"Untitled #2" addresses the threat of oil spills and the potential consequences for marine and coastal ecosystems. The photograph was taken on the Madeleine Islands (Îles de la Madeleine), which are located less than 3 miles off the coast of Dakar. The photograph depicts a capsized ship in the background and a female djinn covered in black tar and feathers in the foreground. Here, Monteiro protests "[p]ollution from petroleum industries [that] is responsible for the disappearance of entire marine ecosystems, for loss of resources, reduction in people's quality of life, and contributes to the disappearance of traditional fishing" ("Ecofund The Prophecy" 00:104:14). The juxtaposition of the figure's tentacle-like limb with her human hand holding a dead bird highlights how oil spills affect both marine and terrestrial life.

"Untitled #3" highlights the pollution of Hann Bay (Baie de Hann) in Dakar. What was once considered one of the most beautiful beaches in the world is now "one of the most polluted bays" as a result of what Monteiro calls "an ecological catastrophe" ("The Prophecy 3rd Photo"). Monteiro shows how a "river of blood" from a nearby slaughterhouse flows directly into the bay, while dead animal carcasses litter the beach (Niedan). Fabrice explains further that "[n]early 80% of household industrial wastes, generated by the 3 million people living in Dakar [. . .] are discharged directly into the Atlantic Ocean without prior treatment," which leads to "the disappearance of marine biodiversity" and the presence of "urban-waste-contaminated fish" ("Ecofund The Prophecy" 00:05:59–00:06:16). Monetiro also comments on the problem of oil going "straight into the ocean," creating a terrible odor on the beach, and turning the sand black (Niedan). Warning of negative impacts to fishing and tourism, "Untitled #3" shows an oversized and ominous creature emerging from the shoreline. On her knees and with her face covered, the female figure has six giant legs made of bound cables protruding from her body.

"Untitled #5" portrays the problems of air pollution, traffic congestion, and urban waste. In the "Ecofund The Prophecy" documentary, Monteiro and Gal explain that "in Dakar and many other African cities the air is loaded with harmful pollutants. Fuel-powered vehicles pollute the air through the release of gases and particles" (00:10:08–00:10:26). Moreover, "[a]s road traffic and the number of vehicles increase, urban transportation is a major cause of air pollution" that leads to "ecological consequences and serious respiratory diseases" ("Ecofund The Prophecy" 00:10:08–00:10:26). Monteiro adds that "[h]ere [in Dakar] the pollution is conspicuous. Tons of old diesel vehicles are constantly ejecting black smoke and toxic gases in the atmosphere" (Juzga 00:04:30–00:04:45). Standing between two vehicles that represent the city (note the Dakar license plate on the car) and the nation (see the Senegalese flag on the truck), the female figure wears a dress made of repurposed bicycle reflectors and seemingly protests the inability to walk and cycle in a car-centered city. Also unable to breathe amidst a cloud of toxic exhaust fumes and carbon emissions, she holds a gas mask to her face, which is already covered by a black plastic bag.

"Untitled #9" underscores "the problem of charcoal" and of "consuming too much wood" in Senegal, which has led to deforestation, soil erosion, and desertification (Monteiro, "Artist's Statement"). Monteiro explains that "[a]pproximately 40,000 hectare of forest disappear every year in Senegal, with 4 million tons of wood used for domestic cooking every year" ("Fire the Imagination"). The consumption of wood and the production and use of charcoal are, in the words of Monteiro, causing the Earth to become "sterile" and the Sahara to move "more and more to the south" (Niedan). Monteiro advocates using the sun and solar panels for energy and heat, rather than "the traditional way of burning, burning, burning, burning" (Niedan). He warns that fire "pollutes the atmosphere," "devastates and sterilizes arable land," and "spews toxic fumes into the atmosphere" ("Artist's Statement"). The featured woman stands tall yet immobile in a dress made of wood and kindling. She exists among what Monteiro calls "a desiccated and burnt" landscape, yet the oversized adornment around her neck suggests a more ecological alternative in solar energy ("Artist's Statement").

"Untitled #10" is the first image in the series to be photographed outside of Senegal. Not wanting "to stigmatize Senegal" and believing that "environmental topics [. . .] affect the whole planet" and represent "a global problem," Monteiro took advantage of the invitation to attend the World Parks Congress in Australia in 2014 to create an Australian prophecy (Stoddard). He insists that making "a prophecy in Australia was a great opportunity for [him] to take it out of African and give it an international dimension" (Juzga 00:16:23–00:16:27). Monteiro explains his goals for "Untitled #10": Australia is

> a rich country and they know that they are destroying the Great Barrier Reef, but they keep on doing it for economic reasons, or whatever. I wanted to talk about the bleaching of the coral, which is created by global warming. The idea was to create a spirit that would represent the whole life of the coral reef, and the image would represent the spirit of the reef leaving the reef, leaving behind this skeleton of the reef where there's no more life. (Stoddard)

The bleached coral in this photograph contrasts starkly with the djinn's colorful adornments. Her colors seemingly represent what once was, but no longer is—as she tries to swim away from the barren undersea landscape.

III   Interpretation

1   What do these six photographs have in common? What visual and thematic elements are repeated? How do the six photographs differ? What are the distinctive features of each? Consider how Monteiro uses the following elements of photographic composition: color and contrast; textures and patterns; lines, curves, and shapes; foregrounding and backgrounding techniques; positive and negative space; symmetry and asymmetry; camera angle, focus, and zoom, stillness and motion; and positioning and framing.

2   Describe the costumes in "Untitled #1," "Untitled #2," "Untitled #3," "Untitled #5," "Untitled #9," and "Untitled #10." What materials are used in their construction? How do the materials used for each costume relate to the theme and setting of the image? In addition to the costumes, what other elements are constructed or staged in each photograph?

3   What elements are living and what elements are dead in each of the six photographs? What elements are natural and what elements are unnatural, artificial, synthetic, or man-made? What commentary does Monteiro make through this juxtaposition of the living and the dead, the natural and the unnatural? Scholars have repeatedly pointed out the lack of human figures in *The Prophecy*, suggesting that the environmental degradation caused by mankind nearly replaces mankind in these images. What commentary does Monteiro make regarding the tension or antagonism between the human and natural environment?

4   What is the effect of using female models for nearly all of the photographs in *The Prophecy* collection and for these six images in particular? What is the effect of using Black models for nearly all of the photographs in *The Prophecy* collection and for five of these six images in particular? What commentary regarding gender or race (or gender or racial discrimination) is made or implied?

5   Most of the images in *The Prophecy* collection show a central figure who cannot walk or move and is stuck, mired, or stagnated *in situ*. What specifically keeps these figures from moving in each instance? What commentary does Monteiro make through the portrayal of a lack of mobility and movement in these images? How might such stagnation be tied to the figure's (implied) gender, race, class, geographic location, or postcolonial status?

6   The female figures in these images are generally alone. The models are also foregrounded and serve as the focal point of each image. What is the effect of portraying a solitary figure of supernatural size in each photograph? What commentary does Monteiro make about isolation, community, coexistence, etc.?

7   The female figures in these images are often looking away from the camera (to the side or down) and their faces are frequently covered or masked by black plastic bags—bags that Monteiro describes as "an aberration" because they are "too thin" to be "reusable" (Juzga 00:02:09–00:02:13). Why might this be and what is the intended effect? What commentary does Monteiro make about our blindness or inability to see? What does Monteiro suggest about our roles as spectators or spectacles?

8   Monteiro admits in an interview that he "was a bit deceived" with *The Prophecy* initially, because he felt like he was "stigmatizing Africa once more [. . .] with this Africa is dirty and there is garbage everywhere" rhetoric, which is why he decided "to create a global prophecy" that is "not from North to South," but "is rooted in Africa and goes all over" (Monteiro "Interview" 00:00:01–00:02:26, 00:07:29–00:07:35). How does Monteiro's photographic series relate to the effects of postcolonialism, the regional challenges for the African continent and the Global South, and the global challenges for the entire planet? Why do you think Monteiro chose Australia's Great Barrier Reef as the site for his first photo shoot outside of Senegal in *The Prophecy* series?

9   What is the effect of not naming each photograph with a specific title other than the word "untitled" and the number in the series? Do you agree with this artistic decision? Why or why not? If not, what titles would you suggest for these six photographs?

10 If the term "prophecy" refers to a prediction of the future, what does Monteiro "prophesize" in *The Prophecy* series in general and "Untitled #1," "Untitled #2," "Untitled #3," "Untitled #5," "Untitled #9," and "Untitled #10" in particular? How does Monteiro's prophecy intersect with the unit themes of this book: planet, people, prosperity, and partnerships?

IV   Planet-Focused Applications to SDGs 6, 7, 12, 13, 14, and 15

1   How does Monteiro engage with SDG 6 (Clean Water and Sanitation) in "Untitled #1," "Untitled #2," "Untitled #3," "Untitled #5," "Untitled #9," or "Untitled #10"? Discuss which of these images promotes the need to "[e]nsure availability and sustainable management of water and sanitation for all" ("SDG Goals 6"). Examine the targets of SDG 6 and discuss which ones are most relevant to Monteiro's photographic series. Consider, for example, Target 6.3 on "improv[ing] water quality by reducing pollution, eliminating dumping and minimizing [the] release of hazardous chemicals and materials" or Target 6.6 on "protect[ing] and restor[ing] water-related ecosystems, including mountains, forests, wetlands, rivers, aquifers and lakes" ("Goal 6 Targets").

2   How does Monteiro address SDG 7 (Affordable and Clean Energy) in the featured photographs from *The Prophecy* series? Discuss which of these images promotes the need to "[e]nsure access to affordable, reliable, sustainable and modern energy for all" ("SDG Goals 7"). How do the images depict the negative consequences of "unaffordable" and "unclean" forms of energy? What solutions, if any, do the images propose? Consider also how concepts related to SDG 7 such as "clean," "renewable," "affordable," "reliable," "sustainable," "modern," and "accessible" relate to Monteiro's photographic collection in contexts other than energy.

3   How do these six photographs from Monteiro's *The Prophecy* series relate to SDG 12 (Responsible Consumption and Production)? How do they highlight (un)sustainable consumption and production patterns or practices? The Oslo Symposium in 1994 defined "sustainable consumption and production" as "the use of services and related products, which respond to basic needs and bring a better quality of life while minimizing the use of natural resources and toxic materials as well as the emissions of waste and pollutants over the life cycle of the service or product so as not to jeopardize the needs of further generations" ("Sustainable Production and Consumption"). Complete the table below with your ideas. Then, compare and contrast your completed table with that of a classmate.

	(Un)sustainable production practices:	*(Un)sustainable consumption practices:*
"Untitled #1"		
"Untitled #2"		
"Untitled #3"		
"Untitled #5"		
"Untitled #9"		
"Untitled #10"		

4   The mission of SDG 13 is to "[t]ake urgent action to combat climate change and its impacts" ("SDG Goals 13"). How does Monteiro address the impacts of climate change in "Untitled #1," "Untitled #2," "Untitled #3," "Untitled #5," "Untitled #9," or "Untitled #10"? What solutions does he propose in these same images?

5   SDG 14 promotes the need "to conserve and sustainably use the oceans, seas, and marine resources" ("SDG Goals 14"). How does Monteiro address concerns with "Life below Water" in "Untitled #2," "Untitled #3," and "Untitled #10"? Which specific sustainability challenges to marine ecosystems and resources does Monteiro depict? Review the targets for SDG 14 and discuss which ones apply most to Monteiro's work.

6   SDG 15 focuses on five primary goals:
   •   "protect, restore, and promote sustainable use of terrestrial ecosystems";
   •   "sustainably manage forests";
   •   "combat desertification";
   •   "halt and reverse land degradation";
   •   "halt biodiversity loss" ("SDG Goals 15").
   Which of these actions does Monteiro promote in *The Prophecy*? How? Which of the six photographs best address issues relevant to SDG 15?

7   In *African Ecomedia: Network Forms, Planetary Politics*, Cajetan Iheka argues that Monteiro's *The Prophecy* series "depicts assemblages of crime scenes" (43). "Consumption is the major crime on display," Iheka explains, since Monteiro "indicts humanity for unbridled consumption" (44, 47). Do you agree with Iheka's interpretation of *The Prophecy*? What are the "crimes" and "crime scenes" put on display in each photograph? Who or what are the victims in each image? Who or what are the culprits in each image?

8   How does the concept of an "ecological footprint" relate to Monteiro's *The Prophecy* collection? An ecological footprint is defined as the measure of environmental impact in terms of the amount of space, environment, or productive land and water required for the production of goods and services and the assimilation of waste required to support a given population or a particular lifestyle or activity. Does Monteiro consider any other "footprints" such as the carbon footprint, the water footprint, the food footprint, the energy footprint, etc.?

9   In "Untitled #1," Monteiro depicts the insufficient or unsuccessful waste management policies and practices in Senegal. According to the World Bank's 2018 publication *What a Waste 2.0: A Global Snapshot of Solid Waste Management to 2050*, "[w]aste disposal practices vary significantly by income level and region" (Kaza, Yao, Bhada Tata, & Van Woerden 34). For example, in the Sub-Saharan Africa region, 69% of waste is openly dumped and often burned, while 24% of waste is disposed of in some form of a landfill, and only 7% of waste is recycled or recovered (Kaza et al., 81). How and why does Monteiro make visible the Global South's inability to properly treat, dispose of, or recycle its own waste? What additional commentary does Monteiro offer on the effects of the "global waste trade," namely, the international exchange or export of hazardous and toxic waste from developed countries in the Global North to developing countries in the Global South? Note that Monteiro said in a 2021 interview: "The only reason Europe doesn't look like this [referring to the Mbeubeuss dump] is because it ships its waste out to us" (Siddons). Finally, how does the practice of "trash picking"—searching for, collecting, sorting, and selling discarded waste for a meager profit—relate to "Untitled #1"? Note that approximately 2,000 rag-pickers, trash dealers, and recyclers worked (and often lived) at Mbeubeuss at the time of "Untitled #1"'s creation in 2013. Does Monteiro praise or condemn the practice of and need for trash picking?

10   How and why do Monteiro and Gal use "upcycling" in *The Prophecy*? Whereas "recycling" involves the destruction of waste in order to create something new, "upcycling" takes waste and creates something new from it in its current state, which makes it a form of reuse that reduces the need for recycling and is an even better option for the environment (Ravenhall). How might the upcycled clothes and repurposed accessories in *The Prophecy* serve to criticize the "wasteful industry" of fashion, which, according to Isadora Italia, "accounts for

10% of global carbon emissions and is the second largest polluter, second to oil" (10)? How do the costumes participate in or recreate haute couture fashion? How do Monteiro and Gal reject "fast fashion" and mass-produced "ready-to-wear" clothing? How do they promote more "sustainable" forms of fashion or what might be called "trashion"?

11 Discuss the significance of the multicultural inclusion of Gaia, Greek goddess of the Earth, and the djinns, animist spirits from nature in the African context. Consider how Monteiro gives voice to Gaia in his "Artist Statement" for Prix Pictet's Global Award in Photography and Sustainability competition: "I am dying. Every day more numerous and more insatiable, the humans make an excessive use of my wealth without thinking of the consequences. It has been many years since they remain deaf in my calls but you, my faithful Djinns, can reach them. Leave, reveal your existence to the humans and alert them of the danger that they incur." Consider also how the "Gaia hypothesis," formulated in the 1970s by chemist James Loveluck and co-developed by microbiologist Lynn Margulis, might relate to this collection. The Gaia hypothesis, also known as the Gaia theory or the Gaia principle, proposes that "all organisms and their inorganic surroundings on Earth are closely integrated to form a single and self-regulating complex system, maintaining the conditions for life on the planet" ("Gaia hypothesis"). If Gaia is dying, according to Monteiro's conception, what does this say about the applicability of the Gaia hypothesis to our contemporary planet?

12 As a viewer, do you find any beauty in Monteiro's photographs? What is the connection between beauty and ugliness in *The Prophecy*? What is the relationship between art and trash? How would you define the "waste aesthetic" employed by Monteiro and Gal?

13 How does Monteiro's *The Prophecy* series relate to the Environmental Justice movement, which aims to address environmental protection inequities? According to the United States Environmental Protection Agency (EPA), environmental justice is "the fair treatment and meaningful involvement of all people regardless of race, color, national origin, or income, with respect to the development, implementation, and enforcement of environmental laws, regulations, and policies" ("Environmental Justice"). In what ways does Monteiro protest environmental injustice? Who suffers these injustices and what are the possible or proposed solutions? Additionally, how does Monteiro's *The Prophecy* series engage the concept of Environmental Racism? Environmental Racism refers generally to "the disproportionate impact of environmental hazards on people of color" and specifically to "the institutional rules, regulations, policies or government and/or corporate decisions that deliberately target certain communities for locally undesirable land uses and lax enforcement of zoning and environmental laws, resulting in communities being disproportionately exposed to toxic and hazardous waste based upon race" ("Environmental Justice & Environmental Racism"). Is Environmental Racism, a term coined in the United States in 1982 by Benjamin Chavis, applicable to the Senegalese or African contexts? Why or why not?

14 Divide the class into six groups and assign one of the SDGs from Part 1 (6, 7, 12, 13, 14, or 15) to each group. Each group will then prepare arguments for a debate in which they maintain that their assigned SDG is the most relevant or central to Monteiro's *The Prophecy* series. (The instructor of the course will decide on the format and length of the debate and facilitate a follow-up discussion with the class upon conclusion of the debate.)

15 Does Monteiro's *The Prophecy* series only reinforce and illuminate the principles under-pinning the UN SDGs and the concept of sustainable development, or does it question any inherent presuppositions, biases, shortcomings, flaws, or gaps in the UN SDG frame-work or in the notion of sustainable development? Explain with details from the featured photographs included in this chapter.

V   Beyond the Planet—Connections to SDGs on People, Prosperity, and Partnerships

Beyond SDGs 6, 7, 12, 13, 14, and 15, what additional SDGs are addressed by Fabrice Monteiro in *The Prophecy* collection? Complete the table below with your ideas. Then compare and contrast your ideas with a classmate.

SDGs:	*Does Monteiro's* The Prophecy *series connect with additional SDGs? If so, which ones and how?*
SDG 1 No Poverty	
SDG 2 Zero Hunger	
SDG 3 Good Health and Well Being	
SDG 4 Quality Education	
SDG 5 Gender Equality	
SDG 8 Decent Work and Economic Growth	
SDG 9 Industry, Innovation, and Infrastructure	
SDG 10 Reduced Inequalities	
SDG 11 Sustainable Cities and Communities	
SDG 16 Peace, Justice, and Strong Institutions	
SDG 17 Partnerships for the Goals	

VI   From Global to Local: On a Personal Level

1   How do you relate personally to Monteiro's *The Prophecy* series? Explain in detail how your own life experiences or personal beliefs intersect with the main ideas and themes of the featured work in this chapter.

2   How does Monteiro's photographic collection relate to your local environment? Explain the global-local connection between Monteiro's *The Prophecy* series and your home or current residence. What place-based considerations permit or prevent the application of the text to your geographical location?

3   Monteiro explains that *The Prophecy* series aims "to motivate an ecological consciousness" and to combine "art and ecology for a change of behavior towards nature" (Juzga 00:02:51–00:02:56; "Ecofund The Prophecy" 00:00:09–00:00:12). What effect did "Untitled #1," "Untitled #2," "Untitled #3," "Untitled #5," "Untitled #9," and "Untitled #10" have on you as a viewer? Did *The Prophecy* series motivate your "ecological consciousness" or cause a change in your "behavior towards nature"? If so, how? If not, why not? In more general terms, what type of response did Monteiro's *The Prophecy* elicit in you? Are you moved to action? Have your viewpoints or attitudes changed? Explain.

VII   Assignments

1   Research

1   Individually or in groups, research two Senegalese movements that may have been inspirational or foundational to *The Prophecy* series: (1) The Baye Fall movement and (2) the Set/Setal movement.

• **The Baye Fall Movement:** Originating in a Sufi branch of the Mouride brotherhood and dating back to the late 19th century, the Senegalese socio-religious movement of the Baye Fall embraces the principles of "humility towards Allah, charity, and rejection of any material dependence" (Matheron 123). The Baye Fall stress "the importance of a humble lifestyle and manual labor," which leads to "a system of sustainable economics" (Crowder). The Baye Fall ethics logically lead to the Baye Fall aesthetics (called Yaye Fall for women), which is characterized by brightly colored patchwork clothing made of recycled fabric (Crowder). In "The Fashion of Devotion of Senegalese Baye Fall," Enrica Picarelli explains that the Baye Fall clothes "were once exclusively fashioned out of retrieved or donated scraps of cloth, since the adherents to the brotherhood relied (and partially still do) on the community for feeding and clothing." "Wearing discarded items of dressing is an act of piety and a profession of humbleness," Picarelli explains further, which allows Baye Fall members "to express their spiritual affiliation and identity," to promote "a form of ethical consumption where recycling also serves as a performative political act," and to exclude their garments "from the economic cycle and the system of wealth and status associated with it." Before beginning *The Prophecy*, Monteiro worked on two photographic collections titled *Portrait of a Baye Fall* and *The Way of the Baye Fall*. Monteiro's interest in the Baye Fall philosophy and aesthetic continues in *The Prophecy*, especially in light of his decision to collaborate with Baye Fall designer Jah Gal. Monteiro explains that he was "inspired" by Gal's habit of "recycling old clothes to make other clothes" and by his "ability to sew any kind of material" (Stone).

• **The Set/Setal Movement:** The Senegalese Set/Setal movement from the early 1990s—which means "Be Clean/Make Clean" in Wolof—was both artistic and social in nature (Fredericks 2). In her 2018 book *Garbage Citizenship: Visual Infrastructures of Labor in Dakar, Senegal*, Rosalind Fredericks characterizes the Set/Setal youth movement as follows: "young men and women throughout the city set out to clean the city, buttress the failing urban waste infrastructure, and purify a polluted political sphere in a frenzied explosion of what came to be billed as *participatory citizenship*" (2). Set/Setal youth aimed to "combat social and urban decay in Dakar," and, in the words of Senegalese historian Mamadou Diouf, "to improve the environment of the neighborhoods, to remove the garbage and dirt [, . . .] to clean up or reform political and social practices" (Iheka 56; qtd in Iheka 56). Specifically, members of this urban youth movement cleaned up the streets, made art out of recycled materials, and promoted "environmental principles by highlighting waste but also repurposing it for artistic means" (Iheka 57).

Going beyond the brief descriptions provided above, explain in detail the Baye Fall and Set/Setal movements and comment on their relevance to both *The Prophecy* collection and to SDGs 6, 7, 12, 13, 14, and/or 15. (The instructor of the course will determine the mode of presentation and delivery—oral presentation, written report, annotated bibliography, or photo essay—for this research assignment.)

2 Since Monteiro began *The Prophecy* series in 2013, Senegal has taken many important steps to improve waste management, to protect ecosystems and prevent deforestation, to ban plastic waste, and to promote renewable energy ("Going Circular" 24). Individually or in groups, research policies and laws in Senegal from 2013 to the present that relate to SDGs 6, 7, 12, 13, 14, and 15 and to the specific planetary issues addressed by Monteiro in "Untitled #1," "Untitled #2," "Untitled #3," "Untitled #5," and "Untitled #9" of *The Prophecy*. Some of the key changes in Senegal's "transition to a green and circular economy" include:

- The Promotion of Integrated Management and Economy of Solid Waste in Senegal (PROMOGED) Program;
- The National Strategy for Economic and Social Development, 2013–2017;
- The "Plan Sénégal Emergent" (PSE);
- The National Strategy for the Promotion of Green Jobs in Senegal (SNPEV) 2015–2020;
- The National Strategic Orientation Document from the Economic, Social, and Environmental Council of Senegal;
- The Priority Action Plan, 2019–2023;
- The Ban on Plastic Waste (Law No. 2020–2004);
- The National Solid Waste Management Program;
- The Green Secondary Cities Development Program;
- The National Action Plan for Energy Efficiency 2015–2020/2030 ("Going Circular" 24–25).

(The instructor of the course will determine the mode of presentation and delivery—oral presentation, written report, short video documentary, digital timeline project, etc.—for this research assignment as well as the number of policies and laws to be included.)

2   Write

1 Write an essay in which you compare and contrast 2 of the 15 images from Monteiro's *The Prophecy* collection in terms of (1) the environmental issue depicted; (2) the (un)sustainable production patterns addressed; and (3) the (un)sustainable consumption patterns addressed. In the concluding paragraph of your essay, discuss which of the two images best relates to SDG 12 and most successfully advocates for sustainable consumption and production patterns. (The instructor of the course will determine the appropriate length for this writing assignment.)

2 Write an essay in which you compare and contrast 2 of the 15 images from Monteiro's *The Prophecy* collection in terms of either SDG 14 (Life below Water) or SDG 15 (Life on Land). In the concluding paragraph of your essay, discuss which of the two images best relates to the chosen SDG (14 or 15) and most successfully advocates for the conservation and sustainable use of marine or terrestrial ecosystems and resources. (The instructor of the course will determine the appropriate length for this writing assignment.)

3   Create

1 Individually or in groups, imagine that you were asked to choose the location and topic for the next photograph in *The Prophecy* series. Where would you choose and why? What would the "environmental crime" be and how does it relate to SDG 6, 7, 12, 13, 14, and/or 15? How would you stage the scene? What costume would you create for the model or djinn? Describe the photographic image as you envision it. (The instructor of the course will determine the mode of presentation and delivery—written proposal, sketch or mockup, oral presentation of the proposed image and location—for this creative assignment.)

2   In groups of three, create a skit in which one student interviews Fabrice Monteiro (played by a second student) and Jah Gal (played by a third student) about *The Prophecy* series and its contributions in the areas of sustainable development and environmental justice. The performance of the interview should include questions and answers about the relevance of *The Prophecy* to SDGs 6, 7, 12, 13, 14, and 15 as well as other topics of interest to the group. For groups of more than three, students could be assigned the role of additional interviewer(s) and/or the model(s) or djinn(s) in the images. (The instructor of the course will determine the mode of presentation and delivery—role play, video project, or interview script—for this creative assignment.)

Works Cited

Crowder, Nicole. "The Roots of Fashion and Spirituality in Senegal's Islamic Brotherhood, the Baye Fall." *The Washington Post*, 23 Jan. 2015, https://www.washingtonpost.com/news/in-sight/wp/2015/01/23/the-roots-of-fashion-and-spirituality-in-senegals-islamic-brotherhood-the-baye-fall/. Accessed 21 Jan. 2022.

"Ecofund The Prophecy #1 to #6 Making of Movie." *YouTube*, uploaded by Ecofund.org, 9 Nov. 2014, www.youtube.com/watch?v=juLucIqEwvo. Accessed 21 Jan. 2022.

"Environmental Justice." United States Environmental Protection Agency, 5 Aug. 2022, https://www.epa.gov/environmentaljustice. Accessed 11 Aug. 2022.

"Environmental Justice & Environmental Racism." Greenaction for Health & Environmental Justice, https://greenaction.org/what-is-environmental-justice/. Accessed 11 Aug. 2022.

"Fire the Imagination: Prix Pictet Announces Shortlist for Prestigious Photographic Prize." *The Telegraph*, 8 July 2021, https://www.telegraph.co.uk/news/2021/07/08/fire-imagination-prix-pictet-announce-shortlist-prestigious/monteiro-untitled9-2015-series-prophecyapproximately-40000-hectare/. Accessed 11 Aug. 2022.

Fredericks, Rosalind. *Garbage Citizenship: Visual Infrastructures of Labor in Dakar, Senegal*. Duke UP, 2018.

"Gaia Hypothesis." *Wikipedia*, https://en.wikipedia.org/w/index.php?oldid=468355554. Accessed 11 Aug. 2022.

"Goal 6 Targets." *Sustainable Development Goals: Goal 6.* United Nations, https://www.un.org/sustainabledevelopment/water-and-sanitation/. Accessed 11 Aug. 2022.

"Going Circular: National Level Processes towards a Circular Economy." *Switch to Green*, 2021, p. 25, https://gcpcenvis.nic.in/PDF/Going_Circular_Towards_a_Circular_Economy.pdf. Accessed 11 Aug. 2022.

Iheka, Cajetan. "Waste Reconsidered: Afrofuturism, Technologies of the Past, and the History of the Future." *African Ecomedia: Network Forms, Planetary Politics*. Duke UP, 2021, pp. 25–63.

Italia, Isadora. "Enacting Gaia and Slow Violence in Fabrice Monteiro's *The Prophecy* Series." *CLAMANTIS: The MALS Journal*, vol. 1, no. 7, 2019, pp. 1–20.

Juzga, Marcia. "The Prophecy / Dakar." *YouTube*, uploaded by Marcia Juzga, 9 Aug. 2015, www.youtube.com/watch?v=mZI_i-LauzY. Accessed 21 Jan. 2022.

Kaza, Silpa, et al. *What a Waste 2.0: A Global Snapshot of Solid Waste Management to 2050*. World Bank, 2018, https://openknowledge.worldbank.org/handle/10986/30317. Accessed 12 Aug. 2022.

Matheron, Aurélie. "Crise environnementale au Sénégal: Fabrice Monteiro et l'ecologie visionnaire de *La Prophétie*." *Nouvelles Études Francophones*, vol. 34, no. 2, 2019, pp. 120–137.

Monteiro, Fabrice. "Artist's Statement." *Prix Pictet: The Global Award in Photography and Sustainability*, https://prixpictet.com/portfolios/fire-shortlist/fabrice-monteiro/statement/. Accessed 11 Aug. 2022.

———. "Interview with Fabrice Monteiro." Interview by Astrup Fearnley Museet. *Alpha Crusis: Contemporary African Art*. YouTube, uploaded by Astrup Fearnley Museet, 17 July 2020, www.youtube.com/watch?v=Y0Ijmpsncuc. Accessed 21 Jan. 2022.

———. "Of Djinn and Man: A Conversation with Fabrice Monteiro." Interview by Evan D. Williams. *Africanah.org Arena for Contemporary African, African-American and Caribbean Art*, 10 May 2020, www.africanah.org/fabrice-monteiro-3/. Accessed 21 Jan. 2022.

———. *Portrait of a Baye Fall. Fabrice Monteiro Photography.* 2015, *viewbook*, fabricemonteiro.viewbook.com/portrait-of-a-baye-fall. Accessed 21 Jan. 2022.

———. *The Prophecy. Fabrice Monteiro Photography.* 2015, *viewbook*, fabricemonteiro.viewbook.com/. Accessed 21 Jan. 2022.

———. *The Way of the Baye Fall. Fabrice Monteiro Photography.* 2015, *viewbook*, fabricemonteiro.viewbook.com/the-way-of-the-baye-fall. Accessed 21 Jan. 2022.

Niedan, Christian. "The Photographic Confrontations of Fabrice Monteiro: An Interview." *The Mantle: Smart Content for the Global Citizen*, https://www.themantle.com/arts-and-culture/photographic-confrontations-fabrice-monteiro-interview. Accessed 11 Aug. 2022.

Picarelli, Enrica. "The Fashion of Devotion of Senegalese Baye Fall." *Afrosartorialism: A Research Project on African Fashion Digitalities*, 7 Feb. 2015, www.afrosartorialism.net/2015/02/07/the-fashion-of-devotion-of-senegalese-baye-fall/. Accessed 21 Jan. 2022.

Ravenhall, Lucy. "What Is the Difference between Recycling and Upcycling?" *The Waste Management & Recycling Blog*, 29 May 2020, www.forgerecycling.co.uk/blog/what-is-the-difference-between-recycling-and-upcycling/. Accessed 21 Jan. 2022.

Siddons, Edward. "Fabrice Monteiro's Best Photograph: A Spirit Emerges from a Rubbish Dump in Senegal." *The Guardian*, 24 Nov. 2021, https://www.theguardian.com/artanddesign/2021/nov/24/fabrice-monteiro-best-photograph-spirit-of-a-rubbish-dump-in-senegal?CMP=Share_iOSApp_Other. Accessed 11 Aug. 2022.

"SDG Goals 6 Clean Water and Sanitation." *United Nations Statistics Division*, 2021, https://unstats.un.org/sdgs/report/2021/Goal-06/. Accessed 11 Aug. 2022.

"SDG Goals 7 Affordable and Clean Energy." *United Nations Statistics Division*, 2021, https://unstats.un.org/sdgs/report/2021/Goal-07/. Accessed 11 Aug. 2022.

"SDG Goals 13 Climate Action." *United Nations Statistics Division*, 2021, https://unstats.un.org/sdgs/report/2021/Goal-13/. Accessed 11 Aug. 2022.

"SDG Goals 14 Life below Water." *United Nations Statistics Division*, 2021, https://unstats.un.org/sdgs/report/2021/Goal-14/. Accessed 11 Aug. 2022.

"SDG Goals 15 Life on Land." *United Nations Statistics Division*, 2021, https://unstats.un.org/sdgs/report/2021/goal-15/. Accessed 11 Aug. 2022.

Stoddard, Jill. "From Environmental Degradation Comes Art: Q&A with Fabrice Monteiro." *International Peace Institute Global Observatory*, 2015, https://theglobalobservatory.org/2015/10/environmental-problems-africa-fabrice-monteiro/. Accessed 11 Aug. 2022.

Stone, Bryony. "Photographer Fabrice Monteiro's Fear-Inducing Prophecy of West Africa's Future." *It's Nice That*, 5 June 2017, www.itsnicethat.com/articles/photographer-fabrice-monteiros-prophecy-west-africas-future-050617. Accessed 21 Jan. 2022.

"Sustainable Production and Consumption." *Sustainable Development Goals Knowledge Platform*, https://sustainabledevelopment.un.org/topics/sustainableconsumptionandproduction. Accessed 11 Aug. 2022.

"The Prophecy 3rd Photo." *Ecofund. Our Future Is Green*, 2014, https://www.ecofund.org/de/news/the-prophecy-3rd-photo.html. Accessed 12 Aug. 2022.

"'We Already Live in a Dystopian World' – Fabrice Monteiro." *Design Indaba: A Better World through Creativity*, 12 Apr. 2018, https://www.designindaba.com/articles/creative-work/we-already-live-dystopian-world-%E2%80%93%C2%A0fabrice-monteiro. Accessed 11 Aug. 2022.

4 Kip Andersen and Keegan Kuhn's *Cowspiracy*

Animal Agriculture and the "Sustainability Secret"

Natalie Khazaal

I   Text

Title	*Cowspiracy: The Sustainability Secret*
Genre	Documentary film
Directors	Kip Andersen and Keegan Kuhn
	Kip Andersen founded Animals United Movement (A.U.M.) Films and Media, a non-profit that promotes awareness and equality for all life. His award-winning work includes the documentaries *Cowspiracy: The Sustainability Secret*, *What the Health* (which became a huge success), and *Seaspiracy*. A graduate of California Polytechnic State University's Business School, Andersen decided to live a more environmentally conscious and ethical life after watching former Vice President Al Gore's climate emergency film *An Inconvenient Truth*. Following an initial focus on recycling, bicycling for transportation, and conserving power and water, he learned of the impact of animal agriculture on the environment.
	Keegan Kuhn is an award-winning documentary filmmaker and professional musician from San Francisco, CA. He has helped nonprofit organizations increase their impact by documenting modern homesteaders in remote areas of Alaska; filming the nation's remaining wild horses in deserts of the American west; and, through a grant from Bloomberg Philanthropies, crafting local nutrition policy in the rural agricultural community of Jackson, MS. His work includes the documentaries *Cowspiracy: The Sustainability Secret*, *What the Health*, *Running for Good*, *They're Trying to Kill Us*, and *The End of Medicine*.
Year	2014–2015
Country	United States of America

Cowspiracy is available on Netflix, through digital downloads via VHX/Vimeo or the film's website (https://www.cowspiracy.com/), and on DVD. *Cowspiracy* DVDs have subtitles available in over 15 languages as well as English Closed Captioning.

Trigger warning: Unlike other movies on the topic, *Cowspiracy* is not a graphic film. However, some viewers might be disturbed by one scene in the film where a duck is slaughtered by a backyard farmer (1:10:16–1:12:23).

DOI: 10.4324/9781003388869-6

Figure 4.1 Movie Poster for *Cowspiracy: The Sustainability Secret,* 2014, Cowspiracy.com.

Figure 4.2 The Butcher Row, *Cowspiracy: The Sustainability Secret,* 2014, Cowspiracy.com.

II   Context

When Kip Andersen saw former Vice President Al Gore's environmental film *An Inconvenient Truth*, he was shocked by the destruction caused by the energy industry and decided to live more sustainably. He started using LED lights, composting, recycling, and biking instead of driving. But a question crept up: Is that enough to save the planet? A 12-minute video about factory farming called "Meet Your Meat," narrated by Alec Baldwin, helped Kip find an answer. Factory farming (the most popular current form of animal agriculture) is the commercial rearing of animals for their flesh, milk, eggs, wool, or skins. Animal agriculture produces three types of greenhouse gases (GHG): methane (from animal belches and manure), nitrous oxide (in manure and fertilizer), and carbon dioxide (from fertilizer, equipment, transport, storage, and processing). Half of all GHG emissions from animal agriculture come from methane, which is 86 times more potent than CO_2 (the main by-product of the oil and gas industry) over a 20-year period ("SDG: The Challenge"). Although this makes animal agriculture a leading cause of environmental destruction, Andersen discovered that most environmental organizations never address it. Discovering this destructive role and its denial gave him a clear vision for how to make a difference in the planet's destiny.

If Andersen's path toward creating *Cowspiracy* started with the environment, for Keegan Kuhn it was social justice. He heard the hard-core punk band "Earth Crisis" talk about the dangers of the meat and dairy industry and became politically active through public speaking, protests, leafleting, and music. Eventually, he realized that film was the most effective tool for reaching a large audience and making an impact on environmental and social justice issues. It took five years to formulate the idea for the award-winning, science-based documentary, but Kuhn, who was also director of photography, shot the film in just ten months on a DSLR 5D mkII (HD) camera with a fully manual lens and triple recording system, using natural light to create an emotional atmosphere.

The final cut is a shocking, yet humorous documentary that "uncovers the most destructive industry facing the planet today [large-scale factory farming]—and investigates why the world's leading environmental organizations are too afraid to talk about it" ("About"). It puts under scrutiny famous organizations like Greenpeace, Sierra Club, Surfrider Foundation, Rainforest Action Network, and Oceana. When Leonardo DiCaprio saw the film, he became obsessed with it and decided to become its executive producer. He personally called Netflix to negotiate its release on the platform, and in 2015, the movie premiered there globally.

Cowspiracy would be unthinkable without the context of recent, industrial-age changes in animal agriculture. For centuries, local family farms allowed small-scale consumption of animal products. However, the 1980s transformed animal agriculture into Concentrated Animal Feeding Operations (CAFOs), which in the USA alone exceed 21,000 (EPA, "NPDES"). CAFOs are damp, dark, freezing, or scorching hangars where millions of animals are packed together on top of feces, urine, and decaying carcasses until they are killed for human food mere months after being born. According to federal data, 70% of cows, 98% of pigs, and 99% of chickens and turkeys are currently raised in CAFOs in the USA ("2017 Census," "US Factory Farming"). CAFOs create over 500 million tons of waste every year and pose a significant contamination threat to surrounding water sources, crops, free-living animals, and human settlements ("National Pollutant Discharge"). Antibiotics are regularly administered to farmed animals to stave off the inevitable diseases that such unhealthy, unhygienic, and extremely confined environments cause, while steroids are injected to induce rapid weight gain. Because of the obvious suffering induced by the living conditions in factory farms, most people avoid acknowledging their part of the impact of animal agriculture upon the planet and other living beings. That is not difficult, as various industry tactics have shielded people from understanding the true impact of routine meals—from hiding CAFOs out of sight (lack of public awareness), false advertisements (e.g., "happy cows," "grass-fed meat," and "eco-farming"), to cognitive dissonance (animals are not morally relevant and do not deserve compassion). When advertisements and hiding fall short, the industry turns to prosecuting whistleblowers who film the gruesome reality of raising and killing animals for human food and its harmful impact on the environment. Because animal agriculture is very expensive, many governments around the world subsidize it with tax-payers' money, making dairy and meat products artificially cheap.

III   Interpretation

1   Can *Cowspiracy* be defined as an activist documentary? A documentary is "a factual film which is dramatic" (Pinkerton). Providing an opinion and a new message together with the facts, a documentary is a "recording" of "any aspect of reality interpreted either by factual shooting or by sincere and justifiable reconstruction, so as to appeal either to reason or emotion, for the purpose of stimulating the desire for, and the widening of human knowledge and understanding, and of truthfully posing problems and their solutions" (Rotha 30–31). Does *Cowspiracy* follow the tradition of documentary filmmaking? Is it factual? Dramatic? Does it appeal to reason and/or emotion? Does it widen human knowledge and understanding? Does it present information that concerns citizens?

2. *Cowspiracy*'s creator Kip Andersen's main goal was to inform those who did not know how animal agriculture operates, not to tell people what to do. Do the film's visual aids enhance or diminish from this goal (consider Figures 4.3–4.5)? How do they demonstrate the effects and scale of emissions from animal agriculture? How do they communicate complex information to viewers? How does one effectively share large-scale and multifaceted information to non-specialists?

Figure 4.3 Film still from *Cowspiracy* showing that all means of transportation combined produce less GHG emissions than animal agriculture (00:04:35).

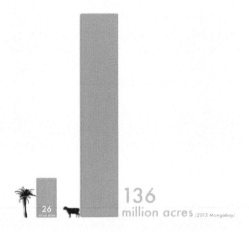

Figure 4.4 Film still from *Cowspiracy* showing that animal agriculture causes over five times more deforestation than palm oil plantations (00:32:38).

Figure 4.5 Film still from *Cowspiracy* showing that animal agriculture produces 130 times more biological waste than all humans (00:40:36).

3   *Cowspiracy* opens with a quotation from Martin Luther King, Jr.: "In the end, we will remember not the words of our enemies, but the silence of our friends" (00:00:17–00:00:27). The following scene depicts an exchange between creator Kip Andersen (KA) and Bruce Hamilton (BH), Deputy Executive Director of the environmental organization Sierra Club:
       [Camera is focused on BH.]
       BH: You know, the world's climate scientists tell us that the highest safe level of emissions would be around 350 ppm of carbon dioxide greenhouse gases in the atmosphere. We're already at 400 [. . .].
       KA: What about livestock and animal agriculture?
       [Background music stops. Camera depth shifts, focused on confused BH face.]
       BH: Uh? Well, what about it? (00:00:29–00:01:54)
     How does Dr. King's quote relate to the scene and to the film's main message? How does *Cowspiracy* use elements of cinematic composition (camera, sound, juxtaposition) in this

sequence to drive the main message? How does *Cowspiracy* frame environmental advocacy organizations? Should they represent the interests of the planet, its inhabitants, or animal agriculture? Does the film frame Anderson as a challenger? Why is he represented as a voice without a body in this scene?

4   In addition to visual aids (question IV. 2) and dialogues that allow audiences to listen to conversations between two people (question IV. 3), many documentaries use narrators. The narrator is the voiceover that tells the audience what is happening on the screen. It is one of the keys to making a good documentary film. Typically, narrators are voiceover actors whose professional abilities engage audiences and allow them to connect to the subject. But many documentary filmmakers are experts or witnesses to the subject they present, which makes them more reliable narrators. What are the advantages and disadvantages of having Kip Andersen as the first-person narrator and Keegan Kuhn take a behind-the-scenes role in the film? Would a third-person narrator have served *Cowspiracy* better or worse? Why? Consider the film stills in Figures 4.6–4.8 in regard to these questions.

Figure 4.6 Film still from *Cowspiracy* showing Kip Andersen in conversation with Demosthenes Maratos of The Sustainability Institute at Molloy College (00:17:30).

Figure 4.7 Film still from *Cowspiracy* showing Kip Andersen in conversation with Michael Besancon, former Whole Foods Market executive (00:16:38).

Figure 4.8 Film still from *Cowspiracy* showing Kip Andersen trying to reach environmental organizations (00:07:37).

5   *Cowspiracy*'s private investors dropped out after realizing that it addresses environmental organizations' inaction, due to their ties to and fear of being critical of these organizations, according to an interview with Andersen ("Kip Andersen" 00:10:22–00:10:50). The documentary was later crowdfunded and is now featured worldwide on Netflix. How have crowdfunding and streaming services changed independent films' visibility and access to viewers? How have they helped films that challenge cultural, economic, or political traditions gain credibility without big-player investors? What are the advantages and disadvantages of crowdfunding and streaming distribution for documentaries like *Cowspiracy* in terms of (1) product control; (2) revenue generation; (3) navigating relationships with funders; (4) message credibility; and (5) attracting interest?

6   The 2000s marked the rise of popular activist documentaries like *Bowling for Columbine* (2002, on gun control), *Super Size Me* (2004, on the damage caused by the fast-food industry), and *Blackfish* (2013, on the abuse and imprisonment of whales for entertainment). Some of them greatly affected social conditions, e.g., after the release of *Super Size Me*, fast-food chains introduced healthier options, while in 2015 SeaWorld reported an 84% drop in profits (Rhodan) and in 2016 announced the end of its whale breeding program (Du Lac and Bever). What is *Cowspiracy*'s place among whistle-blowing documentaries given its popularity and influence, as evidenced in the table below? How do you think it influenced the relationship between environmental organizations and animal advocates? Is the publicity it generates for environmental organizations good or bad? Why?

Cowspiracy's *popularity:*	Cowspiracy's *influence:*
• Audience Choice Award, 2015, South African Eco Film Festival ("*Cowspiracy* Wins") • Best Foreign Film Award, 12th Annual Festival de films de Portneuf sur l'environnement ("Le FFPE") • Nomination for second Audience Choice Award, 2015, Cinema Politica ("Vote for") • 8.1/10 *IMDb* score ("Cowspiracy" *IMDb*) • 88% *Rotten Tomatoes* score ("Cowspiracy" *Rotten Tomatoes*)	• A significant number of social media posts credited the film for switching to a sustainable lifestyle and plant-based diet (e.g., Berry; Ms Riggen; Pritchard; Vegan Future). According to a *Vomad* international survey, "24.6% or 692 people first wanted to go vegan after watching Cowspiracy" (McCormick). • Many attendees at a University of Amsterdam Q&A with Andersen confirmed the same ("Kip Andersen" 48:30–48:58). • *Cowspiracy* inspired the creation of vegan farms and restaurants switching to a 100% plant-based menu (e.g. Pevreall). • *Cowspiracy* inspired a vlogger to make the documentary *Seaspiracy* ("Kip Andersen" 32:52–33:45) and the creation of *Milked*, an indigenous award-winning documentary about the environmental dangers of the dairy industry ("Milked"). • Research study participants reported greater awareness of animal agriculture's environmental impact, more favorable attitudes toward systemic reduction of meat consumption, and strong personal intention to do it (Pabian).

7   How does *Cowspiracy* source the statistics that it cites? Discuss its sources below listed alphabetically for each category.

~ncies and organizations:	Scientific journals, newspapers, magazines, books, print, and online publications
government agencies: US Bureau of Land Management US Energy Information Administration US Environmental Protection Agency (EPA) US FDA: Department of Health and Human Services US General Accounting Office US Geological Service US National Aeronautics and Space Administration US National Oceanic and Atmospheric Administration USDA: Agricultural Waste Management Field Handbook USDA: Economic Research Service USDA: Foreign Agriculture Service USDA: Natural Resources Conservation Center **~ agencies:** FAO: Fisheries and Aquaculture Division (NFI) Food and Agriculture Organization of the United Nations (FAO) The World Bank UN 67th general assembly UN Climate Summit 2014 UN Environment Program UN news center UNICEF **~ernational government organizations:** International Energy Agency	**Scientific journals/academic publications:** 1 *Bioscience* 2 *Cornell Chronicle* 3 *Ecosystems* 4 *Environmental Research Letters* 5 *Georgetown Environmental Law Review* 6 *Journal of Animal Science* 7 *Marine Policy* 8 *Nature* 9 *Nature Communications* 10 *Population and Development Review* 11 *Proceedings of the National Academy of Sciences* 12 *Public Health Reports* 13 *Research Journal of Recent Sciences* 14 *Science* 15 *Science advances* 16 *Science of the Total Environment* 17 *The American Journal of Clinical Nutrition* 18 *Water Resources and Industry* 19 *Yale School of Forestry and Environmental Studies: Global Forest Atlas* **Popular scientific magazines:** 20 *Energy Global* 21 *Phys.org (ScienceX)* 22 *Scientific American* 23 *Smithsonian Magazine* **Books and academic articles:** 24 Allaby, Michael, and Robert Coenraads. *The Encyclopedia of Earth: A Complete Visual* Guide.

Academic institutions:
22   Johns Hopkins Center for a Livable Future
23   Twente Water Center, University of Twente, Netherlands

NGOs:
24   Center for Biological Diversity
25   Environmental Working Group
26   International Livestock Research Institute
27   Pacific Institute
28   Post Growth Institute
29   Predator Defense
30   Water Education Foundation
31   Water Footprint Network
32   World Resources Institute
33   World Wide Fund (WWF)
34   Oceana
35   Shark Savers
36   Animal Welfare Institute
37   Rainforest Relief
38   A Well-Fed World (hunger relief)
39   Action Bioscience
40   Free from Harm

Private foundations and charities:
41   Annenberg Learner (funds non-profits)
42   The Population Institute

Advocacy Organizations:
43   Mighty Earth (environmental)
44   ADAPTT (animal rights)
45   Compassion in World Farming

Business, political, religious organizations:
46   Wisconsin Soybean Marketing Board
47   Earth Save
48   The Sisters of Notre Dame de Namur

25   Jacobson, Michael, and Center for Science in the Public Interest. *Six Arguments for a Greener Diet: How a More Plant-based Diet Could Save Your Health and the Environment.*
26   Oppenlander, Richard. *Comfortably unaware: Global Depletion and Food Choice Responsibility: What You Choose to Eat is Killing Our Planet.*
27   Oppenlander, Richard. *Food Choice and Sustainability: Why Buying Local, Eating Less Meat, and Taking Baby Steps Won't Work.*
28   Robbins, John. *How Your Food Choices Affect Your Health, Happiness and the Future of Life on Earth.*
29   Schwab, Denise, et al. "Grass-fed and Organic Beef: Production Costs and Breakeven Market Prices, 2008–2009."
30   Simon, David. *Meatonomics: How the Rigged Economics of Meat and Dairy Make You Consume Too Much—and How to Eat Better, Live Longer, and Spend Smarter.*
31   Smil, Vaclav. *Harvesting the Biosphere: What We Have Taken from Nature.*

Newspapers:
32   *International Business Times*
33   *The Economist*
34   *The Guardian*
35   *The Huffington Post*
36   *The Independent*
37   *The New York Times*
38   *The Telegraph*

Popular Magazines:
39   *National Geographic*
40   *Nova*
41   *Ocean News*
42   *Slate*
43   *Time*

Online publications:
44   *Business Insider*
45   *Chestsculpting.com* (bodybuilding)
46   *Common Dreams.org* (non-profit news website)
47   *Fishcount.org* (Reef Environmental Education Foundation)
48   *Food Safety News*
49   *Globalagriculture.org*
50   *Inhabitat*
51   *Mongabay* (environmental)
52   *One Green Planet*
53   *Save The Amazon. org*
54   *Shrink that Footprint*
55   *The Vegan Calculator*
56   *Vegetarian Guide*
57   *Wildlife News*
58   *Worldometers* (statistics)

Media outlets:
59   World Watch

Documentaries:
60   *Forks over Knives* ("The Facts")

Consider the sources listed above in terms of:

- legitimacy and trust by experts in their field
- potential bias
- filmmakers' choice to rely on over 100 sources
- filmmakers' choice to rely heavily on government sources
- filmmakers' attempts to defuse controversy
- filmmakers' choice to rely on multiple sources per claim (see Figure 4.9, showing two examples of how *Cowspiracy*'s companion website cowspiracy.com lists all its claims' sources)

2,500 GALLONS OF WATER ARE NEEDED TO PRODUCE 1 POUND OF BEEF.

(NOTE. The amount of water used to produce 1lb. of beef vary greatly from 442 - 8000 gallons. We choose to use in the film the widely cited conservative number of 2500 gallons per pound of US beef from Dr. George Borgstrom, Chairman of Food Science and Human Nutrition Dept of College of Agriculture and Natural Resources, Michigan State University, "Impacts on Demand for and Quality of land and Water.")

Robbins, John. "2,500 gallons all wet?" Earth Save: Healthy People Healthy Planet.

Pimentel, David, et al. "Water Resources: Agricultural and Environmental Issues". BioScience (2004) 54 (10): 909-918. **(New)**

"Water Content of Things: Data Table 19". The World's Water 2008-2009

Beckett, J. L, Oltjen, J. W "Estimation of the Water Requirement for Beef Production in the United States". Journal of Animal Science. 1993. 71:818-826

"Water". Environmental Working Group.

"Water footprint of crop and animal products: a comparison". Water Footprint Network. **(New)**

Oppenlander, Richard A. *Food Choice and Sustainability: Why Buying Local, Eating Less Meat, and Taking Baby Steps Won't Work.* Minneapolis, MN: Langdon Street, 2013. Print

---

ANIMAL AGRICULTURE WATER CONSUMPTION RANGES FROM 34-76 TRILLION GALLONS ANNUALLY. [II] [XV]

"Summary of Estimated Water Use in the United States in 2005". United States Geological Service

Pimentel, David, et al. "Water Resources: Agricultural and Environmental Issues". BioScience. (2004) 54 (10): 909-918

Figure 4.9 Cowspiracy's reliance on multiple sources per claim, https://www.cowspiracy.com/facts (permission granted by *Cowspiracy* creators).

8   The directors include this note before listing all their sources on *Cowspiracy*'s companion website page called "The Facts": "The science and research done on the true impacts of animal agriculture is always growing. The statistics used in the film were based on the best information we had available while producing the film. We will continually update this list with further resources as they become available." Do you agree that they fulfilled their promise (see https://www.cowspiracy.com/facts)? How does their decision to include direct links to sources for transparency affect *Cowspiracy*'s credibility? How does organizing facts by rubrics and direct links empower:

- viewers (lay persons) to verify statistics and understand sources;
- experts to confirm or challenge statistics;
- the factory farming industry to qualify or deny its role in environmental destruction;
- traditional mass media (television, radio, and press) to create thoughtful reports about the movie and the issues it raises;

- politicians to grasp the severity of animal agriculture as a major cause of global warming and environmental destruction and to have ready data to back up new legislation?

9   *Cowspiracy* cites two estimates for animal agriculture's contribution to our climate catastrophe, 18% and 51%. Some have labeled the film propaganda on account of the second statistic, which comes from a 2009 *Worldwatch Institute Report* called "Livestock and Climate Change: What if the Key Actors in Climate Change Are . . . Cows, Pigs, and Chickens" (Goodland and Angang). The report argues that 35%–51% of GHG emissions can be attributed to "land change use" or the conversion of non-farm land like forests to farm land (11). Other statistics published over the past two decades estimate the effects on GHG emissions associated with animal agriculture anywhere between 14.5% and 68%:

- UN FAO's 2006 report "Livestock's Long Shadow" suggests that "Livestock's contribution is enormous. It currently amounts to about 18% of the global warming effect—an even larger contribution than the transportation sector worldwide" (272).
- In their 2013 book *Tackling Climate Change through Livestock,* published by UN FAO, Gerber et al. argue that animal agriculture is responsible for 14.5% of all human-induced GHG emissions (15), although their study uses outdated statistics and represents an underestimate according to Richard Twine (6,276).
- In the 2018 article "Reducing Food's Environmental Impacts through Producers and Consumers" published in *Science*, Joseph Poore and Thomas Nemecek estimate that switching to "a diet that excludes animal products" could lead to a 49% reduction in CO_2 equivalent (5).
- According to Michael Eisen and Patrick Brown's 2022 article "Rapid Global Phaseout," "eliminating animal agriculture has the potential to offset 68 percent of current anthropogenic CO_2 emissions" (caused by humans).

Keeping these statistics in mind, discuss:

- The state of consensus among them. (Should the film be dismissed as propaganda?)
- Whether the filmmakers made the right choice to cite the statistic of 51%. (Did they violate the spirit of documentaries to create "a factual film which is dramatic" (Pinkerton)? Is the inclusion of this statistic doing more harm than good to their goal of raising concern about the negative effects of factory farming? Will their choice be considered controversial 50 years from now?)
- An alternative statistic. (Would citing a lower statistic have caused controversy? If we consider the statistics in the middle or even at the lower end, would animal agriculture cease to be destructive to the environment? What statistic would you have chosen and why?)

10   The name *Cowspiracy* is a play on the words "cow" and "conspiracy." A conspiracy is "a secret agreement to do an unlawful or wrongful act or an act which becomes unlawful as a result of the secret agreement" ("Conspire"). For reference, in the 1970s, international tobacco companies conspired against anti-smoking legislation, promoting "controversy" over data that links smoking to disease (Operation Berkshire); the conspiracy was uncovered more than 20 years later (Francey and Chapman). According to an interview with *Cowspiracy's* filmmakers, environmental organizations, such as Greenpeace or Sierra Club, etc., are guiltier of conspiracy than farmers, because unlike farmers, they are aware of the devastating effects of animal agriculture on the planet but choose not to share this information ("Kip Andersen" 27:20–28:25). Do you agree with the filmmakers that there is a conspiracy to cover up animal agriculture's impact on the planet? Why? Why did the filmmakers use this title? Why did they choose "cow" instead of another farmed animal? Is the title *Cowspiracy* appropriate? Is it effective? Can you think of a more appropriate and/or effective title? What do you think of the subtitle: *The Sustainability Secret*?

IV   Planet-Focused Applications to SDGs 6, 7, 12, 13, 14, and 15

1   *Cowspiracy* depicts animal agriculture as a leading cause of air and water pollution. Agricultural waste disseminates manure, blood, antibiotics, pesticides, steroids, pathogens, endotoxins, allergens, and other contaminants on and beyond agricultural areas. It also runs off into lakes, rivers, and the ocean, affecting negatively many species' drinking water and shelter. How does *Cowspiracy* engage with SDG 6 (Clean Water and Sanitation) and its goal to "ensure availability and sustainable management of water and sanitation for all" ("The 17 Goals")? How does it engage with target 6.6, to "protect and restore water-related ecosystems, including mountains, forests, wetlands, rivers, aquifers and lakes" ("The 17 Goals")?

2   *Cowspiracy* does not directly discuss SDG 7 (Affordable and Clean Energy). Nonetheless, how could a potential decrease in animal agriculture land use contribute to target 7.2, to "increase substantially the share of renewable energy in the global energy mix" ("The 17 Goals")? What renewable energy installations could replace land previously designated to livestock grazing?

3   How does *Cowspiracy* critique animal farming in terms of achieving SDG 12 (Responsible Consumption and Production)? Currently, countries are left to develop their own sustainable production and consumption guidelines because there are no *specific* globally agreed-upon directives. Figure 4.10 shows whether the dietary guidelines of the World Health Organization (WHO) and four countries promote sustainable food consumption, based on a study by Hannah Ritchie et al. The study concludes that current "national dietary guidelines are incompatible with climate mitigation targets" (Ritchie et al. 53). Design better global guidelines for sustainable food consumption, based on Figure 4.10 and *Cowspiracy*. What changes should industries make to respond to such guidelines?

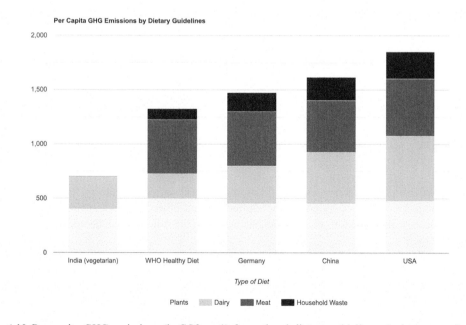

Figure 4.10 Per capita GHG emissions (kgCO2eyr-1) for national dietary guidelines. A close approximation created with data from Hannah Ritchie et al.'s study of the impact of global dietary guidelines on climate change.

4   SDG 13 intends to "take urgent action to combat climate change" ("The 17 Goals"). How do methane, nitrous oxide, and CO_2 emissions from animal agriculture affect climate change, according to *Cowspiracy*? What solutions does it propose?
     Consider the public outcry at the menu of the 2022 climate conference COP27, where attendees feasted on $100 angus beef medallion platters. According to *Reuters*, "meat [was] on the menu, not the agenda," featuring "beef, chicken, fish, and dairy products [. . .] amid calls from eco-activists to cut down on meat to save the planet" (Valdmanis and Cocks). Twitter exploded with pictures of the beef platter, the menu prices, and comments that the conference might as well offer an endangered species. Discuss how *Cowspiracy* can help us understand this public outcry and its connection to animal agriculture and SDG 13.

5   SDG 14 (Life below Water) establishes the goal "to conserve and sustainably use the oceans, seas, and marine resources" ("The 17 Goals"). In "Reducing Food's Environmental Impacts," Poore and Nemecek argue that "[t]he lowest-impact aquaculture systems still exceed [GHG] emissions of vegetable proteins. This challenges recommendations to expand aquaculture" (990). Along similar lines, *Cowspiracy* visually presents data from a UN Food and Agriculture Organization report, which states that one pound of shrimp caught equals 20 pounds of bycatch that includes sharks, dolphins, and turtles (Clucas). What are the main ways that aquatic animals are impacted by fishing, marine travel, and human-generated noise? How do these contribute to ocean dead zones and species extinction (you may consult https://www.cowspiracy.com/facts under the subcategory "Oceans")? Does *Cowspiracy* show another "Sustainability Secret" related to fishing and aquaculture? What is the clash between protecting aquatic animals and using them as a resource?

6   SDG 15 (Life on Land) aims to:

   •   protect, restore, and promote sustainable use of terrestrial ecosystems and forests
   •   combat desertification, land degradation, and biodiversity loss ("The 17 Goals")
     How can these issues be solved according to *Cowspiracy*? How does its solution compare to the one proposed in UN FAO's "Livestock Long Shadow Report":

     Seventy percent of previous forested land in the Amazon is occupied by pastures, and feedcrops cover a large part of the remainder. [. . .] The loss of species is estimated to be running 50 to 500 times higher than background rates found in the fossil record. [. . .] the livestock sector [. . .] is the major driver of deforestation, as well as one of the leading drivers of land degradation, pollution, climate change, overfishing, sedimentation of coastal areas and facilitation of invasions by alien species. (xxi, xxiii)

7   According to *Cowspiracy*, who is ultimately responsible for the systemic environmental degradation caused by animal agriculture? What other players contribute to it? How can those responsible turn into saviors, according to the following meta-analysis:

     Dietary change can deliver environmental benefits on a scale not achievable by producers. Moving from current diets to a diet that excludes animal products has transformative potential, reducing food's land use by 3.1 (2.8 to 3.3) billion hectares (a 76% reduction), including a 19% reduction in arable land; food's GHG emissions by 6.6 (5.5 to 7.4) billion metric tons of CO_2 equiv. (a 49% reduction); acidification by 50% (45 to 54%); eutrophication by 49% (37 to 56%); and scarcity-weighted freshwater withdrawals by 19% (−5 to 32%) for a 2010 reference year. (Poore and Nemecek)

8   What makes many humans reluctant to admit the harmful role of animal agriculture in species extinction, environmental destruction, and generating GHG? What cultural assumptions are typically associated with eating animals and wearing their skins? Why do you think scholars have called historical human societies "hunter-gatherers" rather than "gatherer-hunters" even though women provided the majority of the calories by gathering plants?

9   *Cowspiracy* interviews farmers who employ so-called "eco-friendly" practices like grass-fed beef, organic eggs, eating local, low-carbon chicken, or regenerative grazing. Greenwashing is the "practice of making a product, policy, activity, etc. appear to be more environmentally friendly or less environmentally damaging" ("Greenwashing"). How does greenwashing impact consumer behavior? Why do companies profit more from products labeled eco-friendly, sustainable, or humane than those marketed without such terms?

10 Environmental justice is "the fair treatment and meaningful involvement of all people regardless of race, color, national origin, or income, with respect to the development, implementation, and enforcement of environmental laws, regulations, and policies" ("Learn About"). How does *Cowspiracy* relate to the environmental justice movement, which aims to address these inequities? How does animal agriculture contribute to environmental racism or to situations in which the Global South and US "communities consisting primarily of people of color continue to bear a disproportionate burden of [a] nation's air, water and waste problems" (Bullard)? Consider the following:

- US per capita meat consumption is three times the global average (Poore and Nemecek).
- Slaughterhouses and meat-packing plants are among the most dangerous workplaces; they employ mostly immigrants and undocumented workers (Khazaal).
- Animal agriculture businesses forcefully remove indigenous people from their land (Lowry).
- Animal agriculture pollution displaces indigenous people from their land (Lowry).

11 Do environmentalists who consume animal products harm the environment and send the wrong message? Why? How would *Cowspiracy*'s filmmakers answer this question? Consider the following statement from Poore and Nemecek's meta-analysis of 570 peer-reviewed scientific studies with data covering 38,700 commercial farms in 119 countries representing approximately 90% of global protein and calorie consumption: "[environmental] impacts of the lowest-impact animal products typically exceed those of vegetable substitutes, providing new evidence for the importance of dietary change" (Poore and Nemecek 987).

12 Individually or in groups, pretend to be a policy maker trying to determine the best methods to tackle GHG emissions from the food industry. Come up with a statement of policy recommendations for your state or country that consider the following:

- recommended targets;
- taxes or tax breaks;
- abolishing or adding subsidies;
- monitoring emissions;
- requiring environmental labels for products;
- educational campaigns about the true costs of food.

Be sure to justify each policy recommendation included in the report.

13 For decades, environmental organizations failed to frame animal agriculture as a primary source of environmental destruction, nor did they encourage people to make substantial changes to their diet. Compare the following two instances and comment on changes in Greenpeace's willingness to address animal agriculture's environmental impact:

- In a discussion at the University of Amsterdam on May 17, 2016, Kip Andersen accuses Greenpeace of being more invested in fundraising than the planet's survival. A Greenpeace affiliate denies the allegations: "I'm your ally . . . We ask our members and everybody to eat less meat" ("Kip Andersen" 38:35–39:09). When Andersen asks the affiliate if Greenpeace has posted on their website information on animal-caused global warming, the affiliate shares that they are working on it ("Kip Andersen" 39:10–39:30).

- Since *Cowspiracy*, Greenpeace has published a few posts about the devastating effect of meat consumption. For instance, in the 2015 post "More Meat Threatens the Planet," the organization acknowledges that "[m]ore and more of our supporters are telling us they are really concerned about the impact the world's obsession with meat is having on the environment." In 2020, Katie Nelson writes that "new report links 2020's record-breaking fires in Brazil's Pantanal wetlands to [the] world's biggest meat processor." And during the 2022 UN Climate Change Conference (COP27), Greenpeace's website featured the post "Empty Words Feed No One," which admits: "It is time to think of a near future, a future where emissions peak by 2025, where developed countries drastically reduce meat consumption" (Thöner and Martin).

14 Divide the class into six groups and assign each an SDG from Part 1 (6, 7, 12, 13, 14, or 15). Each group will then prepare arguments for a debate in which they maintain that their assigned SDG is the most relevant to *Cowspiracy*. (The instructor of the course will decide on the format and length of the debate and facilitate a follow-up discussion with the class.)
15 Does *Cowspiracy* only reinforce the SDGs and the concept of sustainable development, or does it question any inherent biases, shortcomings, or gaps in the SDG framework or in the notion of sustainable development? Be sure to analyze the film's subtitle—*The Sustainability Secret*—in this regard.

V   Beyond Planet—Connections to SDGs on People, Prosperity, and Partnerships

Beyond SDGs 6, 7, 12, 13, 14, and 15, what additional SDGs are addressed by *Cowspiracy*? Complete the table below, then compare and contrast your ideas with a classmate.

SDGs:	Does Cowspiracy *connect with additional SDGs? If so, which ones and how?*
SDG 1 No Poverty	
SDG 2 Zero Hunger	
SDG 3 Good Health and Well Being	
SDG 4 Quality Education	
SDG 5 Gender Equality	
SDG 8 Decent Work and Economic Growth	
SDG 9 Industry, Innovation, and Infrastructure	
SDG 10 Reduced Inequalities	
SDG 11 Sustainable Cities and Communities	
SDG 16 Peace, Justice, and Strong Institutions	
SDG 17 Partnerships for the Goals	

VI   From Global to Local: On a Personal Level

1   How do you relate personally to *Cowspiracy*? Explain in detail how your own life experiences or personal beliefs intersect with its main themes?

2   How does *Cowspiracy* relate to your local environment? Explain the global-local connection between *Cowspiracy* and your home or current residence. What place-based considerations permit or prevent its application to your geographical location?

3   What type of response did *Cowspiracy* elicit in you? Are you moved to action? If so, explain. If not, why not? Have your viewpoints or attitudes changed? Explain.

VII   Assignments

1   Research

1   Individually or in groups, research one advocacy organization focused on sustainability, such as the World Wildlife Foundation, Food and Water Watch, Ecology Action, Sierra Club, Surfrider, Greenpeace, or Sea Shepherd. Analyze their efforts and assess how they align with the objectives of effectively mitigating climate change and ecosystem collapse. How seriously do they address animal agriculture's harmful impacts? Are they more concerned with other actions such as recycling, restricting water use, promoting alternate forms of transportation, etc.? How do their aims and objectives intersect with the UN SDGs studied in this chapter: 6, 7, 12, 13, 14, and 15? Back up your conclusions with examples. (The instructor of the course will determine the mode of presentation and delivery—oral presentation, written report, annotated bibliography, etc.)

2   Individually or in groups, research the impact of routine personal choices on the environment. First, compare the water use and GHG emissions of a vegan, vegetarian, and omnivore diet. Second, compare the relationship between personal choices in diet and one's ecological footprint versus personal choices in fossil fuel consumption and one's ecological footprint. Finally, use the information from *Cowspiracy* as well as other online resources or sources referenced in this chapter to help you estimate the carbon and environmental footprint of your own diet and lifestyle. What avenues for improvement do you see? What would be the best incentives for you personally to make progress on lowering your environmental footprint? (The instructor of the course will determine the mode of presentation and delivery—oral presentation, written report, infographic, etc.)

2   Write

1   Based on the goal of responsible consumption and production, write an op-ed (opinion editorial) on the following cultural practices:

- "The Bucket Challenge," where people pour a bucket of milk, ice, or other food over their head and post the footage on social media.
- "Project Runway (2004–present)," the reality show which inspired intense interest in fast fashion and often uses animal-based fabrics (hair, fur, skin, and silk). Note that between the years 2000 and 2014, global clothes production doubled (+100%), but the human population increased by one-fifth (+19%) (Remy, Speelman, and Swartz).
- "Best-by Date," the date when a food item is of the best flavor. It incentivizes people to trash it afterward and ensures higher profit for the producer.

(The instructor of the course will determine the appropriate length for this writing assignment.)

2   Write an essay in which you compare how "sustainable" farming practices on land and sea relate to SDGs 6, 7, 12, 13, 14, and 15. In the concluding paragraph of your essay, discuss whether *Cowspiracy* successfully addresses the problems posed by agricultural practices on land and sea. Discuss any shortcomings and criticisms of its themes and whether the filmmakers argue for a "more sustainable" use of marine or terrestrial ecosystems or the abolition of such practices entirely. (The instructor of the course will determine the appropriate length for this writing assignment.)

3   Create

1   How many methods and sources have humans discovered to produce meat and dairy alternatives that can help lower environmental damage? Choose one and create a marketing slogan and campaign to advertise it. Enter your slogan in a competition against your classmates for the title of "Sustainability Expert." (The instructor will determine the delivery mode—oral presentation, poster, commercial in skit or video form.)

2   Make a short documentary about animal- and plant-based diets at your home school/ university. Share the documentary with your classmates and answer their questions about its content and approach. (The instructor will determine the delivery mode.)

Works Cited

"2017 Census of Agriculture: United States Summary and State Data." USDA, April 2019, https://www.nass.usda.gov/Publications/AgCensus/2017/Full_Report/Volume_1,_Chapter_1_US/usv1.pdf. Accessed March 17, 2023.

"About." *Cowspiracy* website, 2014, https://www.cowspiracy.com/about. Accessed March 1, 2023.

Allaby, Michael, and Robert Coenraads. *The Encyclopedia of Earth: A Complete Visual Guide*. Oakland: University of California Press, 2008.

Andersen, Kip, and Keegan Kuhn. *Cowspiracy: The Sustainability Secret*. A.U.M. Films, 2014.

Berry, Emma. "Cowspiracy Documentary." Intro to Environmental Studies and Sustainability Class Blog, Fall 2016, College of Charleston, https://blogs.cofc.edu/envt-200/2016/10/24/cowspiracy-documentary/. Accessed March 17, 2023.

Bullard, Robert D. "The Threat of Environmental Racism." *Natural Resources & Environment* 7(3), 1993: 23–56.

Clucas, Ivor. "A Study of the Options for Utilization of Bycatch and Discards from Marine Capture Fisheries." *FAO Fisheries Circular* No. 928 FIIU/C928, FAO Fisheries Department, Food and Agriculture Organization of the United Nations, Rome, October 1997.

"Conspire," def. 1. *Merriam-Webster Dictionary*, 2023, https://www.merriam-webster.com/dictionary/conspire. Accessed March 10, 2023.

"Cowspiracy: The Sustainability Secret." *IMDb*, March 14, 2023, https://www.imdb.com/title/tt3302820/.

"Cowspiracy: The Sustainability Secret." *Rotten Tomatoes*, March 14, 2023, https://www.rottentomatoes.com/m/cowspiracy_the_sustainability_secret.

"*Cowspiracy* Wins Audience Choice Award." *The South African Eco Film Festival*, April 9, 2015, https://web.archive.org/web/20150416111332/http://southafricanecofilmfestival.com/2015/04/09/cowspiracy-wins-audience-choice-award/. Accessed March 1, 2023.

Du Lac, J. Freedom, and Lindsey Bever. "Sea World Ends Captive Breeding Program, Says Current Batch of Killer Whales 'Will Be the Last.'" *Washington Post*, March 17, 2016, https://www.washingtonpost.com/news/morning-mix/wp/2016/03/17/seaworld-says-its-current-generation-of-killer-whales-will-be-the-last/. Accessed March 1, 2023.

Eisen, Michael, and Patrick Brown. "Rapid Global Phaseout of Animal Agriculture Has the Potential to Stabilize Greenhouse Gas Levels for 30 Years and Offset 68 Percent of CO_2 Emissions This Century." *PLOS Climate* 1(2), 2022. https://journals.plos.org/climate/article?id=10.1371/journal.pclm.0000010.

Francey, Neil, and Simon Chapman. "'Operation Berkshire': The International Tobacco Companies' Conspiracy." *British Medical Journal* 321(7257), 2000: 371–374.

Gerber, P.J., et al. *Tackling Climate Change through Livestock: A Global Assessment of Emissions and Mitigation Opportunities*. Rome: Food and Agriculture Organization of the United Nations, 2013.

Goodland, Robert, and Jeff Angang. "Livestock and Climate Change: What If the Key Actors in Climate Change Are... Cows, Pigs, and Chickens." *Worldwatch Institute Report* 2009.

"Greenwashing." *Merriam-Webster Dictionary*, 2023, https://www.merriam-webster.com/dictionary/greenwashing. Accessed March 13, 2023.

Jacobson, Michael F., and Center for Science in the Public Interest. *Six Arguments for a Greener Diet: How a More Plant-based Diet Could Save Your Health and the Environment*. Washington, DC: Center for Science in the Public Interest, 2006.

Khazaal, Natalie. "Introduction." In Khazaal, Natalie, and Nuria Almiron. *"Like an Animal": Critical Animal Studies Approaches to Borders, Displacement, and Othering*. Leiden: Brill, 2021, pp. 1–48

"Kip Andersen (Director of Cowspiracy)." Room for Discussion (University of Amsterdam), May 18, 2016, https://www.youtube.com/watch?v=qSIJ6Ou10AM&t=2373s. Accessed March 1, 2023.

"Learn About Environmental Justice." US Environmental Protection Agency (EPA), September 6, 2022, https://www.epa.gov/environmentaljustice/learn-about-environmental-justice. Accessed March 17, 2023.

"Le FFPE récompense les films gagnants de la 12e edition." *Festival de films de Portneuf sur l'environnement*, April 27, 2015.

"Livestock's Long Shadow: Environmental Issues and Options." Food and Agriculture Organization of the United Nations, 2006, https://www.fao.org/3/a0701e/a0701e.pdf. Accessed March 17, 2023.

Lowry, David Shane. *Lumbee Pipelines: American Indian Movement in the Residue of Settler Colonialism*. Lincoln: University of Nebraska Press, 2024.

McCormick, Benjamin. "Why People Go Vegan: 2019 Global Survey Results." *Vomad*, March 4, 2019, https://vomadlife.com/blogs/news/why-people-go-vegan-2019-global-survey-results#:~:text=24.6%25%20or%20692%20people%20first,Forks%20Over%20Knives%20(2011). Accessed March 17, 2023.

"Milked: Awards." *IMDb*, March 15, 2023, https://www.imdb.com/title/tt15567002/awards/?ref_=tt_awd.

"More Meat Threatens the Planet." *Greenpeace*, June 25, 2015, https://www.greenpeace.org/usa/sustainable-agriculture/issues/meat/. Accessed March 11, 2023.

"National Pollutant Discharge Elimination System Permit Regulation and Effluent Limitation Guidelines and Standards for Concentrated Animal Feeding Operations (CAFOs)." *Environmental Protection Agency*. Federal Register vol. 68, no. 29, February 12, 2003, Rules and Regulations, https://www.govinfo.gov/content/pkg/FR-2003-02-12/pdf/03-3074.pdf. Accessed March 17, 2023.

Nelson, Katie. "New Report Links 2020's Record-Breaking Fires in Brazil's Pantanal Wetlands to World's Biggest Meat Processor." *Greenpeace*, March 3, 2021.

"NPDES CAFO Permitting Status Report: National Summary, Endyear 2021." Environmental Protection Agency, July 20, 2022, https://www.epa.gov/system/files/documents/2022-07/CAFO%20Status%20Report%202021.pdf. Accessed March 17, 2023.

Oppenlander, Richard A. *Comfortably Unaware: Global Depletion and Food Choice Responsibility: What You Choose to Eat Is Killing Our Planet*. Minneapolis, MN: Langdon, 2011.

Oppenlander, Richard A. *Food Choice and Sustainability: Why Buying Local, Eating Less Meat, and Taking Baby Steps Won't Work*. Minneapolis, MN: Langdon, 2013.

Pabian, S., et al. "Ninety Minutes to Reduce One's Intention to Eat Meat: A Preliminary Experimental Investigation on the Effect of Watching the *Cowspiracy* Documentary on Intention to Reduce Meat Consumption." *Frontiers in Communication* 5, 2020: 1–7.

Pevreall, Katie. "Cowspiracy Inspires 'Lazy Millennials' to Start Vegan Farm." Livekindly, https://www.livekindly.com/cowspiracy-lazy-millennials-vegan-farm/. Accessed March 17, 2023.

Pinkerton, William. Associated Press News Release, Washington, October 13, 1938. From the personal files of Pare Lorentz.

Poore, Joseph, and Thomas Nemecek. "Reducing Food's Environmental Impacts through Producers and Consumers." *Science* 360, 2018: 987–992.

Pritchard, Matthew. "I Watched." Facebook Post, November 20, 2022, https://m.facebook.com/plantbasednews/photos/a.1574320489487716/3203411836578565/. Accessed March 17, 2023.

Remy, Nathalie, Eveline Speelman, and Steven Swartz. "Style That's Sustainable: A New Fast-Fashion Formula." McKinsey Sustainability, October 20, 2016, https://www.mckinsey.com/capabilities/sustainability/our-insights/style-thats-sustainable-a-new-fast-fashion-formula. Accessed March 17, 2023.

Rhodan, Maya. "Seaworld's Profits Drop 84% after *Blackfish* Documentary." Time, August 6, 2015, https://time.com/3987998/seaworlds-profits-drop-84-after-blackfish-documentary/. Accessed March 1, 2023.

Riggen, Ms. "Veganism 2.0: Inspired by *Cowspiracy* and Tom Brady." Medium, March 23, 2017, https://medium.com/oyster-adams-do-one-thing-project/veganism-2-0-31c24886098c. Accessed March 17, 2023.

Ritchie, Hannah, et al. "The Impact of Global Dietary Guidelines on Climate Change." *Global Environmental Change* 49, 2018: 44–55.

Robbins, John. *Diet for a New America: How Your Food Choices Affect Your Health, Happiness and the Future of Life on Earth*. Second edition. Novato, California: HJ Kramer and New World Library, 2012.

Rotha, Paul. *Documentary Film*. 3d ed. rev. and enl. London: Faber & Faber Ltd., 1956; (U.S. distributors) New York: Hastings House Publishers, 1956.

Schwab, Denise, et al. "Grass-fed and Organic Beef: Production Costs and Breakeven Market Prices, 2008–2009." *Animal Industry Report* 658 no. 1. Iowa State University, 2012.

"SDG: The Challenge." UNECE, https://unece.org/challenge#:~:text=Methane%20is%20a%20powerful%20greenhouses,are%20due%20to%20human%20activities. Accessed March 1, 2023.

Simon, David R. *Meatonomics: How the Rigged Economics of Meat and Dairy Make You Consume Too Much—and How to Eat Better, Live Longer, and Spend Smarter*. Newburyport, MA: Conari Press, 2013.

Smil, Vaclav. *Harvesting the Biosphere: What We Have Taken from Nature*. Cambridge, MA: MIT Press, 2015.

"The 17 Goals." United Nations, Department of Economic and Social Affairs: Sustainable Development, https://sdgs.un.org/goals.

"The Facts." *Cowspiracy* website, 2014, https://www.cowspiracy.com/about. Accessed March 1, 2023.

Thöner, Victorine Che, and Davi Martin. "Empty Words Feed No One." *Greenpeace*, November 16, 2022, https://www.greenpeace.org/international/story/56778/empty-words-feed-no-one/. Accessed March 11, 2023.

Twine, R. "Emissions from Animal Agriculture—16.5% Is the New Minimum Figure." *Sustainability* 13(11), 2021: 6276.

"US Factory Farming Estimates: Animals Alive at Present." Sentience Institute, April 11, 2019, https://www.sentienceinstitute.org/us-factory-farming-estimates. Accessed March 17, 2023.

Valdmanis, Richard, and Tim Cocks, "Meat on the Menu, Not the Agenda." *Reuters*, November 15, 2022, https://currently.att.yahoo.com/att/meat-menu-not-agenda-cop27-111307240.html. Accessed March 13, 2023.

Vegan Future @veganfuture. "Blog: "How Cowspiracy: The Sustainability Secret Inspired Me to Go Vegan."" Twitter, May 27, 2021, https://twitter.com/veganfuture/status/1398076528542597123. Accessed March 17, 2023.

"Vote for the 2015 Audience Choice Award!" *Cinema Politica*, April 6, 2016.

Part II

People

Relating Global Humanities Texts to
UN SDGs 1, 2, 3, 4, and 5

5   Fernando Contreras Castro's *Única Looking at the Sea*

Marginalization, Community, and Politics from a Garbage Dump

Miguel Rosas Buendía

I   Text

Title	*Única Looking at the Sea*
Genre	Novel
Author	Fernando Contreras Castro was born in Alajuela, Costa Rica, in 1963. He earned a degree in Hispanic literature from the University of Costa Rica, where he is currently a faculty member. He is part of a generation of writers who drew international attention to Costa Rican and Central American literature at the turn of the 20th century. His first novel, *Única Looking at the Sea*, was originally published in 1993 and received enthusiastic reviews due to its original approach to topics such as marginalized populations, polluted environments, and political struggles. Contreras Castro has also published novels such as *Los peor* (1995) and *El tibio recinto de la oscuridad* (2000). Both novels have received the Aquileo J. Echeverría National Award, Costa Rica's highest literary honor.
Year	1993 [English translation, 2017]
Country	Costa Rica

Única Looking at the Sea is the story of a marginalized community that inhabits a garbage dump next to Río Azul (Blue River), a fictional suburb near the Costa Rican capital, San José. After losing her mother and her job as a teacher's aide, the eponymous protagonist, Única Oconitrillo, decides to live in the city dump. She joins a community of scavengers or "divers" (*buzos* in Spanish), who were already living there, and starts a new life connected to trash. Única possesses a strong, decisive, and kind personality, which leads her to promote and organize minor but significant community activities that bring together most of the divers. A few weeks after her arrival at the dump, Única finds an abandoned child, Bacán, who becomes her son. Bacán is a kid with congenital abnormalities, but Única embraces not only the maternal responsibility of raising him but also, as a former teacher, the goal of educating him as much as possible. Bacán is in his twenties during the events of the novel. Mondolfo Moya Garro (aka Momboñombo) is the second most important character. Mondolfo attempts to commit suicide by throwing himself onto a passing garbage truck. He ends up in the Río Azul dump and is rescued by Única and other divers. Mondolfo was a night watchman at the National Library but was fired after denouncing the illegal sale of books from this institution to serve as raw material to manufacture toilet paper. The love story between Única and Mondolfo throughout the book is accompanied by a socio-political battle regarding the dump's location. The middle-class neighbors of Río Azul demand that the Government closes and relocates the dump. Initially reluctant, the Government agrees to design a relocation plan after the neighbors' demonstrations create serious interruptions in the system of recollection and disposal of garbage for the whole city. Mondolfo eagerly takes

DOI: 10.4324/9781003388869-8

the role of a leader and tries to convince his fellow divers that they must oppose the Government's plans. Mondolfo's efforts for political organization are not very successful, but he is able to organize a peaceful march to the Presidential Palace. The police severely repress this demonstration and, because of the use of water cannons to disperse protesters, Bacán becomes seriously ill and dies. Following his death, Única and Mondolfo leave the dump and travel to Puntarenas, a coastal town. Única is emotionally shocked and remains silent, while Mondolfo devotedly tries to make her smile. The novel ends with Única looking at the sea and, around her and Mondolfo, a modern urban society continues its cycle of trash production.

Única Looking at the Sea is available in print from numerous online sellers including Amazon and Barnes & Noble. It was originally published in Spanish in 1993 and translated into English in 2017 by Diálogos Books.

II   Context

Contamination in the modern world can be identified in varied settings and by multiple factors; however, the garbage produced by humans in our daily life is a dimension that we often tend to overlook. Contreras Castro's novel deals with garbage as a gateway to environmental and social reflections. Interestingly, Río Azul was the actual name of a city landfill near San José, Costa Rica. It was inaugurated in 1972 and closed in 2002, and it received tons of waste materials over the decades. As Jerry Hoeg indicates in "The Landscape of the Consumer Society. Fernando Contreras Castro's *Única mirando al mar*," "[w]hen it first opened, it was billed as a sanitary landfill but quickly became an open-air garbage dump with neither controls nor treatment facilities" (177). After some years of public controversies due to the uncontrolled use of the dump, the presence of technological waste containing heavy metals and other substances finally expedited its closing. As Rolando Mora Chinchilla and Raúl Mora Amador have identified in "Reseña histórica del relleno sanitario de Río Azul y consideraciones sobre los metals pesados tratados en él y los presentes en nuestros hogares," the mass of metals in this landfill "varies between 70,000 and 100,000 tm, which make it a serious environmental concern" (2003, 57). This actual dump was certainly a reference for Contreras Castro's fictional writing. *Única Looking at the Sea* is a novel rooted in environmental concern over the unrestrained production of garbage and the inappropriate management of it. Indeed, Contreras Castro's novel is part of a late 20th-century wave of artistic productions that aim to force readers to reflect on their direct relationship with garbage production and, more importantly, their intrinsic connection to the capitalist systems of production and consumption. Garbage, dumps, and subsequent contamination do not exist as outsiders to the modern capitalist society; on the contrary, the capitalist system itself originates them and, interestingly, also tries to conceal them from us. As Stephanie Foote and Elizabeth Mazzolini assert in "Introduction: Histories of the Dustheap": "Garbage and waste provide a way to begin to create large-scale models for understanding systems of consumption and production [...] as well as provoking a more finely grained understanding of the ecology of a town, neighborhood, or even individual household" (2–3). Contreras Castro's novel approaches Costa Rican environmental matters on garbage in dialogue with these academic and cultural trends.

In that vein, this novel is primarily a story about a community of people who not only work in the dump but who try to reconstruct a meaningful life from within, even if it is only a fragile and vulnerable effort. In an interview with the Universidad Estatal a Distancia (UNED) from Costa Rica, Contreras Castro states that his novels are usually set up in plausible scenarios "that operate on the margins of a controlling apparatus" (2:03–2:05). *Única Looking at the Sea* is a good example of this aesthetic conviction. The dump in Río Azul is a space where a diverse group of marginalized people has gathered, and therefore, it serves as gateway to explore how modern societies produce and perpetuate the conditions that originally gave birth to the scavenger phenomenon. As the influential thinker Zygmunt Bauman has expressed in *Wasted Lives: Modernity and Its Outcasts*, "[t]he production of 'human waste', or more correctly 'wasted humans', is an inevitable outcome of modernization" (5). Alongside the connection between modernization and marginalized peoples, Contreras Castro's novel is at its core a reflection and an exploration of the human condition and its tragic fate. The Costa Rican author has declared that we tend to see marginalized locations only as places where "people cannot survive although in fact they do" ("Textos y pretextos" 2:12–2:15). Thus, although not heroes, the main characters in his novels are often constructed as ethical, committed, and tragic individuals who, for a moment, envision a better world and try to invent and re-create a meaningful way of life. The main characters of *Única Looking at the Sea*, Única and Mondolfo, are representative of this literary and philosophical exploration. Even though they fail in their efforts and the outcome seems to be cruel, the reader understands the reasons behind the outcome and adopts a more nuanced approach to dumps and scavengers.

Lastly, it is important to highlight that the novel, originally published in 1993, was completely rewritten by Contreras Castro some years later. These editions made the novel more vivid and graphic regarding various narrative aspects such as the portrayal of the rough daily life at the dump, the depictions of the ephemeral moments of joy among divers, and the account of Única's final mourning, among others. In a conversation with teenagers from around the world who had read his works, the author said that the final scene, for instance, was more metaphorical in the first version and that he aimed to communicate a cruder scene after the process of rewriting. He argues that it was necessary to represent the harshness and brutality of contemporary systems of economic exclusion and social stigmatization ("Conversación con Fernando Contreras Castro" 15:20–16:16).

III   Interpretation

1   In *Única Looking at the Sea*, there are constant references to the sea and water images: scavengers are divers, the dump is pictured as "sea tides" (24), the neighborhood is called "Río Azul," among other references. How do you interpret this emphasis? What reflections are these "blue metaphors" looking to stimulate in the reader? How do they contribute to the main messages that the novel seeks to convey?

2   How is the garbage dump described as an urban site? Is it depicted as an isolated area of the city or an integrated part of it? In which ways, does it seem to be isolated and/or integrated? What does the dump description tell you about how contemporary societies perceive dumps and cities?

3   Trash as an intrinsic product of human societies is a sort of character in the novel. How does trash appear throughout the text? What kind of reflection on the production of goods and the consequent production of trash does this novel incite? Among other scenes and passages, think of this phrase by Única: "Of course, trash only exists for people when it begins to get in their way" (80).

4   Dumps are largely seen as marginalized social areas. Describe the representation of the Río Azul dump as a place inhabited by humans. In which ways is it a zone of marginalization? But also, in which ways is it a context to reconstruct lives? Would you consider that pairing social marginalization and life reconstruction constitutes a contradiction? What knowledge and sentiments arise in the community of divers that do not have value outside the dump?

5   Describe what we learn about the lives of Única Oconitrillo and Mondolfo Moya Garro. What were they doing before their arrival to the dump? What relationships did they have with official institutions of the Costa Rican society? What impacts do they have in the community of divers?

6   Why does the existence of the dump in Río Azul become controversial? What are the complaints presented by the middle-class neighbors of Río Azul? Which narrative strategies are used to introduce this issue in the book? What are the different stages through which the proposition of relocating the dump passes and what is the role of official institutions with regard to this issue?

7   How does Mondolfo Moya Garro change throughout the course of the novel? Think of this phrase by the narrator: "The city was not the same seen from the perspective of a diver, which don Mondolfo had become" (66). What is Mondolfo's reaction when he hears about the official plans to remove the dump from Río Azul to another location? What are his strategies and actions to advance a political response from the dump and its community of divers?

8   How does the love story between Única and Mondolfo develop in the novel? Describe their wedding. Through which type of language and tone are the wedding scenes portrayed? Think of this phrase by the narrator: "And the divers ate, drunk and sang, and for a good part of the morning they forgot that happiness has a bar code" (117). What is the metaphorical meaning of their unity as a family? What is the role of Bacán, Única's son, in it?

9   Comment on the final scenes of the novel. Describe the interaction between the divers and the Government? What is the reaction of Mondolfo and Única when the protesters are attacked with water cannons? What is the reaction of the rest of the divers? Why do Única and Mondolfo leave the dump a few days after the failure of the protest and to where do they go?

10 Describe the secondary characters in the novel such as Bacán, Don Retana, Llorona, Oso Carmuco, and the Novios. What roles do they play in the story? Which aspects of life in the dump are developed through these characters? Which of them could be labeled as symbols of marginality, of hope, or both?

IV   People-Focused Applications to SDGs 1, 2, 3, 4, and 5

1   According to the United Nations, the SDGs are "an urgent call for action by all countries—developed and developing—in a global partnership" ("The 17 Goals"). The SDGs, adopted in 2015, have been built over decades and are part of a series of historical resolutions by the UN. One of the most significant resolutions is the *Universal Declaration of Human Rights*, adopted in 1948. As part of his efforts to oppose the relocation of the dump, Mondolfo writes a letter to the President of Costa Rica, and he walks to the Presidential Palace to personally drop off the letter. About the letter, the narrator says: "Who knows what things he scribbled in the hours that it took for him to fill up two sheets of paper, which he came out to show everyone as if he carried under his arm the Declaration of Human Rights" (136). What is the significance of this parallel made by the narrator? Why would it be possible to consider this novel and, particularly, the struggle to oppose the dump relocation as a case of Human Rights? What kind of connection can be made between these two historical UN resolutions through Contreras Castro's novel?

2   SDG 1 aims to eradicate poverty. The objective of target 1.5 is to "build the resilience of the poor and those in vulnerable situations and reduce their exposure and vulnerability to climate-related extreme events and other economic, social and environmental shocks and disasters" ("Goal 1"). Why is it possible to argue that the community of divers in Río Azul represents a resilient community? What types of vulnerabilities do they face? Are these

vulnerabilities created by economic, social, or environmental factors? If all three types play a role, to what extent is one factor more prevalent than the others?

3   As part of the mission to eradicate poverty, target 1.b seeks to "[c]reate sound policy frame-works at the national, regional and international levels, based on pro-poor and gender-sensitive development strategies, to support accelerated investment in poverty eradication actions" ("Goal 1"). In the novel, the local and national governments have to deal with the relocation of the dump. How can we correlate this aspect of the novel with the objective of target 1.b? Can the Government's plans be considered pro-poor development strategies? The issue of relocation is introduced in the text through newspaper headlines and notes; the first headline states: "Río Azul residents ask Government for Solidarity" (72). What does the notion of solidarity used by Río Azul's neighbors entail in this headline? On the other hand, how is solidarity present in the community of divers? What do these conflicting understand-ings of solidarity say about how policy frameworks can involve unfair assumptions?

4   The mission of SDG 2 is ending hunger and promoting sustainable agriculture. The objec-tive of target 2.1 is to "end hunger and ensure access by all people, in particular the poor and people in vulnerable situations, including infants, to safe, nutritious and sufficient food all year round" ("Goal 2"). The divers represent a vulnerable group of people marginalized by modern society and a population facing food insecurity. How does this community tackle the issue of hunger and scarce access to food? What is the role of Única in this? How do solidarity and friendship operate in this precarious context regarding food?

5   Connected to the mission of SDG 2, the Zero Hunger Challenge calls for "[z]ero loss or waste of food," among other ends ("Related SDGs, Goal 2"). Loss and waste of food are related to problems in the global system of food production and are also associated with pat-terns of consumption and waste. This novel includes a reflection on what produces disgust, and food leftovers are included in it. In a telling scene when Única has just arrived in the dump, she asks an old diver about eating food leftovers: "But doesn't it disgust you?," and the diver replies: "It is disgusting not to eat" (28). This phrase is later repeated by Única to Mondolfo. About disgust in the novel, Jerry Hoeg affirms: "All through the novel, Contre-ras Castro attempts to transfer the visceral disgust produced by the various items cast into the landfill to social/moral disgust with the society responsible for their (over)production" ("Evolutionary Theory" 579). Describe how this process of transfer mentioned by Hoeg functions in the novel? Why is disgust an effective emotion through which to explore local and global responsibilities regarding food waste and hunger?

6   The mission of SDG 3 is ensuring healthy lives and promoting well-being for all at all ages. In that vein, target 3.8 emphasizes the need to "[a]chieve universal health coverage" ("Goal 3"). Connected to this goal, the Global Strategy "Every Woman Every Child" is a milestone in UN campaigns for health and has been defined as an unprecedented global movement "that mobilizes and intensifies international and national action by governments, the UN, multilaterals, the private sector and civil society to address the major health challenges facing women, children and adolescents" ("Every Woman"). How do the origin, health con-ditions, and death of the character of Bacán, Única's son, correlate to SDG 3 and the UN Global Strategy "Every Woman Every Child"?

7   The objective of SDG 4 is ensuring inclusive and equitable quality education. The goal of target 4.c is to "substantially increase the supply of qualified teachers" ("Goal 4"). The novel describes Única's occupation before the dump through the following words: "She was one of those recruited by the Department of Public Education when there was a shortage of teachers with degrees" (37). How does Única's life as educator shed light on the obstacles and chal-lenges that target 4.c faces? Likewise, to what extent can Única's impact on the community of divers and life in the dump be interpreted as a broadening of her skills as a qualified teacher?

8   The goal of target 4.6 is to "ensure that all youth and a substantial proportion of adults, both men and women, achieve literacy and numeracy" ("Goal 4"). Mondolfo Moya Garro attended "elementary school up to the sixth grade," enough to develop good reading skills (51). In what ways does Mondolfo's literacy influence the novel's plot? Is it possible to argue that Mondolfo's literacy functions as a gateway to represent the significance and positive effects of target 4.6?

9   SDG 5 aims to achieve gender equality. The goal of target 5.1. is to "[e]nd all forms of discrimination against all women and girls everywhere" ("Goal 5"). Likewise, the goal of target 5.5 is to "[e]nsure women's full and effective participation and equal opportunities for leadership at all levels of decision-making in political, economic and public life" ("Goal 5"). In an interview with Edin Hernández, Contreras Castro stated: "Única is a character that represents the archetypical nature of a Latin American woman: strong, committed to struggle to carry on living" (1994, 2). How does the novel portray Única as female character? What forms of discrimination do she and other female characters face? What kind of leadership does she represent? Consider the following passage for your analysis: "Momboñombo, you know that I have come to the conclusion that trash is also a woman . . . Look, it's trash—in feminine gender. I know about gender because I used to teach it in school. So, it's trash, and in the beginning, it was pleasing to all, when it was nice and new, and as soon as it grows old, then, no one wants it . . . But that's how people are and that's why I prefer to dive here alone" (75). Finally, how do you interpret her final condition of noncommunication? Is it a contradictory ending considering her previous characterization throughout the book?

10   Commenting on how consumerist economy and society are addressed in the book, Jerry Hoeg asserts: "In the novel, from the President of the Republic down to the lowliest human scavenger on the dump, all parties unquestioningly accept a market ideology of economic exchange and trade" ("Evolutionary Theory" 583). On the other hand, Contreras Castro points out that Mondolfo's decision to throw himself in the garbage is "a metaphor for many other possible forms to break with identities that are assigned by social rules" (3:20–3:28). The author adds: "He must empty himself as a subject of the previous system" (5:42–5:50). How is this tension between an inescapable market ideology and the struggle for a liberated identity portrayed in the novel? To what extent is Mondolfo's goal achieved and to what extent is the economic system inexorable as the main structure for human interactions?

11   One of the main twists in the novel's plot is the attempt of Mondolfo to politicize divers and organize their response to the Government's plans to relocate the dump. The narrator observes about Mondolfo's task: "The divers for their part, the real divers, those who had arrived at the dump many years ago with a hollow soul, and who by now had already stuffed it with trash, the authentic divers did not understand Mondolfo's concerns. They were used to living day to day" (82). How do you interpret the attitude of the old divers? Pay attention to the image of the "hollow soul": why this choice of words? Is there a pessimistic interpretation about divers' political capabilities? Or is it a realistic take on their political capital as marginalized people?

12   Edgar Cota in "Reciclaje humano en *Única mirando al mar*" maintains that the exploration of poverty and trash in the novel serves to expose the presence of "dehumanization, because the dump workers have lost their status as human beings before the rest of the local society" (2015, 123). What is more, Jerry Hoeg proposes that "the novel does advocate a change in socioenvironmental relations, namely a change in the way society disposes of its surplus so as to avoid environmental and human degradation" ("Evolutionary Theory" 590). How do you evaluate Cota and Hoeg's approaches? How is dehumanization or human degradation presented and depicted throughout the novel? Comment, for instance, on the following passage in which Mondolfo recognizes a pattern in his fellow divers: "Mr. Mondolfo had already noticed that the divers were good at going about talking to themselves and that it

was difficult for them to hold a conversation for longer than five minutes" (55). Identify similar passages in the novel.

13 For the conceptualization and implementation of the SDGs in any given context, the gathering of scientific data is crucial. Environmental policies, for instance, must rely on trustworthy evidence. In Contreras Castro's novel, regarding the relocation of the dump from Río Azul to the town of Esparza, it is stated: "The results had been political, not scientific, which was why the Government insisted on maintaining that designation" (147–148). How does the novel handle the influence of political agendas in environmental and urban policies? How is the notion of evidence (scientific, sociological, etc.) presented and examined throughout the book?

14 Divide the class into five groups and assign one of the SDGs from Unit 2 (1, 2, 3, 4, or 5) to each group. Each group will then prepare arguments for a debate in which they maintain that their assigned SDG is the most relevant or central to Contreras Castro's *Única Looking at the Sea*. (The instructor of the course will decide on the format and length of the debate and facilitate a follow-up discussion with the class upon conclusion of the debate.)

15 Does *Única Looking at the Sea* only reinforce and illuminate the principles underpinning the UN SDGs and the concept of sustainable development, or does it question any inherent presuppositions, biases, shortcomings, flaws, or gaps in the UN SDG framework or the notion of sustainable development? Explain with details from the text.

V   Beyond People—Connections to SDGs on Planet, Prosperity, and Partnerships

Beyond SDGs 1, 2, 3, 4, and 5, what additional SDGs are addressed by Fernando Contreras Castro in *Única Looking at the Sea*? Complete the table below with your ideas. Then compare and contrast your ideas with a classmate.

SDGs:	*Does Contreras Castro's* Única Looking at the Sea *connect with additional SDGs? If so, which ones and how?*
SDG 6 Clean Water and Sanitation	
SDG 7 Affordable and Clean Energy	
SDG 8 Decent Work and Economic Growth	
SDG 9 Industry, Innovation, and Infrastructure	
SDG 10 Reduced Inequalities	
SDG 11 Sustainable Cities and Communities	
SDG 12 Responsible Consumption and Production	
SDG 13 Climate Action	
SDG 14 Life Below Water	
SDG 15 Life on Land	
SDG 16 Peace, Justice, and Strong Institutions	
SDG 17 Partnerships for the Goals	

VI   From Global to Local: On a Personal Level

1   How do you relate personally to the featured text in Chapter 5? Explain in detail how your own life experiences or personal beliefs intersect with the main ideas and themes of Contreras Castro's *Única Looking at the Sea.*

2   How does the global humanities text featured in Chapter 5 relate to your local environment? Explain the global-local connection between Contreras Castro's *Única Looking at the Sea* and your home or current residence. What place-based considerations permit or prevent the application of the text to your geographical location?

3   What type of response did Contreras Castro's *Única Looking at the Sea* elicit in you? Are you moved to action? If so, explain. If not, why not. Have your viewpoints or attitudes changed? Explain.

VII   Assignments

1   Research

1   Costa Rica is a country globally known for its commitment to environmental action and green policies regarding natural resources, protected areas, and biodiversity. The Central American nation has received the 2019 Champions of the Earth award, the UN's highest environmental honor ("Costa Rica Named"). The UN has not only recognized Costa Rica as a "global pioneer with a strong social conscience" but also as the "ultimate environmental frontier" due to its National Decarbonization Plan ("Costa Rica: the 'Living Eden'"). Individually or in groups, research the history of sustainable environmental policies that have made Costa Rica an exemplary case. Investigate the steps the country has taken over the decades toward fulfilling its vision and policies. How do Costa Rica's programs, policies, and achievements relate to SDGs 1, 2, 3, 4, and/or 5? (The instructor of the course will determine the mode of presentation and delivery—oral presentation, written report, annotated bibliography, short video documentary, digital timeline project, etc.—for this research assignment.)

2   Despite its undeniable achievements, Costa Rica is still facing environmental challenges. *Única Looking at the Sea* offers a critical view of the country when exploring the management of trash and garbage dumps, as well as the social problem around scavengers and other marginalized people. When reflecting on garbage, culture, and politics, the philosopher John Scanlan believes "that garbage is everywhere but, curiously, is mostly overlooked in what we take to be valuable from our lived experiences, and crucially, in the ways we . . . organize the world" (9). Garbage dumps, landfills, and other types of waste disposal are crucial infrastructures for our modern societies; however, as Scanlan points out, we tend to focus on goods and consumption without thinking of where the resulting waste goes after use. The dump of Río Azul in Contreras Castro's novel encourages the reader to think about that issue, even more so since the fictional dump refers to a real one. As Jerry Hoeg indicates about the actual Río Azul dump: "When it first opened, it was billed as a sanitary landfill but quickly became an open-air garbage dump with neither controls nor treatment facilities" ("The Landscape" 177). Individually or in groups, research the history, policies, and laws around garbage dumps and other waste disposal sites in Costa Rica (paying particular attention to the case of Río Azul) and in Central America. How do these initiatives in Costa Rica compare to those in other Central American countries? Which contemporary challenges do all

these countries face? How does the collected information relate to SDGs 1, 2, 3, 4, and/or 5? (The instructor of the course will determine the mode of presentation and delivery—oral presentation, written report, annotated bibliography, short video documentary, digital timeline project, etc.—for this research assignment.)

2   *Write*

1   Aligned with the SDGs, the UN General Assembly adopted at the end of the 20th century a series of resolutions around the concept of "Culture of Peace." Following the foundational values and goals of the UN toward the "transformation from a culture of war and violence to a culture of peace and non-violence" ("Resolution 52/13"), the *Declaration and Programme of Action on a Culture of Peace* explains that peace "not only is the absence of conflict, but also requires a positive, dynamic participatory process where dialogue is encouraged and conflicts are solved in a spirit of mutual understanding and cooperation" ("Resolution 53/243"). Interestingly, since the late 19th century, only two brief periods of violence have marred Costa Rica's democratic development. Likewise, on December 1, 1948, Costa Rica dissolved its armed forces. However, in Contreras Castro's novel, a culture of peace and dialogue between the government and the community of divers is not present. The "Peace March" proposed by Mondolfo receives a strong official response (148). Write an essay in which you discuss the ways in which this novel addresses the concept of "Culture of Peace" and what reflection can we provide about it as readers? (The instructor of the course will determine the appropriate length for this writing assignment.)

2   *Única Looking at the Sea* has been justly interpreted as a caustic critique of the Costa Rican society and government. In turn, it has not only become a best-seller all over Latin America, but, interestingly, it has been included as mandatory reading for all secondary schools in Costa Rica by the Ministry of Education. Regarding this issue, Minor Calderon (2003) has raised a question: if the novel is "so transgressive and inquisitive [about the consumerist society, the government, and the global markets], why has it been institutionalized in school programs by the Ministry of Education?" (174). Write a persuasive essay in which you adopt a position in this debate: does becoming a mandatory reading in schools constitute a contradiction to the novel's message? (The instructor of the course will determine the appropriate length for this writing assignment.)

3   *Create*

1   Individually or in groups, create an infographic about the problem of waste management in Costa Rica and Central America, or design a campaign that promotes awareness of the unstoppable production of waste and how it is related to our patterns of consumption. (The instructor of the course will determine the format and mode of delivery for this creative assignment.)

2   The phenomenon of 'divers' as they are called in Contreras Castro's novel is not exclusive of Costa Rica. Scavengers and pickers are present in many areas, and particularly in developing countries. In Argentina, urban pickers are called *cartoneros*, since cardboard (*cartón* in Spanish) is the most visible of the recyclable materials that they collect. From within the 'cartonero culture,' a publishing phenomenon was born in the beginning of the 21st century in Latin America: the *editoriales cartoneras* [cardboard publishers]. *Editoriales cartoneras* are small, independent publishers that make their books by hand out of recycled cardboard

and sell them at prices lower than those of large publishing houses. The book cover made of cardboard is a very symbolic part of the whole piece since the word "cardboard" (*cartón*) serves to name the pickers, *cartoneros*, and the publishers, *cartoneras*. Individually or in groups, create a *cartonera* book cover for *Única Looking at the Sea*. Search for examples of *cartoneras* books and design the cover according to your thoughts on the novel's message and the SDGs studied in this chapter and in Unit 2. (The instructor of the course will determine the appropriate length, format, and mode of delivery for this creative assignment.)

Works Cited

Audiovisuales UNED. "Textos y pretextos - Fernando Contreras," *YouTube*, uploaded by Audiovisuales UNED, November 22, 2019, https://www.youtube.com/watch?v=D-0CVqUuwvM. Accessed 1 October 2022.

Bauman, Zygmunt. *Wasted Lives: Modernity and Its Outcasts*. Polity Press, 2004.

Biblioteca Nacional Costa Rica, Proyecto Entre libros y autores. "Conversación con Fernando Contreras Castro." *Facebook*, uploaded by Biblioteca Nacional Costa Rica, November 21, 2020, https://www.facebook.com/bibliotecanacional.mcj.cr/videos/fernando-contreras-castro-autor-de-muchas-obras-y-cuyas-obras-los-peor-y-%C3%BAnica-m/384711366064218/. Accessed 30 September 2022.

Calderón Salas, Minor. "*Única mirando al mar*: entre la transgresión y la norma." *Letras*, vol. 35, 2003, pp. 173–184.

Contreras Castro, Fernando. *Única Looking at the Sea*. Translated by Elaine S. Brooks, Diálogos, 2017.

"Costa Rica Named 'UN Champion of the Earth' for Pioneering Role in Fighting Climate Change." *United Nations Climate Change*, 20 September 2019, https://unfccc.int/news/costa-rica-named-un-champion-of-the-earth-for-pioneering-role-in-fighting-climate-change. Accessed 1 October 2022.

"Costa Rica: The 'Living Eden' Designing a Template for a Cleaner, Carbon-Free World." *UN Environment Program*, 20 September 2019, https://www.unep.org/news-and-stories/story/costa-rica-living-eden-designing-template-cleaner-carbon-free-world. Accessed 1 October 2022.

Cota Torres, Edgar. "Reciclaje humano en *Única mirando al mar* de Fernando Contreras." *Káñina: Revista de Artes y Letras*, vol. 39, no. 1, 2015, pp. 119–127.

"Every Woman Every Child." *Department of Economic and Social Affairs. Sustainable Development*, 2022, https://sdgs.un.org/partnerships/every-woman-every-child. Accessed 1 October 2022.

"Food Security and Nutrition and Sustainable Agriculture. Related SDGS, Goal 2." *Department of Economic and Social Affairs Sustainable Development*, 2022, https://sdgs.un.org/topics/food-security-and-nutrition-and-sustainable-agriculture. Accessed 2 October 2022.

Foote, Stephanie, and Elizabeth Mazzolini. "Introduction: Histories of the Dustheap." *Histories of the Dustheap. Waste, Material Cultures, Social Justice*, edited by Stephanie Foote and Elizabeth Mazzolini. The MIT Press, 2012, pp. 1–18.

"Goal 1." *United Nations Department of Economic and Social Affairs Sustainable Development*, 2022, https://sdgs.un.org/goals/goal1. Accessed 30 September 2022.

"Goal 2." *United Nations Department of Economic and Social Affairs Sustainable Development*, 2022, https://sdgs.un.org/goals/goal2. Accessed 30 September 2022.

"Goal 3." *United Nations Department of Economic and Social Affairs Sustainable Development*, 2022, https://sdgs.un.org/goals/goal3. Accessed 30 September 2022.

"Goal 4." *United Nations Department of Economic and Social Affairs Sustainable Development*, 2022, https://sdgs.un.org/goals/goal4. Accessed 30 September 2022.

"Goal 5." *United Nations Department of Economic and Social Affairs Sustainable Development*, 2022, https://sdgs.un.org/goals/goal4. Accessed 30 September 2022.

Hernández, Edin. "Única: la fortaleza de la desesperación." *Signos: Semanario Cultural*, vol. 36, 1994, pp. 1–2.

Hoeg, Jerry. "Evolutionary Theory and Fernando Contreras Castro's *Única mirando al mar*." *Interdisciplinary Literary Studies*, vol. 17, no. 4, pp. 577–592.

———. "The Landscape of the Consumer Society. Fernando Contreras Castro's *Única mirando al mar*." *Reading and Writing the Latin American Landscape*, edited by Beatriz Rivera-Barnes and Jerry Hoeg. Palgrave Macmillan, 2009, pp. 177–185.

Mora Chinchilla, Rolando, and Raúl Mora Amador. "Reseña histórica del relleno sanitario de Río Azul y consideraciones sobre los metals pesados tratados en él y los presentes en nuestros hogares." *Revista Reflexiones*, vol. 82, no. 2, 2003, pp. 47–58.

Scanlan, John. *On Garbage*. Reaktion Books, 2005.

"The 17 Goals." *Department of Economic and Social Affairs Sustainable Development*, 2022, https://sdgs. un.org/goals. Accessed 30 September 2022.

6   Agnès Varda's *The Gleaners and I*

From Waste to Wonder—A Cinematic Odyssey on Food Loss and Gleaning

Stéphanie Boulard

I   Text

Title	*The Gleaners and I*
Genre	Documentary Film
Director	Agnès Varda (1928–2019), a French film director and photographer, was a Paris-based key figure in modern film history, and one of the world's leading filmmakers. Her first film, *La Pointe Courte* (1955), was a precursor of the French New Wave movies of the 1960s. However, her work is distinct from the French New Wave for its crossing of genres, as she is known as much for her feature-length dramas and shorts as for her documentaries. Not limiting herself to the borders of France, her films have been shot in a variety of locations, including the United States, Cuba, and Iran. The themes and issues in her films focus on women's rights, social taboos, and the struggles against political, economic, or social oppression, death, and time. Her films are known for their distinctive experimental style such as her 2000 movie *The Gleaners and I* (*Les Glaneurs et la Glaneuse*), in which she uses a digital camera for the first time. In 2019, director Martin Scorsese described Varda as "one of the Gods of Cinema" (*The Hollywood Reporter*). She has received many prizes for her work and was the first female director to be awarded an honorary Oscar.
Year	2000
Country	Shot in the north of France and in Beauce, Jura, Provence, the Pyrenees and Paris between September 1999 and April 2000, *The Gleaners and I* examines both a historical subculture and a turn-of-the-millennium phenomenon: the gleaners who, by necessity, chance or choice, glean or salvage left-over items discarded by others. Director Agnès Varda, who describes the film as a "wandering-road-documentary" (Varda, "Promotional Materials"), spent several months driving around France with her digital camera, traveling the streets of Paris and rural communities, seeking out different varieties of gleaners wherever she could, collecting images about food poverty, food wastage, and overconsumption. At first, the gleaners' life conditions and their reasons for gleaning seem unrelated; but over the course of the film, Varda draws remarkable social and political connections between them, encouraging the spectator to connect their various motives, such as poverty and adversity, but also more unexpected ones, such as resourcefulness, tradition, art, and activism. With her handheld camera, Varda ultimately tells her own story, highlighting that filmmaking is itself a form of gleaning. The film was entered into competition at the 2000 Cannes Film Festival and won awards around the world, including the European Film Award, the BSFC Award and the Chicago International Film Festival for Best Documentary, the LAFCA Award or the Critics Award of French Syndicate of Cinema Critics (2001) for Best Film. In 2016, the film appeared at No. 99 on BBC's list of the 100 greatest films of the 21st century. Two years later, she made a sequel entitled *The Gleaners and I: Two Years Later* (*Deux ans après*, 2003).

DOI: 10.4324/9781003388869-9

Students who are interested in watching the film, *The Gleaners and I*, have several options available to them. They can visit their local library and check if the DVD is available for borrowing. Alternatively, they can purchase the DVD from online vendors such as Amazon or eBay. For those who prefer to stream the movie, it is available on various platforms including The Criterion Channel, DocAlliance Films, and Amazon Prime Video (although availability may vary). Additionally, students can rent the movie from Netflix or DocAlliance Films.

During the 2023 Cannes Film Festival, Varda's daughter, Rosalie Varda, accompanied by Martin Scorsese, announced the launch of a unique educational and heritage project, which Netflix has chosen to support. This ambitious initiative aims to restore and make available to students worldwide the entirety of the footage from the documentary feature, *The Gleaners and I*. It involves a platform established by France's National Audiovisual Institute (INA), where young filmmakers can study Agnès Varda's editing technique and engage with the raw material to create their own version of the film. For Netflix and Ted Sarandos, the Co-CEO, this innovative project holds particular importance as it targets the young generation of filmmakers and aims to spark interest in the language of cinema. "Agnes Varda was a real trailblazer of cinema," Sarandos told *IndieWire*,

> [h]er amazing work inspired the filmmakers who created the French New wave and in turn influenced generations of artists around the world. She was a creative bridge between cultures, generations and cinema movements. She leaves behind a remarkable body of work that will serve as the foundation of this exciting program for students that will keep her timeless legacy alive. (Kohn)

In light of this remarkable project, students who are passionate about *The Gleaners and I* now have an extraordinary opportunity to delve deeper into Varda's creative process and study her editing technique while engaging with the raw footage to craft their own interpretations of the film. This educational endeavor not only pays tribute to Varda's influential contributions to cinema but also aims to ignite a passion for the language of film in the younger generations. It is a testament to Varda's status as a cinematic pioneer and a bridge between cultures and generations.

II   Context

1   *Food Loss and Waste*

Les Glaneurs et la Glaneuse is a French documentary by Agnès Varda about food poverty, hunger, food wastage, ecology, art, and autobiography shot in digital video. Her movie project was triggered by a scene of food poverty in Paris. In her interview with Melissa Anderson, Varda recalls the moment when she saw an old woman at the marketplace, struggling to bend down to reach discarded vegetables or bread and she thought, "Oh my God, these poor people." Varda admits, "I felt bad for them," and this sentiment, the emotional impact that this suffering provoked, prompted Varda to make the film (Anderson 24). Agnès Varda thus started filming *The Gleaners and I* in 1999 with a question: Who are those who eat what we throw away in these times of overconsumption? The first part of the film investigates the term and concept of gleaning as practiced in France since the 19th century, while the remainder of the film considers the concrete function that encompasses a range of activities from recuperation, to human trash-picking or dumpster diving, to art built on the use of recycled materials. Varda's "nomadic cinema," which uses iconic traveling shots such as when she squeezes trucks on the highway between her fingers and makes them appear even smaller than car figurines (see 00:41:00–00:41:58) takes us to multiple locations in France (Powrie 68). She films modern-day gleaners, in town or in the countryside, who depend on gleaning to survive. Rather than filming food wastage in some distant "developing" country, Varda's gaze, directed at food poverty in metropolitan France, is central to its *affective* force (Topping 4).

In 2019, a study by the United Nations Environment Program (UNEP) estimated that 913 million tons of food or 17% of the total food available was thrown away in households, retail, restaurant, and other food service trash. According to the International Food Policy Research Institute (IFPRI), the total reduction of losses and wastage would make it possible to feed approximately 2 billion people. In *The Gleaners and I*, Varda shows tons of potatoes discreetly dumped in a field by producers because they are incorrectly sized or shaped. She also depicts representatives of the food production industry and supermarket employees destroying out-of-date produce so that it cannot be gleaned. These disturbing sequences cause discomfort and lead to the demand for an ethical position. While Varda's movie shows in multiple scenes and interviews a society that allows vast quantities of food to be wasted in the name of progress and market values, the film "marks a fundamentally humanist stance in that it recognizes the value of individuals in their own right and their compassion and creativity" (Topping 9). Varda's gleaners have different motivations, but all have in common an acute awareness and a strong ecological conscience. Losing what the earth offers seems to them an insult to nature; throwing away what can be used or repaired or contributing to polluting the planet in a way that will affect the well-being of future generations who will inherit a weakened, even hostile environment appears to them unacceptable. Varda and the gleaners argue that the act of gleaning helps reduce food loss and waste and is also essential to ensure food security.

2   *A Sociological and Environmental Study in Postmodern Consumerism*

The Gleaners and I presents us with both a sociological study and a lesson on cinema and its changing essence in the postmodern universe of consumerism and individualism. In this way, the film reinscribes the filmmaker in the community. Compassion, fragility, and the need to look differently, particularly at the margins, are some emerging themes that interconnect the film as a whole (Topping 11).

Although when it comes to editing the footage of her movie she is "strict and trying to be structured," Varda explains that she also tries to be "instinctive" such as when she meets a group of marginalized young people who got into trouble with the law in Prades, in the South of France (Mayer). They are accused of having vandalized the bins of a supermarket where bleach had been poured on unsold products. Another instance of such instinctive filming is when she meets Alain, the street newspaper seller (Alain sells *L'Itinérant*, a street newspaper intended to help the homeless), who feeds on vegetables gleaned at the end of the market, directly on the asphalt. But over the course of her meetings with Alain, Varda discovers that he lives in a home for precarious workers in the Paris suburbs and gives literacy courses to non-Francophone immigrants in the evening. Alain, who has a Master's degree in Biology, opts for selfless aid and gives what he has, that is to say, his knowledge. Given the importance of language proficiency for social inclusion, the value of this gift is immense.

Agnès Varda's film also features François, who scavenges from garbage cans for political reasons, not out of economic necessity. François expresses his strong ideas about waste and its connection to the Erika boat disaster, highlighting the negative impact of a consumerist society (00:55:02). The shipwreck caused an unprecedented ecological catastrophe in France resulting in the spillage of over 30,000 tons of fuel oil into the Atlantic Ocean, which polluted 400 km of coastline and caused the deaths of up to 300,000 birds. The incident halted fishing, banned shellfish consumption, and caused economic devastation for local beach resorts. The Erika trial, which constituted a watershed moment for environmental groups, was one of France's most significant environmental cases to be brought to court. It acknowledged that a polluter could be held accountable for the ecological harm caused by oil spills. Despite initially not seeing a connection between the Erika disaster and gleaning, Varda included François's commentary in the film, highlighting the societal issue of mass, cheap production, and the economic necessity of gleaning. This link underscores the cultural and political significance of the film as a critique of consumerism and mass production, while also showcasing the ingenuity and resourcefulness of marginalized individuals who glean for political reasons. Ultimately, Varda was pleased with the inclusion of this connection in her film (Anderson 25).

3   *The Various Faces of Gleaning: From Michelin Star Chefs to
      Eco-Artists and Legal Vagueness*

In the movie, not all of the gleaners that she interviews are poor: some are not driven by poverty or hunger but are instead legally gleaning (in French: *glaner*) or picking fruit (in French: *grappiner*) for pleasure or for ecological or artistic reasons. Consider the case of Éduard Loubet, born in 1970, who was, at the time of *The Gleaners and I*, the youngest French master chef to have earned two stars in the Michelin guide. Varda stops to visit Édouard Loubet's restaurant in Southern France in the Provence-Alpes-Côte d'Azur region. According to Varda, he is "inventive and thrifty" (00:18:48). While he offers a gourmet menu, unlike many upscale restaurants, he does not have a lot of leftovers because he is economical. He not only cultivates his own vegetable garden which supplies the raw materials for the restaurant, but he is also a "born gleaner" or a "born picker" who regularly gleans herbs and fruits in the fields surrounding his restaurant because he prefers fresh ingredients "rather than refrigerated produces from Italy" (00:19:58). Varda, by including the master chef Loubet in her film about detritus, juxtaposes the homeless with an elitist cultural attitude toward food and the master chef sharing his recipes for good health and well-being (Loubet). And then come the artists, some very famous, who build their artistic vision and work on abandoned trash or the leftovers of other people's lives.

However, there is a kind of legal vagueness surrounding the right to glean. Even if the lawyers consulted by Varda formally confirm the right to glean—a lawyer (the "Maitre") cites a text dating back to 1545 and another judge educates viewers on the law of making curbside trash one's own by reclaiming abandoned fridges or televisions—, the facts show that gleaning is frequently prohibited locally. Gleaning is defined in the Penal Code only implicitly, through the conditions under which it is prohibited. "It's allowed without being too much. At least it's not illegal," explains an oyster gleaner (00:44:02). Agnès Varda has fun highlighting the lack of knowledge and vagueness surrounding this centuries-old right. The sequence shot at the Passage du Gois de Noirmoutier shows that no one knows exactly what the law says, neither about the distance to be respected from the parks nor about the authorized weight: "Ten- fifteen meters from the parks," said one (00:44:10); "Twenty-five yards," said the other (00:44:12). "Three kilos" (00:44:19), "five kilos per person" (00:44:24), and "three dozen per person" (00:44:35) are all responses given to her question on how much one can glean. Varda's facetious editing shows that no one really knows the legal texts. Finally, Varda suggests that gleaning has more to do with kindness, generosity, and brotherhood than with the law. To allow gleaning is to recognize the need to share a little of one's wealth with those who have nothing, to resist a world where profit and profitability tend to replace any form of a social bond.

4   *A Hybrid Approach to Documentary Filmmaking*

The film combines two approaches: first, the so-called traditional documentary approach of filming with a small team on professional support with prior location scouting and a concrete filming schedule; second, a more spontaneous and unplanned documentary approach with the sequences shot by Varda alone with a lightweight hand-held camera, one of "the more sophisticated of the amateur models [the Sony DV CAM DSR 300]" (Anderson 24). Although the Sony DSR-300 may seem like a relic today, Varda's hand-held digital camera was at that time a groundbreaking way of filming that allowed a lot of freedom, gave the capacity to capture fleeting moments, and facilitated less intrusive filming conditions. Forgetting very quickly that they are being filmed, the gleaners that Varda meets open up more easily. As Agnès recalled during a round table organized by the *Cahiers du cinema* with the filmmakers Alain Cavalier and Raymond Depardon:

> A technique is always linked to a project, to a subject. I knew that to deal with the subject of the gleaners, I was sometimes going to meet people in extremely precarious situations [. . .]. There is an intimacy, a proximity to this little camera which makes it possible to look very closely and to watch alone. (*Cahiers*)

But the female gleaner of the title is obviously Agnès Varda herself who playfully replicates the pose of the gleaner in Breton's painting, clearly presenting that she gleans images "both of the world and of herself" (Vesey 172). The digital camera and "the mobilization of herself as a gleaned image" (Powrie 79) allow her to combine a personal reflection on the world with a playful self-portrait (Rosello 33). She explains that this more personal footage of herself was necessary: "I felt that I was asking so much of these people to reveal themselves, to speak to me, to be honest with me, that I should reveal something of myself too" (Anderson 24). If Varda is aware of the perilous nature of the gleaning metaphor and does not want to compare her artistic gleaning to those who glean food to stay alive without minimizing their ordeal—"you cannot push the analogy [. . .] it's too heavy" (Meyer 2001)—, she focuses on increasing social aware-ness of this societal "waste and trash" by pushing that more important, compassionate question: "Who finds a use for it?" (Bonner), and by reflecting on the artistic expression as a response to marginalization, exclusion, or oppression as the work of art has "the potential to lead to mean-ingful action for social, economic and policy transformation" (Topping 17). In the end, Varda's interviews of those ignored by society and oppressed by corporations and governments allow her always to return to larger political issues such as the immoral dimensions of France's agri-cultural industry, waste, hunger, and poverty.

III   Interpretation

1   At the beginning of the film, Varda takes us to the fields where newly harvested potatoes have just been dumped. One potato gleaner explains that many potatoes are rejected because they are "misshapen" (00:09:48). He shows some of them to the camera and comments that they look like hearts. Varda immediately requests: "Give me the heart-potato" (00:09:51). Why do you think she insists specifically on having the heart-potato (see Figure 6.1)? What is the symbolism of the heart-shaped potato? Do you think it is important to have that scene at the beginning of the movie? Why? When do we see the heart-potato again later in the movie and why might such repetition be important? When filming these heart-shaped potatoes, consider how Varda uses the following elements of cinematographic composi-tion: color and contrast; lines, curves, and shapes; camera angle, focus, zoom, stillness, and motion; positioning and framing. What makes her filming technique singular?

Figure 6.1 Film still of heart-shaped potatoes collected by Varda from Varda's *The Gleaners and I* (00:10:31).

2   Driven by chance encounters, Varda interviewed dozens of gleaners. A documentary involves not only questioning people but also showing them. Reflect on the following topics regarding Agnès Varda's choices as director:

   a.   Where were the people interviewed generally filmed?
   b.   Who were the interviewees that were filmed at home, and why?
   c.   Were the people named, or did they remain anonymous?
   d.   What type of clothing did the gleaners wear during filming? How did Varda stage it into her documentary?
   e.   Who are the gleaners? Choose two to compare and contrast.
   f.   What choices did Varda make as a filmmaker, such as camera angles, low-angle shots, and close-ups?

3   Varda's investigation leads from forgotten corners of France to the famous restaurants featured in the Michelin Guide. Comment on Figures 6.2 and 6.3. What is particular about this gleaner? Do you think it is important that the film's engagement with the real occurs alongside sensorial and gastronomical immersion? Do you think that Varda is "enacting a multisensory experience" (Topping 14)? Why or why not?

4   The gleaners are often filmed and interviewed alone. However, Varda is also interested in a group of young people (see Figure 6.4). How does she film them? Comment on this sequence in the film: 00:50:45–00:53:10. Can we say that Varda films everyone—the young people, the manager of the supermarket, and the prosecutor—in the same way? What are the different symbols of authority that appear in this sequence? Does the surveillance camera

Figure 6.2 Film still of chef Édouard Loubet picking fruits in the fields surrounding his restaurant from Varda's *The Gleaners and I* (00:20:03).

Figure 6.3 Film still of chef Édouard Loubet in front of his famous restaurant featured in the Michelin Guide from Varda's *The Gleaners and I* (00:18:51).

seem threatening to you? Why or why not? What does the progression of this sequence inspire in you? What do you think is the outcome of this situation at the time? Would the outcome be the same today, in France? Why? What would be the outcome in your country?

Figure 6.4 Film still of youngsters gathered on a square from Varda's *The Gleaners and I* (00:50:44).

5   François (00:53:25) has been a gleaner for 10–15 years and speaks candidly about his life and economic situation. In comparison to the other gleaners, what sets François apart? Why does François wear boots? What commentary does François make about society and consumerism? Do you agree with it? How did Varda film François' commentary, and what is the intended effect? Through the portrayal of François, what commentary does Varda make about the capitalist economy and its logic?

6   The film's structure consists of about 20 "chapters." Can you provide a title for each of the chapters in *The Gleaners and I* including those on the film stills shown: Figures 6.1, 6.3–6.6? For example, The Credits; The Origins of Gleaning; Potatoes, etc. Why do you think Agnès Varda included the chapter "The Erika" in her movie (00:54:48–00:55:17)? What is its significance in the film? Can you comment on Varda's filming techniques in "The Erika" chapter? Specifically, what type of shots did Varda use to film the birds, and what might be the reasoning behind her selection of these shots?

7   Compare and contrast two interviews: the lawyer (00:28:44–00:30:20; Figure 6.5) and Alain (1:11:18–1:16:32; Figure 6.6). What is the relationship between the interviewee and the interviewer in each situation? Do these two interviews have anything in common? What are the distinctive characteristics that Varda finds in both interviewees that she likes? Why? Why do you think it is important that Alain teaches the word "success" to these non-French speakers or migrants who are learning the language?

Figure 6.5 Film still of a lawyer (the "Maître") from Varda's *The Gleaners and I* (00:28:47).

Figure 6.6 Film still of Alain teaching from Varda's *The Gleaners and I* (01:15:24).

8   In the press notes for *The Gleaners and I*, Varda argues that documentary is "a discipline that teaches modesty" (Varda, "Promotional Materials"). How do you understand that statement? After watching Varda's documentary, would you agree? What impression does this film give of the profession of director? Is it different from the impression given by other films, interviews, etc. that you know? Explain.

9   The title *The Gleaners and I* (*Les Glaneurs et la Glaneuse*) is reminiscent of the titles of many paintings of gleaning dating back to the 19th century. You can find some of them on the Internet by typing the following names into a search engine: Jean-François Millet, *The Gleaners* (*Les Glaneuses*, 1857); Georges Laugée, *The Gleaners* (*Les Glaneuses*, 1895); Jules Breton, *The Recall of the Gleaners* (*Le Rappel des glaneuses*, 1859); Pissarro, *The Gleaners* (*Les Glaneuses*, 1889); Léon Augustin Lhermitte, *The Gleaners* (*Les Glaneuses*, 1887 and 1898). In what ways are the many paintings on gleaning from the 19th century reminiscent of the title of the film *The Gleaners and I*? One hundred and fifty years after these paintings, Agnès Varda makes her film. What does it tell us about the practice of gleaning? How does Agnès Varda's film continue this tradition of depicting gleaning in art?

10   The transitions in this film are often abrupt. There are also many digressions and even accidents that are recovered as discoveries (images without dialogue or sound, for example). How do the techniques, images, and sound used in *The Gleaners and I* reinforce the idea of encounters and chance and the act of gleaning? Despite the film's primary theme of gleaning, Varda interjects playful digressions and art references, drawing parallels between herself and artists such as Rembrandt, Antoni Tàpies, Cai Guo-Qiang, or Étienne-Jules Marey. What is the significance of Varda playfully mimicking the pose of Breton's "La Glaneuse" (Figure 6.7), carrying a bundle of wheat on her shoulder (Figure 6.8), and dropping it in favor of her digital camera (Figure 6.9)? Why is it significant that she adopts the pose of

Figure 6.7 Film still of Breton's painting *The Gleaner* (*La Glaneuse*, 1877) from Varda's *The Gleaners and I* (00:04:22).

Figure 6.8 Film still of Varda's self-portrait as a female gleaner copying the proud posture of Breton's painting from Varda's *The Gleaners and I* (00:04:30).

Figure 6.9 Film still of Varda's self-portrait as a filmmaker from Varda's *The Gleaners and I* (00:04:38).

the *subject* of the painting here, the gleaner herself? Do these autobiographical episodes interfere with the social aspects of the documentary? Can you find a connection between her self-portrait and the gleaners in the interviews? How does Varda break down the barriers between the filmed subjects and the filmmaker in *The Gleaners and I*? In what ways is the film not only a reflection of gleaning but also a reflection upon cinema itself?

IV   People-Focused Applications to SDGs 1, 2, 3, 4, and 5

1   In the context of sustainable development, SDG 1 (No Poverty) aims to eradicate poverty in all its forms, ensure equal rights to economic resources, build the resilience of the poor and those in vulnerable situations, and provide access to basic services, among other targets. With this in mind, to what extent does Varda engage with the various targets of SDG 1 (No Poverty) in 6.4, 6.5, and 6.6? Do you think there have been any changes in the current situation regarding poverty since Varda's time? Additionally, how does Varda's documentary on gleaning intersect with the unit themes of this book: planet, people, prosperity, and partnerships? What did you "glean" from the film?

2   In *The Gleaners and I*, Varda presents shifting viewpoints and multiple interviewees of gleaners either culling left-over food from fields after the harvest or salvaging food and wares from city markets and trash dumpsters. How does Varda's documentary film about the legalized practice of gleaning and the newer practices of urban gleaning address issues related to SDG 2: "end hunger, achieve food security and improved nutrition and promote sustainable agriculture" (UN SDG Goal 2, 2022)? Complete the table below about the multiple gleaners interviewed in the film. Then, compare and contrast your completed table with that of a classmate. What do the gleaners glean, and why (for fun, out of necessity, for art, for ideology, etc.)? Would you say that these diverse people and their different reasons for gleaning are unrelated or connected? In the film, are there situations or people that surprise you? Which ones? Explain.

Name of character	Time code	What is he/she gleaning?	What are his/her motivations or reasons for gleaning?	What is the most related SDG: 1, 2, 3, 4, or 5?
Claude	0:12:05			
Édouard Loubet, the Master Chef	0:17:40			
Hervé/VR, the artist	0:33:40			
François, "the man with the boots"	0:53:26			
Salomon	0:57:58			
Alain	1:11:28			
Agnès Varda				

3   According to the Food and Agriculture Organization of the United Nations, a specialized agency that leads international efforts to defeat hunger, the global volume of food wastage is estimated at 1.6 billion tons of "primary product equivalents" (FAO, "Food wastage: Key facts and figures"). The total food wastage for the edible part of this amounts to 1.3 billion tons a year, which means that about one-third of the food produced and packaged for human consumption is lost or wasted, while 10% of people in the world are chronically undernourished. The U.S. Department of Agriculture estimates that the United States discards 30 to 40% of the entire US food supply, which corresponds to approximately 133

billion pounds in total or 219 pounds of waste per person ("Food Waste FAQs"). As depicted in Varda's film, wholesome food that could have helped feed families in need is sent to landfills. In France, food loss and waste represent 10 million tons of product per year, representing 66 pounds per person per year ("Food loss and waste"). How does *The Gleaners and I* address the problem of food waste? Does the film only show the problem, or does it also offer solutions?

4   In her exploration of gleaning, Varda brings attention to the issues of poverty, hunger, and waste that prevail in a consumer-driven society and highlights the political and economic decisions that lead to these challenges. While some people glean as a means of survival, others adopt it as a way of life or to challenge the culture of consumerism and excess. How does Varda emphasize the critical significance of addressing politics and poverty through the experiences of the gleaners in her film? Who among the gleaners denounces the waste-fulness of corporations and governments? Finally, does Varda approve or disapprove of gleaning, and what evidence from the film supports your view?

5   The mission of SDG 3 is to "[e]nsure healthy lives and promote well-being for all at all ages" (UN SDG Goal 3, 2022). When Agnès Varda discovers the pile of potatoes discarded because they are too big or too small, she immediately thinks of contacting the French charity *Les Restaurants du Cœur* (soup kitchens called "The Restaurants of the Heart" or "The Restaurants of Love"), whose main activity is to distribute food packages and hot meals to those in need (00:10:36). How does Varda address the impact of poverty, food waste and hunger on health, well-being, and age in that scene? Furthermore, to what extent does the film suggest that art, aesthetic endeavor or pleasure, and community play a role in achieving this SDG 3 mission, and how do these factors intersect with other aspects of SDG 3?

6   SDG 4 promotes the need "to ensure inclusive and equitable quality education and promote lifelong learning opportunities for all" (UN SDG Goal 4, 2022). Do you think the movie addresses that goal? Which specific education challenges and learning opportunities does Varda show?

7   In addition to her interviews that describe the hardships of gleaning, Varda also integrates light-hearted stories and tales of the delights of gleaning, resourcefulness, art, and activism. She visits the following contemporary artists who glean to make art from found objects: the artist named VR/Hervé who makes art from garbage (Figure 6.10); Bodan Litnanski, a Russian stonemason who has created a "palais idéal" (ideal palace) with cemented remnants and discarded and broken dolls; French collage artist Louis Pons (Figure 6.11), who explains to Varda his artistic process of creating reliefs and assemblages made entirely from discarded objects, in which what others see as "a cluster of junk" are for him "a cluster of possibilities"; or American artist Sarah Sze, who makes large-scale sculptures and immense mobiles utilizing everyday materials, found objects, photographs, and wiring. This practice of enhancing the aesthetics of recovered objects while giving them a new "utility" has been coined "upcycling." The term was first used in 1994 by German engineer Reiner Plitz and detailed in 2002 in William McDonough and Michael Braungart's book *Cradle to Cradle: Remaking the Way We Make Things*. Do you think that, in her way, Varda in *The Gleaners and I* already encourages upcycling or the switch from a "cradle-to-grave" pattern to a "cradle-to-cradle" pattern? If yes, how? How does her film teach the spectator that objects can gain value and life in circulation? How does this connect to SDG 3 and SDG 4? How does Varda's camera educate the viewer? What does it mean to draw attention to the visual and material similarities between street creations and gallery arts? How do these urban scavengers "reiterate the question of value or usefulness first raised in connection with food" (Tyrer 168)?

Figure 6.10 Film still of VR/Hervé's artistic creation made with rubbish from Varda's *The Gleaners and I* (00:34:50).

Figure 6.11 Film still of Louis Pons explaining his artistic process from *The Gleaners and I* (00:39:54).

8   In her movie, Varda recalls the rules and traditions of gleaning practices from the past widely known today through various 19th-century paintings. Was there an opposition between men and women in the gleaning process as portrayed historically in art? If yes, who were the gleaners in the past, and who are the gleaners today in Varda's film? Relate your answers to SDG 5 on "achieving gender equality and empowering all women and girls" (UN SDG Goal 5, 2022). Keeping these distinctions in mind, expand your answer to include an interpretation of the film's title—both the French original and the English translation. There is an important discrepancy between the French and English titles. The French title, *Les Glaneurs et la Glaneuse*, can be roughly translated in English as "The Gleaners and The Female Gleaner," with the masculine plural noun juxtaposed to the feminine singular noun. The English title, *The Gleaners and I,* mutes the gender distinction and sets up an implicit opposition between "The Gleaners" as "the people who glean" and the filmmaker as "I," whereas the French title links them, asserting that she (*la glaneuse*) is one of them (*les glaneurs*). Do you think this linguistic distinction that seems to be virtually built into the two languages could tell us something about the French sense of community and the Anglo-American sense of individuality? Or would you consider rather that the "I" of the English title engages Varda in a conversation with the gleaners as well as with the spectator? Which title is more supportive of SDG 5 and why?

9   Discuss the scene in which Varda praises the *Musée en Herbe*'s program, *Poubelle ma belle* ("My Beautiful Garbage Can") (0:56:17–0:57:06), which teaches children to appreciate that which is not brand new and to recycle or even create new objects. How does that scene connect to SDGs 1, 2, and 4? What are the conventional forms of modern recycling presented in that scene? How do you understand the narrative voice's comment at the end of that scene: "In all museums, trash is small, cute, clean and colorful. But have these children ever seen brooms in action, or have they ever shaken hands with a garbage collector?" (00:57:49).

10 What is your opinion regarding the statement made by Rosello where she asserts that "For Varda, gleaning is not the (good) opposite of (bad) waste but a practice that redefines social exchanges" (Rosello 30)? Do you agree or disagree with this statement, and why? Do you think that Varda herself would agree with this statement, and why? Additionally, how do you think this concept of gleaning defined by Rosello as a practice that redefines social exchanges relates to SDG 3, which focuses on promoting good health and well-being for all individuals?

11 In a 2003 interview, Agnès Varda discusses the ethical challenges represented by her film. She explains her approach, which was to situate the documentary within a global framework so as to examine the boundaries between so-called "developing" countries and a Western European nation:

> What I can tell you is that this film *The Gleaners* has been shown more or less everywhere in France and across the world. It raises the same question everywhere. And that's not the question of economic sustainability or of fair trade; it's the question of a society organized around "dosh," ["fric" in French, familiar word for "money"] "whatever you can get," excessive production, excessive consumption, excessive rubbish, and thus waste. The battle needs to be fought at all levels. We can try to slow down the systematic "trashing" of natural resources. We can produce a report on those in dire poverty in South Africa, India or South America. But what I was interested in saying was: "Look. I live in France, it's a civilized, "cultured," rich country and there are people who live off what they find in our bins." It's shaken up many a French person to see that. (Varda, Cité Internationale de la Bande Dessinée et de L'image, translation by Topping)

In what way might it be "shocking" that Varda highlights oppression and exclusion in a Western society known for the ideals of "liberté, égalité, fraternité"? Discuss how Varda's film offers "a powerful critique of the circulation of people, goods, and ideologies of consumption" (Topping 6) while at the same time suggesting new models of community. Discuss how Varda's question—"Can one live on the leftovers of others?" (Varda, *Promotional materials*)—can be examined on a global scale?

12 An entire segment of *The Gleaners and I* focuses on Varda's aging body as Varda includes close-ups of her white hair (Figure 6.12) and her aging hands (Figure 6.13).

In many interviews, such as the one with Julie Rigg in 2005, Varda commented on her self-portraiture and her visual self-explorations:

> I enjoy traveling, but I'm aging. And that came like I say, like the gleaning ideas, images, and emotions; it's like gleaning also first impressions. I allow myself to live in the film, to "let in" the film, because I thought by making a film like this I don't want to be separate from it, to live in another world than those who speak so honestly, so clearly about themselves, and speak about situations in which they could be ashamed or wish to hide or wish to say "don't bother with me." I thought I have to be part of that, I should not back out of it. And it came naturally that I should be part of the film. (Rigg 184)

Scholars have repeatedly pointed out that Varda's presence and digressions in *Les Glaneurs* could be considered as a "Portrait of the Artist as an Old Lady" (Rosello). How does the digital camera and "the mobilization of herself as a gleaned image" allow Varda to combine a personal reflection on the world with a playful self-portrait that forms new visual and

Figure 6.12 Film still Varda's white hair from *The Gleaners and I* (00:05:22).

Figure 6.13 Film still Varda's aging hands from *The Gleaners and I* (00:05:48).

narrative grammars of old age (Powrie 79)? Do you agree with Rosello that the film can thus be seen "as a statement, or rather a reverie on connections between gleaning, filming and the fragility of human life" (Rosello 33)? Is it accurate to say that the film is "structured around the gaze of a woman and the roaming of that woman as she gazes" (Powrie 80)? She explains that this more personal footage of herself was necessary: "I felt that I was asking so much of these people to reveal themselves, to speak to me, to be honest with me, that I should reveal something of myself too" (Anderson 24). Commenting on Varda's aesthetic choice, Rosello argues that Varda not only "questions both the cultural definition of female beauty and the cultural imperative that makes beauty mandatory in our representational universe," but also that by filming her own body—that of an older woman— "the result is the exact opposite of the predatory fragmentation characteristic of a fetishizing masculin-ist gaze," since "it also brings to mind a classic feminist intertext" (35). By questioning what society deems worthy of respect and revaluing the physical signs of age that society chooses to malign (Bonner), filming the "horror" of aging as "dispossession of the self" ["I feel as if I am an animal, worse, I am an animal I don't know"], the film's voice-over, close framings and cutting, combine ecological concerns with feminist ones and open the path to an eco-feminist reading. Eco-feminism is a philosophy that intersects environmental-ism and feminism, recognizing the interconnectedness of the exploitation of women and the natural environment. Eco-feminists believe that by prioritizing the natural world and respecting women's rights, we can create a more sustainable and equitable society. Through her films, Agnès Varda challenges conventional power structures and emphasizes the impor-tance of amplifying the voices of those who have been historically marginalized, particu-larly women. By filming what others would ruthlessly eliminate, "that which mainstream cultural production excludes" (Cruickshank 124), by revaluing "the used, the aged, even the unsightly" (Bonner), how does Varda's cinema embody a kind of eco-feminist subversion of aesthetics? Moreover, how can her approach be linked to Sustainable Development Goal 5, which aims to achieve gender equality and empower all women and girls?

13 Two years after *The Gleaners and I*, Varda met with some of the gleaners again and asked them what they thought of the film. One of them, Alain, criticizes her for the place she granted

herself in her film. He explains, "I think your self-portrait is [. . .] unnecessary" (*The Gleaners and I: Two Years Later*, 2002). He adds that Varda's hands and hair are digressive elements that are an obstruction to the film's political message, suggesting that the film would have been stronger if it included solely a discourse of gleaning as a political act against poverty, hunger, and inequalities. In some ways, Alain wants a focus on many of the UN SDGs covered in this unit. Do you agree with his judgment? Do you think that Varda's moments of self-disclosure are just the film's "digressions" (Tyrer 162)? How does Agnès Varda fit in as a character in her own film? Does her self-portrait or self-analysis relate to SDGs 1, 2, 3, 4, and/or 5?

14 Divide the class into five groups and assign one of the SDGs from Unit 2 (1, 2, 3, 4, or 5) to each group. Each group will then prepare arguments for a debate in which they maintain that their assigned SDG is the most relevant or central to Agnès Varda's *The Gleaners and I*. (The instructor of the course will decide on the format and length of the debate and facilitate a follow-up discussion with the class upon the conclusion of the debate.)

15 Does Varda's *The Gleaners and I* solely support and clarify the principles of the UN SDGs and sustainable development concept? Or does it also challenge any implicit assumptions, prejudices, deficiencies, weaknesses, or gaps within the UN SDG framework or the idea of sustainable development? Explain with details from the featured documentary treated in this chapter.

V   Beyond People—Connections to SDGs on Planet, Prosperity, and Partnerships

Beyond SDGs 1, 2, 3, 4, and 5, what additional SDGs are addressed by Agnès Varda in *The Gleaners and I*? Complete the table below with your ideas. Then compare and contrast your ideas with a classmate.

SDGs:	Does Varda's The Gleaners and I *connect with additional SDGs? If so, which ones and how?*
SDG 6 Clean Water and Sanitation	
SDG 7 Affordable and Clean Energy	
SDG 8 Decent Work and Economic Growth	
SDG 9 Industry, Innovation, and Infrastructure	
SDG 10 Reduced Inequalities	
SDG 11 Sustainable Cities and Communities	
SDG 12 Responsible Consumption and Production	
SDG 13 Climate Action	
SDG 14 Life below Water	
SDG 15 Life on Land	
SDG 16 Peace, Justice, and Strong Institutions	
SDG 17 Partnerships for the Goals	

VI   From Global to Local: On a Personal Level

1   How do you relate personally to Agnès Varda's *The Gleaners and I*? Explain in detail how your own life experiences or personal beliefs intersect with the main ideas and themes of the featured work in this chapter. Additionally, if you consider yourself a gleaner, how would you categorize yourself in relation to the different types of gleaners depicted in the film, and why?

2   How does Varda's documentary film relate to your local environment? Explain the global-local connection between Varda's *The Gleaners and I* and your home or current residence. What place-based considerations permit or prevent the application of the text to your geographical location?

3   What effect did Varda's *The Gleaners and I* have on you as a viewer? What type of response did the documentary elicit in you? Are you moved to action? Have your viewpoints or attitudes changed? Explain.

VII   Assignments

1   Research

1   The title of Varda's documentary is reminiscent of the titles of many paintings of gleaning dating back to the 19th century. Individually or in groups, research and identify the differences between the gleaning practiced in the past and modern practices of gleaning and connect them to SDGs 1, 2, 3, 4, 5. What technical and social developments have changed the habits of gleaners? (Generalization of agricultural machinery, the emergence of supermarkets, calibration standards, etc.) What are we gleaning today? In the fields? And in cities? Look in the film for the different attitudes of the owners toward gleaning (those who willingly let things happen; those who let things happen, but with a strict framework; those who let things happen, but don't like it very much; those who forbid it). What does the law say? Reconstruct the history of the right to glean through the centuries and explain how, over the centuries, the law encourages, regulates, authorizes, or prohibits the right to glean. Be sure to research an important law passed in France on May 21, 2015, concerning unsold food from supermarkets.
(The instructor of the course will determine the mode of presentation and delivery—oral presentation, written report, annotated bibliography, timeline project, or photo essay—for this research assignment.)

2   In the film, attention to words is omnipresent; they also participate in the progress of the documentary as "words give rise to new ideas and call for new images" (Varda, "Promotional Materials"). Varda has fun forming lexical associations. This relationship to the text also passes through popular culture as Varda uses the art of rhyme specific to rap to convey a message. She also worked with several musical collaborators whose music is included in the score. There are 11 distinct pieces of music that comprise the film's score. For this research project, you will analyze how words and music are utilized in the film to convey the message and progress of the documentary. Your first task is to research and identify the different musical genres used in the film and find when Varda utilizes jazz or a poem by French poet Joachim du Bellay. Next, rewatch the scene that includes the song "Rap de Récup'" by Agnès Bredel and Richard Klugman (00:02:40–00:03:33) and compare and contrast the message of the song to the film's overall message. In particular, pay attention to the song's interest in how gleaning is from another age or "may be extinct" (00:02:44),

but how it remains unchanged in our society. Consider also the song's distinction between gleaning and begging, its commentary on shame, and its comparison to street sweepers. Then, research where else in the movie we can hear once again this rap song and in what context. Finally, discuss also how the lyrics from this rap song might connect to the SDGs in ways that are similar to and/or different from the film. (The instructor of the course will determine the mode of presentation and delivery—oral presentation, written report, musical contribution or photo essay—for this research assignment.)

2   Write

1   Write a diary, film review, or response essay recording your reflections and personal reactions to the film's themes and ideas. Be sure to include your reactions to this film, analyze the cinematic features of the film, discuss the main issues, and outline the most related SDGs. At the end, incorporate a list of questions or comments you would like to mention or discuss in class. Make sure to also answer the following questions: Which gleaner interests you the most? Why? What examples of waste do we see in the film? What is your reaction to these examples of waste? Which SDG is the most important in the film? (The instructor of the course will determine the length and format of this writing assignment.)

2   Agnès Varda calls her film a "wandering-road-documentary" (Varda, "Promotional Materials"). Others have seen in this film a social commentary, a documentary on the capitalist system and consumer society, a film on ecology and recycling, a poetic and artistic film on fraternity, or even a self-portrait. Write an essay in which you summarize and analyze the film by choosing *only one of these aspects* of the film and connecting it to one of the SDGs treated in this unit. (The instructor of the course will determine the appropriate length for this writing assignment.)

3   Create

1   Create a self-portrait that you will film using a mobile phone. The exercise is not to take a simple animated selfie, but to describe yourself through objects that are dear to you, to document your own recycling or gleaning practices while focusing on a detail in the manner of Agnès Varda (hands, eyes, etc.), or to adopt the posture of a work of art with which you identify, such as Agnès Varda and her sheaf of wheat imitating a gleaner by Jules Breton. For students who are not enthusiastic about self-filming, make a short portrait of a few minutes of a person who has a job related to the practice of gleaning or recycling. Here again, you can take inspiration from certain sequences of *The Gleaners and I*, such as those of the lawyer in the cabbage field or of chef Édouard Loubet. (The instructor of the course will determine the mode of presentation and delivery for this creative assignment.)

2   Create a storyboard. In a group of 2 to 4 students, imagine a film about gleaning, recycling, waste, or mass consumption that you would like to shoot. Think especially of three aspects of the film: (1) the portrait of the filmmaker and the filmmaker's personal relationship with the subject of gleaning, recycling, waste, or mass consumption; (2) the trip or the "road-movie" aspect; and (3) the people who are to be interviewed. Then prepare a storyboard that you will present to the class, giving the title of your film and a summary of five to ten episodes. For each episode, include the following: location, subject, and people to be interviewed. (The instructor of the course will determine the mode of presentation and delivery for this creative assignment.)

Works Cited

Anderson, Melissa, "The Modest Gesture of the Film-maker: An Interview with Agnès Varda," *Cinéaste*, vol. 26, no. 4, 2001, pp. 24–27.

Bonner, Virginia. "Beautiful Trash: Agnès Varda's *Les Glaneurs et La Glaneuse*." Senses of Cinema, 24 November 2007, www.sensesofcinema.com/2007/feature-articles/glaneurs-et-glaneuse/. Accessed 1 April 2023.

Cavalier, Alain, Raymond Depardon, and Agnès Varda. "Le numérique, entre immédiateté et solitude: Entretien." *Cahiers du cinéma* n° 559, juillet-août 2001, pp. 62–65.

Cruickshank, Ruth. "The Work of Art in the Age of Global Consumption: Agnès Varda's *Les Glaneurs et la glaneuse*." *L'Esprit Créateur*, vol. 47, no. 3, 2007, pp. 119–132.

"Food Loss and Waste." Permanent Mission of France to the United Nations in Rome (FAO, IFAD, WFP), 10 September 2021, https://onu-rome.delegfrance.org/Food-loss-and-waste. Accessed 1 April 2023.

"Food Wastage: Key Facts and Figures." *The Food and Agriculture Organization* (*FAO*), https://www.fao.org/news/story/en/item/196402/icode/. Accessed 1 April 2023.

"Food Waste FAQs." USDA US Department of Agriculture, https://www.usda.gov/foodwaste/faqs. Accessed 1 April 2023.

"Goal 2." *United Nations Department of Economic and Social Affairs Sustainable Development*, 2022, https://sdgs.un.org/goals/goal2. Accessed 1 April 2023.

"Goal 3." *United Nations Department of Economic and Social Affairs Sustainable Development*, 2022, https://sdgs.un.org/goals/goal3. Accessed 1 April 2023.

"Goal 4." *United Nations Department of Economic and Social Affairs Sustainable Development*, 2022, https://sdgs.un.org/goals/goal4. Accessed 1 April 2023.

"Goal 5." *United Nations Department of Economic and Social Affairs Sustainable Development*, 2022, https://sdgs.un.org/goals/goal5. Accessed 1 April 2023.

Kohn, Eric. "How Scorsese and Netflix Inspired a New Effort to Restore Agnes Varda's Work." *Indiewire*, 23 May 2023, https://www.indiewire.com/news/festivals/netflix-scorsese-agnes-varda-1234867034/. Accessed 7 June 2023.

Loubet, Édouard. *Un printemps en Luberon.* Hachette Pratique, 2002.

McDonough, William and Michael Braungart. *Cradle to Cradle: Remaking the Way We Make Things.* New York: North Point Press, 2002.

Meyer, Andrea, "Interview: "Gleaning" the Passion of Agnès Varda," *Indiewire*, 8 March 2001, https://www.indiewire.com/2001/03/interview-gleaning-the-passion-of-agnes-varda-agnes-varda-81092/. Accessed 1 April 2023.

Powrie, Phil. "Heterotopic Spaces and Nomadic Gazes in Varda: From 'Cléo De 5 à 7' to 'Les Glaneurs Et La Glaneuse.'" *L'Esprit Créateur*, vol. 51, no. 1, 2011, pp. 68–82.

Rigg, Julie. "*The Gleaners and I* by Agnes Varda." *Agnès Varda: Interviews*, edited by Kline, T. Jefferson, University Press of Mississippi, *ProQuest Ebook Central*, 2013, pp. 183–190.

Rosello, Mireille. "Agnès Varda's *Les Glaneurs et La Glaneuse*: Portrait of the Artist as an Old Lady." *Studies in French Cinema*, vol. 1, no. 1, 2001, pp. 29–36.

"Telluride: Martin Scorsese Calls Agnes Varda One of the Gods." *The Hollywood Reporter*, 31 August 2019, https://www.hollywoodreporter.com/news/general-news/telluride-martin-scorsese-calls-agnes-varda-one-gods-at-fest-tribute-1235935/. Accessed 3 May 2023.

Topping, Margaret. "Fighting Food Poverty through Film: Or Why Global Challenge Research Needs the Arts and Humanities." *Humanities*, vol. 9, no. 3, 114, 2020, pp. 1–26.

Tyrer, Ben. "Digression and Return: Aesthetics and Politics in Agnès Varda's *Les Glaneurs et la glaneuse* (2000)." *Studies in French Cinema*, vol. 9, no. 2, pp. 161–176.

Varda, Agnès. *Les Glaneurs et la Glaneuse, d'Agnès Varda: Propos Glanés*. Cité Internationale de la Bande Dessinée et de L'image, 2020, http://www.citebd.org/spip.php?page=imprimir_articulo&id_article=4367. Accessed on 1 April 2023.

———. *Promotional materials for Les Glaneurs et la glaneuse*. Paris: Ciné-Tamaris and the Groupment National des Cinémas de Recherche, 2000.

———. *The Gleaners and I: Two Years Later*. C.N.D.P, Canal+, and Ciné Tamaris 2002.

Vesey, Alyxandra. "Waste Not: *Les Glaneurs et la glaneuse* and the Heterogenous Documentary Film Score." *Studies in French Cinema*, vol. 14, no. 3, pp. 167–179.

7 Agustina Bazterrica's *Tender Is the Flesh*

Devouring Each Other in Consumerist Society

Mirla González

I   Text

Title	*Tender Is the Flesh*
Genre	Science fiction novel
Author	Agustina Bazterrica was born in Buenos Aires in 1974 and earned an undergraduate degree in Fine Arts from the University of Buenos Aires. A central figure in the Buenos Aires literary scene, as a novelist and short story writer, she has received several awards for her writing. *Tender Is the Flesh* received the Premio Clarín in 2017. The idea for her novel arose after spending time at her brother's restaurant, Ocho Once, in Buenos Aires which specializes in organic food.
Year	2017
Country	Argentina

Tender Is the Flesh is the story of a dystopian society in which a virus infects animals. Given the high demand for meat, inability to safely consume livestock, and reluctance to turn to plant-based diets, society normalizes cannibalism. Butcher shops that once sold traditional cuts of beef and pork resort to selling items including lower and upper extremities and brochettes made of ears and fingers, all referred to as "Special Meat." The primary targets are vulnerable groups such as the poor, indigenous populations, immigrants, and women. Insidiously, the government also sees cannibalism as a solution to overpopulation, poverty, and crime. *Tender Is the Flesh* is available in print and audiobook from numerous online sellers including Amazon and Barnes & Noble.

Trigger Warning: This novel contains violent content (violence, rape, femicide, cannibalism, and mutilation), which may be difficult for some readers.

II   Context

In the *Irish Times,* Bazterrica writes,

> I have always believed that in our capitalist, consumerist society, we devour each other. We phagocyte each other in many ways and in varying degrees: human trafficking, war, precarious work, modern slavery, poverty, gender violence are just a few examples of extreme violence. Objectivising and depersonalising others allows us to remove them from the category of human being (our equal) and place them in the category of a mere 'other,' whom we can be violent to, kill, discriminate against, hurt, etc. ("I have always believed")

Bazterrica goes on to say that this violence and indifference extends to other sentient beings. She explains: "It may sound exaggerated, for sure. But to many Argentinians, a meat dish is

DOI: 10.4324/9781003388869-10

not seen as a being, but merely as protein. In my country, meat is part of our national identity. Barbecues are basically considered sacred rites" (Bazterrica, "I have always believed"). The *asado* is not merely a barbeque with hamburgers and hot dogs. Along with the main cuts of meat, an *asado* also typically includes chorizo and morcilla (blood sausage) which are served in bread as *choripán* and *morcipán*. In "The 'asado'—an Argentine Ritual," *Turismo Buenos Aires* states that an *asado* "is more than just a meal, it's a moment in which the key ingredients are friendship and camaraderie." It is a social ritual. Given how ingrained the *asado* is in Argentinian life, Bazterrica argues:

> Despite the fact that I actually am a vegetarian, meat is also part of my identity and I am part of a society that eats meat and unflinchingly accepts animal cruelty with the same brutal indifference shown towards vulnerable groups such as the poor, indigenous populations and women. ("I have always believed")

Through her novel, Bazterrica offers a critique of industrialized farming as well as consumerist society.

Moreover, regarding vulnerable groups in our society today, Bazterrica calls attention to the crisis of violence against women. "Through this book, through these words," she states,

> I wish to move the energy of a non-violent, caring culture, to think of a world where we respect differences with equal rights, a world where one woman isn't killed every 18 hours in acts of gender-based violence, a world where symbolic or real cannibalism is just fiction. ("I have always believed")

Though *Tender Is the Flesh* depicts a society that has taken extreme measures post-pandemic; the parallels with modern society make it all feel sickeningly real.

III   Interpretation

1   Does the novel use heterodiegetic or homodiegetic narration? Is the narrator omniscient or third-person limited? How does this perspective affect our interpretations of the characters, events, and story?

2   From the first page of the novel, the importance of words is made clear: "His [Marcos's] brain warns him that there are words that cover up the world. [. . .] There are words that are convenient, hygienic. Legal" (Bazterrica, *Tender Is the Flesh* 3). What images, ideas, concepts, actions, etc. do you traditionally associate with the words below?

- Change, Transformation, Shift, Transition
- Human, Person, Female, Animal
- Flesh, Skin, Head, Body, Meat, Food
- Product, Property, Merchandise
- Natural, Artificial, Synthetic, Modified
- Name, Identity, Special

How are these words above used in the novel? What meanings do they convey? Which words are used interchangeably? What euphemisms are present in the novel (for example, in the butcher shops), and how are they used? What effect do these euphemisms have on the reader? Beyond euphemisms, what other purposes does language serve in this society?

3   What are some of the characteristics of a dystopia? How are these elements present in the novel? Describe the dystopian society in the novel. How is it structured? What laws allow society to function? What role do gender, race, and class play in this society? What is the role of the inspectors? Who are the scavengers and what do they do at the end of the novel?

4   What are the various theories regarding GGB? What was the official story? What was the theory proposed by the most eminent zoologist and why? What were the benefits of the purge? What role do institutions like the government, universities, the Church, and the media play during the outbreak and how do they influence public opinion? What does Marcos think about the origin of the virus? What is the relationship between the government and the Church?

5   Describe the breeding centers. Why are the heads kept in separate cages? What is a First Generation Pure (FGP)? What is the role of artificial insemination? What is the purpose of the teaser stud? How has El Gringo diversified the breeding center? In what other businesses has he invested?

6   How does the processing plant operate? Describe what happens to the head at each of these stages: unloading yard, resting cage sector and antemortem inspection, blue vs. red cages, the box sector, slaughter sector, cutting and storage room, offal room, and cooling room. Why aren't the diseased heads treated or returned to the breeding center? What industries does the processing plant supply and what are the various uses of the human body/"head"?

7   How does Marcos (El Tejo) change throughout the course of the novel? How does he react when he is gifted the female? What actions does he take toward the female? Eventually, how does he transform the house to protect her? How does his attitude toward her change throughout the novel? What do his actions at the end of the novel reveal about his character?

8   Compare and contrast the various female figures in the novel: Spaniel (the butcher), Cecilia (Marcos's wife), Marisa (Marcos's sister), Jasmine (the FGP), and Dr. Valka. How do they change as a result of the outbreak and how do they evolve over the course of the novel? How does Spaniel's shop transform over time? What prejudices does Dr. Valka face as a female scientist?

9   In Greek mythology, what is the story of Icarus and what does it represent? How does Marcos's father interpret the story of Icarus? How does the story of Icarus connect to the novel?

10   The original Spanish novel is titled *Cádaver exquisito*, which translates to *Exquisite Corpse.* The 2020 English version was published as *Tender Is the Flesh*. Compare and contrast both titles. Which title do you prefer and why? What other titles would be appropriate for the content of this novel?

IV   People-Focused Applications to SDGs 1, 2, 3, 4, and 5

1   SDG 1 aims to eradicate poverty. Target 1.4 focuses on providing equal rights to resources. The goal of target 1.5 is to "build the resilience of the poor and those in vulnerable situations and reduce their exposure and vulnerability to climate-related extreme events and other economic, social and environmental shocks and disasters" ("Goal 1"). What examples illustrate the economic disparity present in the novel?

2   The mission of SDG 2 is ending hunger and promoting sustainable agriculture. When the virus made animals poisonous to eat, thereby causing the extinction of the meat industry, society turned to cannibalism in order to survive. Identify examples from the story that show food disparity. How is food related to social inequality? Think of the black market, the scavengers, the meal enjoyed by the hunters, and the farewell service hosted by Marisa.

3   Some of the targets of SDG 3 include ending epidemics and communicable diseases, reducing "the number of deaths and illnesses from hazardous chemicals and air, water and soil pollution and contamination," and supporting "the research and development of vaccines and medicines for the communicable and non-communicable diseases" ("Goal 3"). How does the novel depict the epidemic? What challenges does society face regarding public health? What solutions do they come up with?

4   The goal of SDG 4 is "ensuring inclusive and equitable quality education" ("Goal 4"). When Marcos is caring for Jasmine, the narrator recalls his inner thoughts: "He wishes he could teach her to read, but what's the point if she can't speak and will never be part of a society that sees her only as an edible product?" (126). What role does education play in the novel? How do gender and class affect education?

5   SDG 5 seeks to achieve gender equality. How does the novel portray a world in which gender equality has been dismantled? How are women treated in society and what factor does class play? What are the various uses of the female body in this dystopian society? How are female bodies altered and why? What overall commentary does Bazterrica make in terms of gender (in) equality?

6   In his reading of the novel, Sebastian Williams argues that "the viral outbreak in the narrative is often understood in Malthusian terms; that is, many suggest it is the result of overpopulation. Bazterrica challenges this idea, showing that overconsumption and poor resource distribution are greater issues" (11). Do you agree with Williams's interpretation? How does the novel highlight overconsumption and poor resource distribution? How does the novel critique modern-day capitalism? Does the novel also critique overpopulation?

7   How does the novel criticize industrial livestock production? What are the parallels between industrialized cannibalism in the novel and factory farming in our world today? In "What's Wrong With Eating People?" David Tierney comments: "When humans begin to be eaten, it's the same people who suffer in our world who go first. 'Immigrants, the marginalized, the poor.' Labels are blurred. We ignore facts and similarities between different humans, and between humans and animals, so that we can see the world in a way that allows us to be happy." In your view, what is the difference between eating an animal and eating a human? Do you think our society is capable of cannibalism? Why? In the novel, what is society's position on slavery and what are the laws regarding domesticated females? How does society's view on slavery compare with their position on cannibalism? Does the outlaw of slavery and normalization of cannibalism reflect a more advanced society?

8   In her article in the *Irish Times*, Bazterrica writes: "Although my book contains clear criticism of the meat industry, I also wrote the novel because I have always believed that in our capitalist, consumerist society, we devour each other. We phagocyte each other in many ways and in varying degrees: human trafficking, war, precarious work, modern slavery, poverty, gender violence are just a few examples of extreme violence [. . .]. Thus, we devour each other because we are generally blind to our kinship with others. When faced with their suffering, we look the other way" ("I have always believed"). The novel's dystopian world is plagued by overpopulation and a scarcity of resources. Those most affected are "immigrants, the marginalized, the poor. They were persecuted and eventually slaughtered [to satisfy the demand for meat]" (Bazterrica, *Tender Is the Flesh* 6). In one instance, the press recounts a story of two unemployed Bolivians who were barbecued by a group of neighbors. What other examples in the novel highlight society's indifference toward the vulnerable, the poor, and marginalized communities? In this post-pandemic world in the novel, where do we see society's complicity in violence and oppression toward the Other?

9   A pregnant body is highly valued and can serve many purposes. What precautions does Marcos take when he discovers that Jasmine is pregnant and why? A more extreme version of exercising caution is through the maiming of impregnated women at the breeding centers. Why is this action taken? Pregnant females are also used on hunting reserves as the exchange between Urlet and Marcos reveals. Urlet states, "I don't want any more females that haven't been impregnated. They're idiotic and submissive" (140). Marcos replies, "That's fine. Impregnated females cost three times as much. From four months on, the cost goes up further" (140). Urlet responds, "Not a problem. I want a few with the fetus developed, so it can be eaten afterwards" (140). What do these examples say about society's view and treatment of the maternal body? What are the parallels between the objectification of women in the novel and in contemporary life?

10 On the topic of language and patriarchy, Bazterrica writes in the *Irish Times*: "Language gives us an identity; it speaks of who we are. In my country, in my language, a language I share with 22 other nations and 572 million people, we say 'dog'—perro—to speak about man's best friend. When we use the feminine noun *perra* it becomes synonyms with *puta* (whore). When we speak about someone who is daring—*atrevido*—we are talking about a fearless man. When we utter the feminine form *atrevida* we are referring to a *puta* (whore). The synonyms we use in Spanish for puta are many (101, to be precise), but there is no negative equivalent to talk about a man who has sex with many women. Because using the masculine form *puto* constitutes an insult to refer to a homosexual man. Men who have sex with lots of women are considered desirable. There is no derogative word to define them and that is a clear sign of the social construction that is patriarchy" ("I have always believed"). Just as language is important, so is the unwritten word. She adds: "When we do not talk about femicide, for example, we give room to impunity, to thinking that women's lives are worthless. By naming acts of violence and understanding them, we give them entity and can work towards preventing them [. . .]. Through this book, through these words, I wish to move the energy of a non-violent, caring culture, to think of a world where we respect differences with equal rights, a world where one woman isn't killed every 18 hours in acts of gender-based violence, a world where symbolic or real cannibalism is just fiction" ("I have always believed"). Human trafficking is a local and global issue. In the dystopian novel, while the hunters are feasting on the day's catch, they discuss Lulú's cabaret: "He's using code words because it's known that the place is a seedy club involved in human trafficking, with one minor difference: after paying for sex, a client can also pay to eat the woman he's slept with. It's extremely pricey, but the option exists, even if it's illegal. Everyone is involved: politicians, the police, judges. Each takes their cut because human trafficking has gone from being the third largest industry to the first" (147). What other scenes call attention to issues of violence against women, including rape? How does the author treat these sensitive issues?

11 Bazterrica stopped eating meat in 2014 after watching the documentary *Earthlings*. She also had a revelation while walking through a butcher's shop in Buenos Aires. She states, "I saw the corpses. I thought, here in Argentina we eat cows and pigs and chickens but in India, they don't eat the cow because it's sacred. In China, once a year they have a festival where they kill dogs and eat them. So I thought: 'the meat that we eat is cultural—we could eat each other'" (Kim). Elizabeth Sulid Kim, who herself grew up a "vegetarian in a carnivorous world," adds that "the way in which her imagined society blinds itself to human suffering reflects the way ours can be blind to the realities of animal killing. There's the same normalisation of eating flesh; the same euphemisms around what is being consumed (to the consumer, they're always sausages and burgers, not chunks of dead pig and

cow).″ Delicacies in the novel include "a starter of fingers in a sherry reduction with candied vegetables" (147) and "the tongue of Ulises Vox marinated in fine herbs, served over kimchi and lemon-dressed potatoes" (148). How does the novel challenge the food and the ideas that people consume daily? Can fiction change our cultural attitudes toward what we choose to eat? Do you think a novel can convert readers to veganism or vegetarianism? Has a book ever caused you to alter your behavior? What is the role of literature, art, and fiction?

12 One of the references to Argentina is through the character of Dr. Valke, whom people called "Dr. Mengele" behind her back. Dr. Josef Mengele, who became known as the "Angel of Death," was a Nazi scientist who conducted inhumane medical experiments on prisoners at Auschwitz with a focus on twins. As Barbier points out in *Spies, Lies, and Citizenship: The Hunt for Nazi Criminals*, "Mengele was not interested in just mass producing twins; he also wanted to eliminate particular genetic traits from the Aryan gene pool. Eradication of the DNA that produced dwarfism would result in a population of tall, strong Germans who could fulfill the Third Reich's destiny" (77–78). He also participated in ophthalmic research, which "not only solidify Mengele's reputation as an angel of death but also show the symbiosis that existed between the concentration camp physicians and others in the Nazi medical establishment" (Halioua and Marmor 744). After the war, Mengele evaded capture and settled in Argentina. "The large German community in Argentina knew who he was but did not expose him even though an 'international manhunt' for him had begun. The situation for Mengele and other former Nazis in Argentina changed, however, in 1955, when Perón unwillingly left office. No one knew how receptive the new Argentine leader would be to the German community, which had become a refuge for former Nazis" (Barbier 86). Eventually, Mengele fled to Paraguay. In the novel, what experiments are carried out at Valka Laboratories? How do you interpret the connection made between Dr. Valke and Dr. Mengele? What ethical questions does the novel raise? Where do we see displays of moral ambiguity?

13 Bazterrica's novel depicts horrific events that in a film would require a warning to the audience. How does the author treat these sensitive topics? Does the story glorify violence or cause desensitization? Do you empathize with some of the characters? One technique that helps break up the vivid descriptions and terrifying scenes is the use of dark humor. Identify examples of this in the novel.

14 *Tender Is the flesh* presents a fictional representation of zoonotic disease in which the virus becomes a catalyst for violence, mass hysteria, fear, and lies. As the narrator explains: "After GGB, the world changed definitively. They tried vaccines, antidotes, but the virus resisted and mutated. He remembers articles that spoke of the revenge of the vegans, others about acts of violence against animals, doctors on television explaining what to do about the lack of protein, journalists confirming that there wasn't yet a cure for the animal virus. A scratch meant death.

[. . .] He remembers the groups in yellow protective suits that scoured the neighborhoods at night, killing and burning every animal that crossed their paths" (4–5). Then there are those who question the legitimacy of the virus, such as one of the teenagers at the zoo who says, "Don't be an idiot. Can't you see they're controlling us? If we eat each other, they control overpopulation, poverty, crime" (153). Though the novel depicts a dystopian society that has taken extreme measures post-pandemic, one finds traces of the challenges posed by Covid-19 and our present-day reality. What commentary does the novel offer about viruses, overpopulation, public health discourse, and stereotypes about Asian cultures?

15 Divide the class into five groups and assign one of the SDGs from Part 1 (1, 2, 3, 4, or 5) to each group. Each group will then prepare arguments for a debate in which they maintain

that their assigned SDG is the most relevant or central to Bazterrica's *Tender Is the Flesh*. (The instructor of the course will decide on the format and length of the debate and facilitate a follow-up discussion with the class upon conclusion of the debate.)

V   Beyond People—Connections to SDGs on Planet, Prosperity, and Partnerships

Beyond SDGs 1, 2, 3, 4, and 5, what additional SDGs are addressed by Agustina Bazterrica in *Tender Is the Flesh*? Complete the table below with your ideas. Then compare and contrast your ideas with a classmate.

SDGs:	*Does Bazterrica's* Tender Is the Flesh *connect with additional SDGs? If so, which ones and how?*
SDG 6 Clean Water and Sanitation	
SDG 7 Affordable and Clean Energy	
SDG 8 Decent Work and Economic Growth	
SDG 9 Industry, Innovation, and Infrastructure	
SDG 10 Reduced Inequalities	
SDG 11 Sustainable Cities and Communities	
SDG 12 Responsible Consumption and Production	
SDG 13 Climate Action	
SDG 14 Life below Water	
SDG 15 Life on Land	
SDG 16 Peace, Justice, and Strong Institutions	
SDG 17 Partnerships for the Goals	

VI   From Global to Local: On a Personal Level

1   How do you relate personally to Agustina Bazterrica's *Tender Is the Flesh*? Explain in detail how your own life experiences or personal beliefs intersect with the main ideas and themes of the featured work in this chapter.

2   How does Bazterrica's novel relate to your local environment? Explain the global-local connection between Bazterrica's *Tender Is the Flesh* and your home or current residence. What place-based considerations permit or prevent the application of the text to your geographical location?

3   What type of response did Bazterrica's *Tender Is the Flesh* elicit in you? Are you moved to action? If so, explain. If not, why not? Have your viewpoints or attitudes changed? Explain.

VII   Assignments

1   Research

1   While Argentina once had one of the wealthiest economies in the world and attracted immigrants from Europe and Latin America, the country has seen a rise in class inequality. *The Economist* has described Argentina's economy as being in a "a century of decline" ("A century of decline"). According to the CIA's *The World Factbook*, in 2019, 35.5% of the population lived below the poverty line. As reported in an article by Julián Pilatti in *People's Dispatch*, "[a] piece of information that did not receive mainstream media attention, but that paints a picture of a country that is modifying its cultural habits due to the suffering economy (or rather, the deep social inequality): According to the Rosario Stock Exchange, in 2021 an average of 47.8 kilos of beef was consumed per capita, the lowest amount of consumption since 1920." Individually or in groups, research two organizations and social responsibility programs fighting poverty and hunger in Argentina. What actions has Argentina taken toward ending poverty (SDG1)? (The instructor of the course will determine the mode of presentation and delivery—oral presentation, written report, annotated bibliography, etc.—for this research assignment.)

2   Historically, Argentina has been recognized worldwide as a top exporter and consumer of grass-fed beef given the vast plains of the *pampas*. Unfortunately, in recent decades, the country has seen an increase in feedlots (Shute). Through this practice, rather than consuming natural grass, cattle are given high-protein, high-energy feed via troughs across corrals each holding hundreds of animals (Forero). Rodrigo Troncosco, general manager of the Argentina Feedlot Chamber, "explains that 45% of the national cattle slaughter now spends some time in one of the country's 2,100 registered feedlots. It's quite a switch from a decade ago when 90% of the cattle in Argentina were strictly grass finished" (Peck). Troncoso sees feedlots as an important part of Argentina's future: "The truth is that we produce beef [with] grass, also we produce beef with grain. We are known [for grass-fed beef] historically. We have to show the world that we can do all kinds of beef" (Forero). Individually or in groups, research sustainable agricultural practices in Argentina. Investigate the steps the country has taken toward fulfilling the targets of SDG 2, specifically 2.4 which looks to "ensure sustainable food production systems and implement resilient agricultural practices that increase productivity and production, that help maintain ecosystems, that strengthen capacity for adaptation to climate change, extreme weather, drought, flooding and other disasters and that progressively improve land and soil quality" ("Goal 2"). How do the initiatives in Argentina compare to those in Uruguay and Brazil, which also rely heavily on their cattle production? (The instructor of the course will determine the mode of presentation and delivery—oral presentation, written report, annotated bibliography, short video documentary, digital timeline project, etc.—for this research assignment.)

2   Write

1   Write an essay in which you compare and contrast two of the female characters in the novel in relation to SDG 5 (gender equality). (The instructor of the course will determine the appropriate length for this writing assignment.)

2   Tied to Argentina's socioeconomic inequalities are the regional disparities in its education system. Write a persuasive essay in which you convince the reader that SDG 4 should be the top priority for Argentina. What are the main challenges that the education system faces?

What initiatives has the government taken toward improving the education system? What effect does a weak education system have on the other SDGs studied in this chapter and in Part 1? (The instructor of the course will determine the appropriate length for this writing assignment.)

3   *Create*

1   Individually or in groups, create a pamphlet educating the class about factory farming, sustainable farming, veganism, or vegetarianism. (The instructor of the course will determine the appropriate length, format, and mode of delivery for this creative assignment.)
2   Individually or in groups, create an infographic that teaches the class about the problem of gender-based violence and femicide in Argentina or design a campaign that fights gender-based violence or human trafficking in Argentina. (The instructor of the course will determine the format and mode of delivery for this creative assignment.)

Works Cited

"A Century of Decline; The Tragedy of Argentina." *The Economist*, vol. 410, no. 8874, 15 Feb. 2014, p. 18(US). *Gale Academic OneFile*, https://go.gale.com/ps/i.do?p=AONE&u=gainstoftech&id=GALE|A358534439&v=2.1&it=r&sid=bookmark-AONE&asid=c2595e38. Accessed 29 July 2022.

"Argentina." *The World Factbook*, Central Intelligence Agency, 20 July 2022, https://www.cia.gov/the-world-factbook/countries/argentina/#economy. Accessed 12 August 2022.

Barbier, Mary Kathryn. *Spies, Lies, and Citizenship: The Hunt for Nazi Criminals*. Potomac Books, 2017.

Bazterrica, Agustina. "I Have Always Believed that in Our Capitalist, Consumerist Society, We Devour Each Other." *The Irish Times*, 21 Feb. 2020, https://www.irishtimes.com/culture/books/i-have-always-believed-that-in-our-capitalist-consumerist-society-we-devour-each-other-1.4179631. Accessed 27 July 2022.

———. *Tender Is the Flesh*. Translated by Sarah Moses, Scribner, 2020.

Forero, Juan. "Argentine Cattle No Longer Just Home On The Range." NPR, 14 Sept. 2009, https://www.npr.org/templates/story/story.php?storyId=112767649. Accessed 30 August 2022.

"Goal 1." *United Nations Department of Economic and Social Affairs Sustainable Development*, 2022, https://sdgs.un.org/goals/goal1. Accessed 30 August 2022.

"Goal 2." *United Nations Department of Economic and Social Affairs Sustainable Development*, 2022, https://sdgs.un.org/goals/goal2. Accessed 30 August 2022.

"Goal 3." *United Nations Department of Economic and Social Affairs Sustainable Development*, 2022, https://sdgs.un.org/goals/goal3. Accessed 30 August 2022.

"Goal 4." *United Nations Department of Economic and Social Affairs Sustainable Development*, 2022, https://sdgs.un.org/goals/goal4. Accessed 30 August 2022.

Halioua, Bruno and Michael F. Marmor. "The Eyes of the Angel of Death: Ophthalmic Experiments of Josef Mengele." *Survey of Ophthalmology*, vol. 65, no. 6, 2020, pp. 744–748, *Science Direct*, https://doi.org/10.1016/j.survophthal.2020.04.007. Accessed 27 July 2022.

Kim, Elizabeth Sulis. "Can a Book Make You Vegan?" *BBC Culture*, 26 Apr. 2020, https://www.bbc.com/culture/article/20200424-can-a-book-make-you-vegan. Accessed 12 August 2022.

Peck, Clint. "Two Countries Two Directions." *Beef*, 1 Apr. 2020. https://www.beefmagazine.com/foreign-trade/beef_two_countries_two. Accessed 30 August 2022.

Pilatti, Julián. "Climbing Inequality in Argentina as Poverty and Inflation Soars." *People's Dispatch*, 30 June 2022, https://peoplesdispatch.org/2022/06/30/climbing-inequality-in-argentina-as-poverty-and-inflation-soars/. Accessed 28 July 2022.

Shute, Nancy. "Farewell to Argentina's Famed Beef." *NPR*, 8 Dec. 2011, https://www.npr.org/sections/thesalt/2011/12/08/143362233/farewell-to-argentinas-famed-beef. Accessed 28 July 2022.

Tierney, David. "What's Wrong with Eating People? *Tender Is the Flesh* by Agustina Bazterrica." *Headstuff*, 30 Apr. 2020, https://headstuff.org/culture/literature/agustina-bazterrica/. Accessed 27 July 2022.

"The 'Asado'—An Argentine Ritual." *Turismo Buenos Aires*, https://turismo.buenosaires.gob.ar/en/article/asado-argentine-ritual. Accessed 28 July 2022.

Williams, Sebastian. "Self-Consumption: Cannibalism and Viral Outbreak in Agustina Bazterrica's *Tender Is the Flesh*." *Interdisciplinary Studies in Literature and Environment*, 2021, https://doi.org/10.1093/isle/isab007. Accessed 12 August 2022.

8 Kief Davidson and Pedro Kos's *Bending the Arc*

Public Health Pioneers Fight for Universal Health Equity and Global Justice

Seung-Eun Chang

I Text

Title	*Bending the Arc*
Genre	Documentary film
Directors	Kief Davidson (born in Brooklyn, New York) is an Academy Award®-nominated director who makes films that both inspire and entertain. The film, *Bending the Arc*, executive produced by Matt Damon and Ben Affleck in collaboration with the Sundance Institute and Skoll Foundation, follows Dr. Paul Farmer and his organization *Partners In Health*. Pedros Kos (born in Rio de Janeiro, Brazil) is a director and Emmy Award®-winning film editor. His feature documentary directorial debut *Bending the Arc* premiered at the 2017 Sundance Film Festival.
Year	2017
Country	The film is a U.S. production by Directors Kief Davidson and Pedro Kos (Brazilian-American). Mainly set in Haiti, the film offers a global health focus that also takes viewers to Peru and Rwanda. The leading figures are Dr. Paul Farmer (American), Dr. Jim Yong Kim (Korean-American), and activist Ophelia Dahl (British-American).

The text for this chapter is the award-winning documentary film *Bending the Arc* (2017).

Davidson and Kos's *Bending the Arc* depicts the inspiring struggle, beginning in the 1980s, of the non-profit health organization Partners In Health (pih.org) to deliver basic healthcare to people in a rural Haitian village (Cange) through the narratives of Dr. Paul Farmer, Dr. Jim Yong Kim, activist Ophelia Dahl, and the other extraordinary doctors and patients who participated in this endeavor. The film highlights how a humble, idealistic, and courageous local effort by a couple of young, ambitious advocates (barely out of their teens) has been developed into a global health movement in Haiti, Peru, and Rwanda. Their initial effort to treat tuberculosis (TB) and HIV/AIDS among the Haitians who lacked access to even the most rudimentary medical help encountered tremendous obstacles. However, these challenges led them to build a revolutionary community-based healthcare model, in collaboration with the community and patients themselves, called the *accompaniment system*: training Haitian villagers to serve as community healthcare workers.

The official website of the film is https://bendingthearcfilm.com/, and the film is available to watch on both Netflix and ProQuest.

II Context

Ophelia Dahl visited Haiti in 1983 as an 18-year-old volunteer for an ophthalmic group running outreach clinics. She met Paul Farmer (then 23 years old), who had not yet started medical school. Images of Haiti in the 1980s when they met are provided in the film (see Figure 8.1).

DOI: 10.4324/9781003388869-11

Farmer met Jim Kim in 1983 in Boston while participating in the same medical training program. They immediately clicked with each other based on their similar reason and motivation for attending medical school—"social justice" (00:11:30).[1] These three young people became very close friends and spent many late nights talking about the fundamental question: "What is the nature of our responsibility in the world?" (00:11:50).

Figure 8.1 Haiti in the 1980s, film still from *Bending the Arc* (00:04:01).

While witnessing the collapse of poor countries after the decision made at the World Bank Annual Meeting in Washington D.C. in 1981, Dahl says, "We realized that poor countries weren't poor because of some kind of moral failing, and we felt that we needed to use our own opportunities to do something about it" (00:13:28–00:13:38). These young people began to feel that they needed to use their own opportunities to do something to improve the outlook of the citizens in these impoverished countries. The film begins by featuring a young Haitian woman at death's door due to her TB, who then starts to get better. Dahl narrates that "[h]er healing was not because of the magic recipe but was the treatment that's been available for decades and decades to many people in other countries. It was just basic medical healthcare, but it is still not accessible to some people" (00:02:03–00:02:36). She felt it did not have to be this way.

Co-Directors Kief Davidson and Pedros Kos and writer and producer Cori Stern began to film *Bending the Arc* in 2010, right after the terrible earthquake in Port-au-Prince, Haiti. Kos explained that the story of Partners In Health resonated on a very personal level because he came from a family of doctors in Brazil and firmly believes that access to healthcare is a human right, which is a value that was instilled in him from a very young age. When he learned about Dr. Paul Farmer, Dr. Jim Yong Kim, and Partners In Health, he felt an incredibly strong connection to their story and knew he had to tell it (Roston). The following statement by Kos addresses clearly what he hoped to achieve through this film:

> I very much hope that the film will help change many of the conversations around what is possible, especially in the world of global health. As Dr. Paul Farmer and Dr. Jim Yong Kim have said numerous times, the main obstacle to expanding access to healthcare and treatment is the resistance from establishments, either because something is too costly or too difficult

to achieve. If we keep within our entrenched ideas, we will never use our imaginations to rethink the impossible. And that is my big hope for *Bending the Arc*, that it will inspire the imaginations of people to rethink the impossible—especially in the global health establishment and governments around the world—and show that if you really put your mind (and imagination) to it, you can change the world, provide access to medical care, and save lives. (Roston)

Kos's goals for the documentary intersect perfectly with the ideas of Dr. Agnes Binagwaho, former Minister of Health in Rwanda, who says in the last part of the film: "We dream big without having anything" (01:29:47).

The three young people's passion turned into a movement backed by the philanthropy of Thomas White, who enabled the Partners In Health clinic to be established in Haiti. This film tells their story. The subjects and concerns portrayed are not only directly related to the health issue in Haiti, Peru, and Rwanda but also apply to poverty, hunger, education, gender equality, social justice, and global partnerships in any community in the world.

III   Interpretation

1   The root of the word documentary is *docere* in Latin, meaning "to teach" (Ellis 4). According to Jack Ellis in *The Documentary Idea: A Critical History of English-Language Documentary Film and Video*, documentaries are distinctive from the other types of film in terms of five characteristics: (1) subjects; (2) purposes, points of view, or approaches; (3) forms; (4) production methods and techniques; and (5) the sorts of experiences they offer audiences (1–3). Complete the table below to demonstrate how the Bending the Arc reflects these five elements of documentaries based on Ellis's description.

Characteristics	Description	Bending the Arc
(1) subjects	What is the film about?	
(2) purpose, point of view, or approach	What are the filmmakers trying to say about the subjects? How and why do they inform and/or persuade the audience to hold some attitude or take some action in relation to their subjects?	
(3) form	What is important about the formative process, which includes the filmmakers' original conception, the sights and sounds selected for use, and the structures and organization employed.	
(4) production method and technique	What is significant about the ways in which the images are shot, the sounds recorded, and the two aspects edited together? What is significant about the use of non-actors and the shooting on location?	
(5) audience experience	What is your experience as an audience member in terms of both the aesthetic elements of the documentary and any resulting attitudes or actions?	

2   Documentaries generally derive from reality, are limited to actuality, and confine themselves to extracting from and arranging what already exists (Ellis 2). As a result, documentaries do not always follow the conventional progression of dramatic or fictional works from exposition to complication to discovery to climax to denouement (Ellis 3). Discuss the progression of major events and critical moments in *Bending the Arc*. What are the most important moments, how do they impact the movement and its leading figures, and how does the film highlight the importance of these key events?

3   What was the historic event held in Alma-Ata in 1978, and what was the revolutionary promise on healthcare made in the event? (See 00:03:03–00:03:40 in the film.) Subsequently, Dahl narrates that "larger forces from wealthier countries created plans that crippled the once-rising nations. They ushered in poverty, disease, and chaos" (00:03:41–00:04:04). Do you agree with Dahl's view? Why or why not? How do "the larger forces" have an enormous and terrible impact on the people in poor countries such as Cange, Haiti?

4   Documentaries use non-actors ("real people" who "play themselves") rather than actors (who are cast, costumed, and made to play "roles") and real locations rather than stages or studios with constructed sets (Ellis 3). Considering the year, the people who appeared in the film, and the locations in which the film occurs, what challenges and difficulties can you imagine arose while shooting this documentary?

5   The film covers the stories of three countries: Haiti, Peru, and Rwanda. What do the three countries have in common, and how are they different in terms of diseases, difficulties, and solutions to these difficulties? Consider also the most meaningful achievement or contribution of the non-profit organization, Partners In Health, for each of these three countries. Fill in the blanks in the table below. Then, discuss your completed chart with a classmate and compare the answers for each country.

Country	Disease(s)	Difficulties faced	Solving strategies	Achievements
Haiti				
Peru				
Rwanda				

6   The film's basic story includes the tragedy and disaster of poor countries and their people, but the scenes in the film are not gloomy or dark. How do Davidson and Kos brighten the film's mood? Are any scenes humorous or light hearted? If so, explain.

7   Explain the community-based healthcare model called the *accompaniment system*. How has this model been developed, and how does the organization specifically educate people and advance people's health awareness, both on the individual and public levels? How has this model been applied to and evolved in each of the three countries?

8   Some debate surrounds the relative importance of prevention vs. treatment of TB and/or HIV (see 00:55:24–00:58:03 in the film). What are the pros and cons of each position? Which party supports which position and why? What is your own view on the subject?

9   The healthcare model of Partners In Health is applied globally, but it initiates from a place-based and locally rooted approach, and local knowledge is essential to this model. There are several comments in the film related to Paul's deep linguistic and cultural interest in Haiti: Paul says, "I already had this deep interest in Haiti, and Haitian culture [. . .] It was just fascinating." (00:05:23–00:05:32); Dahl mentions that "[w]hen Paul arrived in Haiti, he listened very, very carefully, and was eager to learn from those people who were living there"

(00:07:42–00:07:49); Father Fritz Lafontant also says that "Paul could speak Haitian Creole and also French, so we could communicate very easily" (00:08:08–00:08:18). How important are linguistic and/or cultural interests and expertise in the Partners In Health model and approach? How does linguistic and cultural competence contribute to the community-based approach? Can you find any other similar figures or instances in the case of Peru and/or Rwanda? Explain.

10   What does the film's title, *Bending the Arc*, imply? Consider the initial quotation from a 19th-century clergyman and abolitionist Theodore Parker that opens the film: "I do not pretend to understand the moral universe, the arc is a long one . . . / But from what I see I am sure it bends towards justice" (00:00:37). Compare and contrast the previous citation with the film's closing statement: "The arc of the moral universe bends towards justice. Together, we bend it faster" (01:35:27). It may also be important to note that Dr. Martin Luther King Jr. re-quotes Theodore Parker in his "Remaining Awake Through a Great Revolution" speech given at the National Cathedral on March 31, 1968: "We shall overcome because the arc of the moral universe is long, but it bends toward justice" ("Dr. Martin Luther King Jr."). According to the documentary, who should bend the arc, how should it be bent, and why should it be bent? How does this "bending" of the arc relate to the unit themes of this textbook: planet, people, prosperity, and partnerships?

IV   People-Focused Applications to SDGs 1, 2, 3, 4, and 5

1   Does the *Bending the Arc* engage with SDG 1 on "No Poverty: End poverty in all its forms everywhere" ("Goal 1")? If so, in what ways? In particular, consider how the film intersects with Target 1.4 of SDG 1: "By 2030, ensure that all men and women, in particular the poor and the vulnerable, have equal rights to economic resources, as well as access to basic services, ownership and control over land and other forms of property, inheritance, natural resources, appropriate new technology and financial services, including microfinance" ("The Global Goals: 1 No Poverty"). In what ways is the documentary concerned with (1) "equal rights to economic resources" and (2) the lack of "access to basic services" for "the poor and vulnerable" men and women? Do you think Target 1.4 intends to include healthcare as either an "economic resource" or as a "basic service?" Why or why not?

2   *The Sustainable Development Goals Report 2021* has announced that 2.37 billion people are without food or unable to eat a healthy balanced diet on a regular basis ("SDG Goals 2"). How does the healthcare system contribute to or impact the hunger issue? How do the local, national, and global healthcare movements, as highlighted in the film, relate to SDG 2: "Zero Hunger: End hunger, achieve food security and improved nutrition, and promote sustainable agriculture" ("Goal 2")?

3   SDG 3 emphasizes the importance of "ensur[ing] healthy lives and promot[ing] the well-being for all at all ages" ("Goal 3"). A series of pictures of sick Haitians who improved with treatment are given in Figures 8.2–8.7. The film stills on the left show the patients before being adequately treated for their disease, while the film stills on the right depict them after treatment. Adeline Merçon is now a mother, educator, and health rights activist. Joseph is a healthy and proud father. St. Ker François is a passionate advocate for health justice. How do you interpret these before-and-after photos of the patients? How does the film address the impacts of the healthcare system on people's ability or inability to lead healthy lives and attain well-being? What solutions does the film propose?

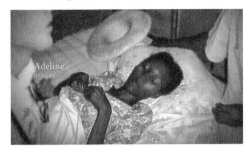

Figure 8.2 Film still of Adeline before treatment (00:53:30).

Figure 8.3 Film still of Adeline after treatment (00:53:35).

Figure 8.4 Film still of Joseph before treatment (00:54:05).

Figure 8.5 Film still of Joseph after treatment (0054:09).

Figure 8.6 Film still of St. Ker before treatment (00:54:33).

Figure 8.7 Film still of St. Ker after treatment (00:54:37).

4   The mission of SDG 4 is to "ensure inclusive and equitable quality education and promote lifelong learning opportunities for all" ("Goal 4"). The film emphasizes the importance of the health education system, including international aid training the next generation and doctors training doctors (01:18:43–01:19:40). How does the healthcare movement depicted in the film connect people's education to healthy lives?

5   SDG 5 aims to "achieve gender equality and empower all women and girls" ("Goal 5"). Does the film address any issues of gender-specific disease? If so, what diseases arise, and why have they become an issue? According to *The Sustainable Development Goals Report 2021*, almost one-third of women of reproductive age globally suffer from anemia, in part due to nutritional deficiencies ("SDG Goals 2"). Does the film propose any solutions to women-related diseases? Does the movement in the film include equal participation of women? Explain how gender equality is portrayed and dealt with in the film. Discuss the connection between health equality and empowerment and gender equality and empowerment.

6   How and why does the movement in the film urge the active support and/or revision of government- and international-wide policies on healthcare? How does the government- and international-wide systematic healthcare initiative relate to the other themes of Part 2, such as poverty, hunger, education, and gender?

7   Do you agree with Farmer's statement in the film: "Appropriate technology, basically, in the end, they were all used to punish poor people" (00:11:58–00:12:16)? How does the film depict the connection between technological advancement and the healthcare system or between technological advancement and poverty on an individual, national, or global scale? A possible example is given in Figures 8.8 and 8.9. These film stills show the contrast between the well-built water dam in Haiti and a citizen's house after being forced into the hillsides due to the dam project. Does the film propose any solutions to this gap between advanced technology and the lives of the poor? How was the technology used positively or successfully in the case of Rwanda?

Figure 8.8 Film still of water dam project in Haiti (00:08:36).

Figure 8.9 Film still of a Haitian's home after being displaced by the dam project (00:09:26).

8 Paul, Jim, and Ophelia criticize the negative impacts of the massive power of the wealthier countries on poor countries (00:03:41–00:04:04). Ironically, during the middle of this health-care movement, Jim became the president of the World Bank, which is obviously one of the "larger forces" (01:20:45–01:21:43). How does the film portray the role of this huge influential world organization in changing the hopeless situation of the neglected countries and advancing SDGs 1–5 for them? You may wish to refer to the Ebola epidemic case (01:26:13–01:28:14). How does the leadership change of the World Bank affect its direction and vision?

9 The film also discusses the debate on treating multiple-drug-resistant (MDR) TB in Peru. After the successful treatment of MDR TB patients, the team thought they had to do something to change the way people thought about MDR TB treatment (00:41:53). Their first question was, "Is it possible to treat MDR TB patients in resource-poor settings?" (00:42:00). Watch the arguments from the two parties (i.e., the academic community and the Partners In Health team) and develop your own opinions about this debate (00:42:06–00:44:49).

10 The drugs for HIV cost $12,000 per year, per patient (00:56:32). Kim mentions that "the notion that you would invest resources in HIV treatment in Haiti or in Africa, just seemed like an idea from outer space" (00:56:35). The U.S. Agency for International Development (USAID) argues that "[h]alf of the budget is for antiretrovirals. If we had them today, we could not distribute them. We could not administer the program because we don't have the doctors, we don't have the roads, and we don't have the cold trains" (00:56:45–00:56:54). He also said, "If you've traveled to rural Africa, you know this. People do not know what watches and clocks are. They do not use Western means for telling time. They use the sun. These drugs have to be administered during a certain sequence of time during the day. And when you say, 'Take it at ten o'clock,' people will say, 'What do you mean by ten o'clock?'" (00:57:10–00:57:27). Also, a U.S. Representative explains that "[t]he dollars available are limited. I have to ask you if it isn't more effective to concentrate almost entirely on the prevention part of this thing" (00:57:34–00:57:44). A man from the World Bank, which had not been endorsing AIDS treatment, said: "Prevention, that's the only thing that works. I conclude government should pay more attention to prevention" (00:59:28–00:59:53). Share your ideas on these arguments. Do you agree or disagree with these arguments? The instructor may wish to have the class debate this topic.

11 Discrimination against poor countries is mentioned several times in the film, especially in the case of Rwanda. Dr. Agnes Binagwaho explains: "This debate is because they are from a poor country, [that] they should not have access to treatment make[s] me furious" (01:17:39). She also mentions, "There are people who just say, 'Too expensive for you' [. . .]. They don't believe that we have an equal right to life, an equal right to dignity, an equal right to say what is our own future" (01:18:06, 01:20:12–01:20:33). What exactly was the debate that Binagwaho mentioned? What is your stance on this debate? How can you support your opinion?

12 The documentary includes comments from an array of critics who do not find the work of Partners In Health to be "sustainable." One critic says: "Maybe it's a good idea, but where and when and for how long? We need to think about sustainability" (00:44:00). Someone else comments: "I want to emphasize 'sustainable.' Do what you can with what you have where you're at" (01:17:57–01:18:02). In contrast to these uses of the terms "sustainability" and "sustainable," Paul insists: "I've never seen this debate play itself out among patients, saying, 'Uh, I don't really think I'm sustainable'" (00:44:07). Jim also notes: "The only time that I hear talk among people like us, academics, of shrinking resources is when we talk about things that have to do with poor people" (00:44:14). Paul summarizes the "expert opinion" from the "scientific community," which was that providing treatment in low-resource, poor countries is "too expensive" and is neither "cost-effective" nor "sustainable" (00:56:09). Examine the different rhetorical uses of the terms "sustainable" and "sustainability." Explain the message

of the documentary *Bending the Arc* as well as the leading doctors and activists featured in the film with regard to the correct use and understanding of these key terms. Consider also the film's insistence on the importance of "love," "hope," and "optimism" in this regard.

13 The official website of the film states that "[r]eaching far beyond the issue of healthcare, *Bending the Arc* shows how moral imagination, strategy, and sheer will together can change the trajectory of the world, bending the arc of the moral universe closer to justice" ("Bending the Arc"). Do you agree that the film expands the healthcare issue to larger issues of morality and justice? If so, give some examples of this. Do you agree with this expanded definition of healthcare? Why or why not?

14 Divide the class into five groups and assign one of the SDGs from Part 2 (1, 2, 3, 4, or 5) to each group. Each group will then prepare arguments for a debate in which they maintain that their assigned SDG is the most relevant or central to the film *Bending the Arc*. (The course instructor will decide on the format and length of the debate and facilitate a follow-up discussion with the class upon the conclusion of the debate.)

15 Does the featured text in this chapter only reinforce and illuminate the principles underpinning the UN SDGs and the concept of sustainable development, or does it question any inherent presuppositions, biases, shortcomings, flaws, or gaps in the UN SDG framework or the notion of sustainable development? Explain with details from the text.

V   Beyond People—Connections to SDGs on Planet, Prosperity, and Partnerships

Beyond SDGs 1, 2, 3, 4, and 5, what additional SDGs do Davidson and Kos address in *Bending the Arc*? Complete the table below using your ideas. Then compare and contrast your ideas with a classmate.

SDGs:	Does Davidson and Kos's Bending the Arc *connect with additional SDGs? If so, which ones and how?*
SDG 6 Clean Water and Sanitation	
SDG 7 Affordable and Clean Energy	
SDG 8 Decent Work and Economic Growth	
SDG 9 Industry, Innovation, and Infrastructure	
SDG 10 Reduced Inequalities	
SDG 11 Sustainable Cities and Communities	
SDG 12 Responsible Consumption and Production	
SDG 13 Climate Action	
SDG 14 Life below Water	
SDG 15 Life on Land	
SDG 16 Peace, Justice, and Strong Institutions	
SDG 17 Partnerships for the Goals	

VI   From Global to Local: On a Personal Level

1   How do you relate personally to the featured text in Chapter 8? Explain in detail how your own life experiences or personal beliefs intersect with the main ideas and themes of Kief Davidson and Pedro Kos's *Bending the Arc*.

2   How does the global humanities text featured in Chapter 8 relate to your local environment? Explain the global-local connection between Davidson and Kos's *Bending the Arc* and your home or current residence. What place-based considerations permit or prevent the application of the text to your geographical location?

3   What type of response did *Bending the Arc* elicit in you? Are you moved to action? If so, explain. If not, why not. Have your viewpoints or attitudes changed? Explain.

VII   Assignments

1   Research

1   Individually or in groups, research one documentary or feature film regarding the lives of the people in Haiti, such as Rachelle Salnave's *La Belle Vie: The Good Life*, Jean Jean's *If God Wants Yuli*, or Noland Walker's *Égalité for All: Toussaint Louverture and The Haitian Revolution*. Provide the following information: director(s); subjects, purposes, points of view or approaches, forms, production methods and techniques, and audience experience(s) (Ellis 1–3). Also, discuss why you or your team selected this film and how the film relates to one or more of the issues and themes of *Bending the Arc* and one or more of the People SDGs treated in Part 2 of this textbook. (The course instructor will determine the mode of presentation and delivery—oral presentation, written report, film review, etc.—for this research assignment.)

2   Individually or in groups, research one non-profit organization in Haiti, Peru, or Rwanda that relates to SDGs 1–5 of Part 2. Provide the following information: name and founder(s) of the organization; the year it was established; its specific mission or purpose(s); its roles and activities; and its impact. Also, discuss why you or your group selected this organization. (The instructor of the course will determine the mode of presentation and delivery—oral presentation, written report, short documentary, informational brochure— for this research assignment.)

2   Write

1   Davidson and Kos's *Bending the Arc* mainly focuses on healthcare issues and seems to be most relevant to SDG 3: Good Health and Well-Being. Write an essay about how this health-care matter is intertwined with the other Sustainable Development Goals of Part 2: (SDG 1) No Poverty, (SDG 2) Zero Hunger, (SDG 4) Quality Education, and/or (SDG 5) Gender Equality. In the concluding paragraph of your essay, discuss which of these four SDGs is best reflected in the film. (The instructor of the course will determine the appropriate length for this writing assignment.)

2   Partners In Health's website explains in the "Our Founders" page that this "Boston-based nonprofit health care organization [was] founded in 1987 by Paul Farmer, Ophelia Dahl, Thomas J. White, Todd McCormack, and Jim Yong Kim" ("Our Founders"). For this writing assignment, choose one of the five founders and write a detailed biography about his/her

life. If you choose Paul Farmer, who recently passed away in Rwanda in 2022, you have the option of writing a eulogy or a biography. In your final paragraph, describe how Partners In Health has evolved and expanded since the period covered in the film, especially in relation to the chosen founder's initial vision and contributions. (The instructor of the course will determine the appropriate length for this writing assignment and the required number of sources.)

3   Create

1   Individually or in groups, imagine that you are creating a non-profit organization to support remote and poor countries. What would the mission or purpose of your organization be? Where would you focus your efforts and why? (Note: You may choose Haiti, Peru, or Rwanda if your organization has a different focus than Partners In Health.) How do you relate your organization to SDGs 1, 2, 3, 4, and/or 5? How do you connect your academic major or special skills or talents to the activities of the proposed organization? (The instructor of the course will determine the mode of presentation and delivery—written proposal, oral presentation, flyer, website, and short video—for this creative assignment.)
2   In groups, create a debate show in which your team chooses one or two topics from the film to discuss. Determine each member's position and justify your stance. Why is your selected debate topic significant and what are the implications of each position? Sample topics could include the relative importance of prevention vs. treatment of disease or whether universal access to healthcare should be guaranteed as a right. (The course instructor will determine the length and format—video project or in-class oral debate—for this creative assignment.)

Note

1   Unless otherwise noted, all references to time stamps are from the documentary film treated in this chapter: Davidson and Kos's *Bending the Arc*.

Works Cited

Bending the Arc. Directed by Kief Davidson and Pedros Kos, Impact Partners, 2017, https://www.netflix.com/watch/80170312?source=35.
"Bending the Arc." Partners In Health, 2020, https://bendingthearcfilm.com/.
"Dr. Martin Luther King Jr." Smithsonian Institute, https://www.si.edu/spotlight/mlk?page=2&iframe=true. Accessed 5 July 2023.
Ellis, Jack. *The Documentary Idea: A Critical History of English-Language Documentary Film and Video*, Prentice Hall, 1989.
"Goal 1." *United Nations Department of Economic and Social Affairs Sustainable Development*, 2022, https://sdgs.un.org/goals/goal1. Accessed 15 September 2022.
"Goal 2." *United Nations Department of Economic and Social Affairs Sustainable Development*, 2022, https://sdgs.un.org/goals/goal2. Accessed 15 September 2022.
"Goal 3." *United Nations Department of Economic and Social Affairs Sustainable Development*, 2022, https://sdgs.un.org/goals/goal3. Accessed 15 September 2022.
"Goal 4." *United Nations Department of Economic and Social Affairs Sustainable Development*, 2022, https://sdgs.un.org/goals/goal4. Accessed 15 September 2022.
"Goal 5." *United Nations Department of Economic and Social Affairs Sustainable Development*, 2022, https://sdgs.un.org/goals/goal5. Accessed 15 September 2022.

"Our Founders." *Partners In Health*, https://www.pih.org/our-founders. Accessed 15 September 2022.

Roston, Tom. Interview with Pedro Kos. "You Never Know Where Your Allies Are Going to Come from: Bending the Arc." *Salon*, 8 Oct. 2017, https://www.salon.com/2017/10/08/you-never-know-where-your-allies-are-going-to-come-from-bending-the-arc/.

"SDG Goals 2 Affordable and Clean Energy." *United Nations Statistics Division*, 2021, https://unstats.un.org/sdgs/report/2021/goal-02/. Accessed 15 September 2022.

"The Global Goals: 1 No Poverty." *The Global Goals*, https://www.globalgoals.org/goals/1-no-poverty/. Accessed 7 March 2022.

Part III

Prosperity

Relating Global Humanities Texts to
UN SDGs 8, 9, 10, 11, and 16

9   Aravind Adiga's *The White Tiger*

Stagnation or Social Mobility in Modern India

Smita Daftardar

I   Text

Title	*The White Tiger*
Genre	Novel
Author	Aravind Adiga was born in India in 1974, where he grew up. After completing his secondary education in Mangalore, in southern India, he moved to Australia. Adiga studied English literature at Columbia University, New York, and obtained his Master's in Philosophy at Magdalen College, Oxford. Since 2000, he has worked as a journalist, starting as a financial correspondent in New York. He moved back to India in 2003 to work as a correspondent for *TIME* magazine, where he also worked on his debut novel, *The White Tiger*. *The White Tiger* was published in 2008 and won the Man Booker Prize for Fiction that same year. Adiga currently lives in Mumbai and has published short stories and novels. His latest novel, *Amnesty*, was published in 2020.
Year	2008
Country	India

The White Tiger is the story of Balram, a promising young man born in poverty in a small village in the Indian state of Bihar, one of the most under-developed regions of India. The story is written as a series of letters by Balram to the Chinese Premier who is on an official visit to India. The letters describe the journey of Balram's life—from working in a small teashop as a child to becoming an entrepreneur in Bangalore. Through Balram's letters, we learn of the struggles of the poorest section of society in terms of the lack of access to the necessities of life: education, employment, and decent living conditions. Balram presents both the moneyed class and the supposedly democratically elected government as corrupt and exploitative. The novel suggests that there is no hope for a better life or for social mobility for the likes of Balram. The story, written from Balram's point of view, takes an extremely dark view of Indian society and institutions.

The White Tiger is available in print and as e-book on online platforms such as Amazon Kindle. The book has been adapted into a film of the same name, which is available on Netflix.

Trigger Warning: This novel contains some violent content (physical violence, murder) and explicit or crude language (references to sexual intercourse and prostitution), which may be too intense or disturbing for some readers.

II   Context

Set in modern India, Adiga's novel *The White Tiger* portrays the black hole of poverty, the dismal condition of state-funded education, unemployment, and cold-blooded exploitation that stem from the unequal distribution of wealth, resources, and opportunities. The novel portrays

DOI: 10.4324/9781003388869-13

the contradictions of a nation that aspires to become a global power while still in the shackles of corruption. Adiga takes an extraordinarily dark view of the Indian system—whether familial, social, political, or economic. This fictional account from the perspective of the anti-hero, Balram, shows the plight of the weakest section of society that has slipped through the cracks into a dark abyss, with crime as the only path to a life of dignity and prosperity. The reader is left to analyze where and why the system fails Balram and if there could have been a different outcome.

The White Tiger has both received accolades and faced sharp criticism for its stark and sordid portrayal of modern India. In his defense, Adiga clarifies that he has not written a "social activist novel," but rather "a work of literature" (Kidd). In interviews, Adiga is at pains to clarify that his book is a work of fiction: "The book is a novel: it's fiction. Nothing in its chapters actually happened and no one you meet here is real. But it's built on a substratum of Indian reality [. . .]. I've tried hard to make sure that anything in the novel has a correlation in Indian reality" ("Aravind-Adiga Interview"). Nonetheless, he does want his book to be a warning and a call to action to change the status quo. He explains that he chose to write about the poorer sections of Indian society because he feels that the reality of their lives and aspirations are mostly invisible to the rest of the world and justifies his dark depiction of Balram as a way to break away from the "sentimentalized, condescending portrait of the poor" found in most books and films (Kidd).

Michael Portillo, Chair of the Man Booker Jury, has called *The White Tiger* "extremely readable" and lauded Adiga's attention to "important social issues: the division between rich and poor, and issues on a global scale" (Higgins). Not all reactions to Adiga's novel have been positive. In his article "Roars of Anger," Stuart Jeffries recounts a conversation with Adiga in which he asks the author about *The White Tiger* "causing offence in Adiga's homeland for its defiantly unglamorous portrait of India's economic miracle," and if he "might come across as a literary tourist ventriloquizing others' suffering and stealing their miserable stories to fulfil his literary ambitions." Adiga defends his rationale for *The White Tiger*:

> At a time when India is going through great changes and, with China, is likely to inherit the world from the west, it is important that writers like me try to highlight the brutal injustices of society. That's what writers like Flaubert, Balzac and Dickens did in the 19th century and, as a result, England and France are better societies. That's what I'm trying to do – it's not an attack on the country, it's about the greater process of self-examination. (Jeffries)

Deirdre Donahue in her review "Roundup: Debut Novels" for *USA Today*, called *The White Tiger* "one of the most powerful books" and an "amazing and angry novel about injustice and power" that highlights "the vast economic inequality between the poor and the wealthy elite" and depicts Balram's India as "a merciless, corrupt Darwinian jungle where only the ruthless survive." While this "merciless, corrupt Darwinian jungle," described from Balram's point of view, is a place of utter hopelessness, the reality of India is not quite as dark. Issues such as dowry and caste-based discrimination, although not eliminated completely from the social fabric of India, have long been declared illegal and carry a significant penalty and/or jail time. There exists a system of affirmative action, guaranteed by the Constitution of India, called caste-based reservation, which provides representation to historically disadvantaged groups in "the form of quotas in government jobs, educational institutions, and electoral seats at each level of government" that is "being constitutionally enshrined," "is practically irreversible," and "cannot be challenged legally" (Deshpande 19). Also, India is the world's largest democracy and has a multiparty political system, both at a national and state levels. An Election Commission established in 1950 conducts and regulates elections. Lastly, even though in *The White Tiger*,

Balram's relatives are the reason for his downward spiral, family has historically been, and remains today, a very strong institution in India. Discussing the role of family in psychotherapy, Rakesh K. Chadda and Koushik Sinha Deb claim in their article "Indian family systems, collectivistic society and psychotherapy" that "despite the changes in the social scenario," the Indian family was still "capable of fulfilling the physical, spiritual and emotional needs of its members; initiate and maintain growth, and be a source of support, security and encouragement" (S308). Similarly, "Religion and Living Arrangements Around the World," a 2021 Pew Research report, shows that extended families make up 54% of household types in India (29). Only about 5% of children are likely to live in single-parent homes and only 4% of adults over the age of 60 years live alone ("Religion and Living," 83, 88). That being said, readers of *The White Tiger* mostly agree that Balram's (or Adiga's) description of corruption and the conditions of poor in India is not far from the truth.

III   Interpretation

1   What qualities make Balram an anti-hero? How does narrating from an anti-hero's perspective amplify or enhance the story's message? What are the effects of not using a traditional hero as the protagonist? Does Balram have any "heroic" qualities? How does the epistolary nature of the novel aid Adiga in developing the story in general and Balram's character in particular? Why does Balram choose the Chinese Premier Wen Jiabao as the recipient of his letters?

2   Which secondary characters have the most influence—positive and/or negative—on the trajectory of Balram's life? Explain the importance of these secondary characters in shaping Adiga's protagonist: Balram's father Vikram, grandmother Kusum, brother Kishan, the school inspector, the old driver who teaches him the trade, the bus conductor turned politician Vinod, the Stork, Mr. Ashok, the Mongoose, and Pinky Madam. Did Balram have any positive mentors or role models?

3   Write a character analysis of the main female characters in the novel, namely, the women in Balram's family and Pinky Madam. Which female characters are empowered? Which ones lack autonomy? Does Balram's narration present all women—rich or poor; educated or illiterate; and urban or rural—as non-players in Indian society? Does the author or the novel reject or adopt the stance of the narrator-protagonist with regard to these women? Explain.

4   Indian culture is typically considered collectivistic, while Western cultures are often deemed individualistic. According to Rakesh K. Chadda and Koushik Sinha Deb in "Indian family systems, collectivistic society and psychotherapy": "Unlike the western society, which puts impetus on 'individualism,' the Indian society is 'collectivistic' in that it promotes interdependence and cooperation, with the family forming the focal point of this social structure" (S299). Which characters in *The White Tiger* are collectivistic and which characters are individualistic? What are some examples of collectivistic and individualistic behavior in the novel and what are the outcomes and consequences of these behaviors?

5   In "Collectivism: An Indian Perspective," Ritu Tripathi and Uday Vijayan share their view of social collectivism in India: "We owe allegiance to implicitly defined in-groups such as family members, neighbors, community members and close others. This runs parallel to the process of isolation and indifference towards the *out-group.*" In *The White Tiger*, a seemingly compassionate Ashok repeatedly lets down Balram's hopes, and the reader's hopes, that he will do the right thing by Balram. How might Tripathi and Vijayan's description of this particular brand of collectivism in Indian society relate to Ashok's behavior toward Balram? What are the effects of in-group "allegiance" and out-group "isolation and indifference" in the fictional world of the novel and in society more generally?

6   "*Tamaso ma jyotirgamaya*," which means "lead me from darkness to light," is a well-known Sanskrit chant or invocation from Brihadaranyaka Upanishad, an ancient Hindu scripture ("Brihadaranyaka Upanishad"). Darkness represents ignorance, while light signifies knowledge or enlightenment. Many Indian traditions involve lighting a symbolic lamp to dispel ignorance and spread knowledge, to empower, and set one free. Balram believes that his boss, Ashok, is in the Light, while he, Balram, is from the Darkness. How does Adiga use metaphors of darkness and light throughout the novel? Analyze the following statements from Balram:

- "Like all good Bangalore stories, mine begins far away from Bangalore. You see, I am in the Light now, but I was born and raised in Darkness" (11).
- "Things are different in the Darkness. There, every morning, tens of thousands of young men sit in the tea shops, reading the newspaper, or lie on a charpoy humming a tune, or sit in their rooms talking to a photo of a film actress. They have no job to do today. They know they won't get any job today. They've given up the fight" (45).
- "poor bastards had come from the darkness to Delhi to find some light —but they were still in the darkness" (115).
- "Now, G.B. Road is in Old Delhi, about which I should say something. Remember, Mr. Premier, that Delhi is the capital of not one but two countries—two Indias. The Light and the Darkness both flow into Delhi. Gurgaon, where Mr. Ashok lived, is the bright, modern end of the city, and this place, Old Delhi, is the other end" (214).

How does Balram's understanding of light and darkness differ from the classical meaning of light and darkness captured in "*Tamaso ma jyotirgamaya*?" Is the affluent, American-educated Ashok in light or darkness? Is Balram able to leave the darkness and embrace the light? Is *The White Tiger* the story of Balram's journey from his Darkness to his Light? Explain with textual examples from the novel.

7   How does Adiga's novel or Balram's narration critique Indian democracy, government, and politics? Consider the significance of the character of "the Great Socialist," described as "the boss of the Darkness" (81). Discuss the importance of each of the following passages from the novel:

- "You see, a total of 93 criminal cases—for murder, rape, grand larceny, gun-running, pimping, and many other such minor offenses—are pending against the Great Socialist and his ministers at the present moment. Not easy to get convictions when the judges are judging in Darkness, yet three convictions have been delivered, and three of the ministers are currently in jail but continue to be ministers. The Great Socialist himself is said to have embezzled one billion rupees from the Darkness, and transferred that money into a bank account in a small, beautiful country in Europe full of white people and black money" (81).
- "Like eunuchs discussing the Kama Sutra, the voters discuss the elections in Laxmangarh" (82).
- [. . .] "Mr. Ashok shrugged. 'Didn't we already pay those bastards off?'
'The minister wants more. It's election time. Every time there's elections, we hand out cash. Usually to both sides, but this time the government is going to win for sure. The opposition is in a total mess. So we just pay off the government, which is good for us. I'll come with you the first time, but it's a lot of money, and you may have to go a second and third time too. And then there are a couple of bureaucrats we have to grease. Get it?'
'It seems like this is all I get to do in Delhi. Take money out of banks and bribe people. Is this what I came back to India for?'" (204)

8   The national motto of India, displayed under the national emblem, is the Sanskrit phrase
    "*Satyameva Jayate*" meaning "Truth Alone Wins," from the *Mundaka Upanishad*, an
    ancient Hindu scripture. In stark contrast to this faith in truth, Balram sees deception and
    crime as the only way to a life of dignity. He feels that his actions are completely justified.
    Upon rereading the following citations, discuss how and why Balram blurs the boundaries
    between right and wrong, ethical and unethical, and justice and injustice:

    •   "The strangest thing was that each time I looked at the cash I had made by cheating him,
        instead of guilt, what did I feel?
        Rage.
        The more I stole from him, the more I realized how much he had stolen from me" (196).
    •   "*Go on, just look at the red bag, Balram—that's not stealing, is it?*
        I shook my head.
        And even if you were to steal it, Balram, it wouldn't be stealing.
        How so? I looked at the creature in the mirror.
        *See—Mr. Ashok is giving money to all these politicians in Delhi so that they will excuse
        him from the tax he has to pay. And who owns that tax, in the end? Who but the ordinary
        people of this country—you!*" (208)
    •   "'the fault is mine. Not the driver's. The police have let me off. That is the way of this
        jungle we live in. But I accept my responsibility. I ask for your forgiveness.'
        I pointed to the brown envelope lying on the table.
        'There are twenty-five thousand rupees in here. I don't give it to you because I have to, but
        because I want to. Do you understand?'" (268)
    •   "The real nightmare you get is the *other* kind. You toss about in the bed dreaming that you
        haven't done it—that you lost your nerve and let Mr. Ashok get away—that you're still in
        Delhi, still the servant of another man, and then you wake up.
        The sweating stops. The heartbeat slows.
        You did it! You killed him!" (269)
    •   "And then I'll have to come up with an answer—or kill him, I suppose. But that question
        is still a few years away. Till then we'll have dinner together, every evening, Dharam, the
        last of my family, and me" (271).

    Considering all that Balram has had to face in his life, should one believe in "*satyameva jay-
    ate*" or not? Identify some incidents in the story that compel the reader to sympathize with
    Balram or to understand how his ends justify his means.
9   *The White Tiger* includes two separate incidents of automobile accidents. How are the
    accidents similar and how are they different? What is distinct about the ways in which
    those in power deal with the accidents? How do these accidents differentiate Balram,
    the boss, from Ashok, the boss? Who comes across as a better person and what does this
    suggest? Justify your position with concrete examples or citations from the novel.
10 Examine Adiga's use of the Rooster Coop analogy in the novel. Balram insists that "[t]he
    greatest thing to come out of this country [India] in the ten thousand years of its history is
    the Rooster Coop" (147). He explains further:

    [. . .] The roosters in the coop smell the blood from above. They see the organs of their
    brothers flying around them. They know they're next. Yet they do not rebel. They do
    not try to get out of the coop.
        The very same thing is done with human beings in this country. (148)

How do Balram's many reflections on "The Great Indian Rooster Coop" serve to explain or even justify his later actions (149)? Examine Balram's efforts to "rebel," to "break out of the coop," to escape "perpetual servitude," and to gain "a man's freedom" (148, 150, 149, 212). Why does it "take a White Tiger" to succeed (150)? What is your reaction to Balram's self-proclamation: "*I've made it! I've broken out of the coop!*" (275)? Do you agree? Why or why not?

IV Prosperity-Focused Applications to SDGs 8, 9, 10, 11, and 16

1 *The White Tiger* is set in several places, starting in the small village of Laxmangarh in Bihar and moving first to the mid-sized city of Dhanbad and later to the cosmopolitan centers of Delhi and Bangalore. In each location, Balram tries to make a living and shake off the poverty into which he is born. How does Balram's journey highlight the need for SDG 8 (Decent Work and Economic Growth)? Research the specific targets for SDG 8. Then, discuss the connection between the targets and Balram's life situation, paying particular attention to the need for: sustained "per capital economic growth" (8.1); "higher levels of economic productivity through diversification, technological upgrading and innovation" (8.2); "decent job creation" (8.3) and "full and productive employment and decent work for all women and men" (8.5); decoupling "economic growth from environmental degradation" (8.4); reducing "the proportion of youth not in employment, education or training" (8.6) and having a "global strategy for youth employment" (8.C); protecting "labour rights" and "safe and secure working environments" (8.8); and strengthening "the capacity of domestic financial institutions to encourage and expand access to banking, insurance and financial services for all" (8.A) ("Goal 8"). How does Adiga's novel advocate for the need of SDG 8 and its targets? According to the novel, what are the impediments toward successful or eventual achievement of SDG 8 and its targets?

2 What is the significance of the name "The White Tiger" in the novel and how has this name influenced Balram's life—from being given the name "White Tiger" by the school inspector to becoming the owner of "White Tiger Drivers?" One of the targets of SDG 8 is to "secure the prohibition and elimination of the worst forms of child labour," and "by 2025[, to] end child labour in all its forms" ("Goal 8"). What should being called "White Tiger" have meant for young Balram had he been able to stay in school and get a formal education? Discuss the perils of not eradicating child labor, and its long-term implication on an individual's potential, their ambitions, and choices they make in life, in the context of *The White Tiger*.

3 According to Diane Holt in *Exploring Youth Entrepreneurship*, a report published by UNDESA in 2020, an informal economy is defined as the "unregulated non-formal portion of the market economy that produces goods and services for sale or for other forms of remuneration" (24). Holt explains that the informal economy corresponds to "precarious labor environments" that "support millions, many through running small businesses, of which many are likely to be youth entrepreneurs" (23). The informal economy thus includes "the institutional space in which households across the developing world earn an income and trade on a daily basis" (23). Holt estimates that "70% of the world's population may live in such marketplaces excluded from employment and the market" (23). According to *Exploring Youth Entrepreneurship*, the informal market "is often conceived negatively in terms of undeclared labor, tax evasion, unregulated enterprises, and illegal but not criminal activities" (Holt 24). Nonetheless, Holt explains, "[t]he informal economy is a socially resilient and enduring institution. Far from shrinking in size, in many developing and emerging economies it has remained a strong component of the day-to-day livelihood of millions. When young people cannot find employment in the developing world, they are likely to

engage in some form of business in the informal economy" (23). What evidence of this informal economy do you see in *The White Tiger*? How does the novel portray India's informal economy and Balram's participation in such an "unregulated" and "precarious" marketplace? How and in what ways might SDG 8 support the labor force of the informal economy and provide a path to upward social mobility for a person like Balram?

4   Consider the relevance of SDG 9 (Industry, Innovation, and Infrastructure) to *The White Tiger*. How does Adiga's novel address the need to "[b]uild resilient infrastructure, promote inclusive and sustainable industrialization and foster innovation" ("Goal 9")? Note instances in the novel that depict poor infrastructure, unsustainable industrialization, or a lack of innovation. How might improvements in the target areas of SDG 9 change the lives of characters such as Balram and Kishan?

5   The objective of SDG 10 is to "[r]educe inequality within and among countries" ("Goal 10"). Why is SDG 10 important to the novel? What incidents in the lives of Balram and other characters in *The White Tiger* highlight the existing inequalities in society? What causes these inequalities? Are the problems depicted "within" or "among" countries—or both? Consider in this regard the importance of Mr. Ashok's and Pinky Madame's experiences in America versus India. In what ways could SDG 10 help improve the lifeworld of the novel?

6   India has its own form of affirmative action, which is a caste-based reservation or quota system that is meant to help historically disadvantaged groups get representation in education, government jobs, and electoral seats in government. This reservation system has existed since pre-independence days and has since been guaranteed by the Constitution of India (Deshpande 10, 19). Currently, there is a 50% quota or reserved seats in "all government services as well as technical and professional institutions, both in the Center [Federal] and the States" for historically disadvantaged groups identified as "socially and educationally backward classes" (Mandal 64, iii), as recommended by the Mandal Commission. In the context of *The White Tiger*, what is the role of caste in the growth of people like Vikas and Balram? To truly achieve the mission of "Reduced Inequalities" as defined in SDG 10, should the focus in India be on caste, poverty, corruption, or something else? Explain. Consider the following quotations from the novel in this regard:

  • "Vijay's family were pig-herds, which meant they were the lowest of the low, yet he had made it up in life" (26).
  • "To sum up—in the old days there were one thousand castes and destinies in India. These days, there are just two castes: Men with Big Bellies, and Men with Small Bellies. And only two destinies: eat—or get eaten up" (54).
  • "'Are you from a top caste or bottom caste, boy?'
    I didn't know what he wanted me to say, so I flipped both answers—I could probably have made a good case either way—and then said, 'Bottom, sir'" (54).

7   Mahatma Gandhi has famously said that "India lives in its villages" (*Voice of Truth* 280). He shares his vision of an ideal village: "My ideal village will contain intelligent human beings. They will not live in dirt and darkness as animals. Men and women will be free and able to hold their own against anyone in the world" (Gandhi, *Voice of Truth* 280). Describe how this vision is in stark contrast to the village in which Balram grows up, citing examples from the novel to support your ideas. Now consider the fact that Narendra Modi, India's Prime Minister since 2014, has proposed the "Model Village Plan," a program put in place by the Indian government to make villages self-sufficient. The initiative lays down targets such as reduction (elimination, ideally) in poverty, 100% adult literacy, education for children, healthcare and sanitation, housing for all, all-weather roads, among other things, for

the village to qualify as a model village (Pradhan Mantri Adarsh Gram Yojana). How do the objectives of this program align with the prosperity-related SDGs (8, 9, 10, 11, and 16)? Discuss how this strategy could potentially transform Balram's village and the destinies of its residents.

8   In "Urbanization in India: An Impact Assessment," Neelmani Jaysawal and Sudeshna Saha outline some unique features of Indian urbanization: "[r]apid urbanization leads to massive growth of slums followed by misery, poverty, unemployment, exploitation, inequalities, degradation in the quality of urban life. Urbanization occurs not due to urban pull but due to rural push factors. Distress migration initiates urban decay" (62). Human migration is typically attributed to push and pull factors—factors (mostly negative) that push one away from one's native land, and factors (mostly positive) that pull one to a new place. Yet, as Jaysawal and Saha point out, the rural-to-urban migration in India is due to the negative push factors in the rural setting and not positive pull factors in the urban setting: "Poverty induced migration occurs due to rural push factors [. . .] Illiterate, low-skilled or unskilled migrants from rural areas are absorbed in poor low-grade urban informal sector at a very low wage-rate and urban informal sector becomes inefficient and unproductive" (62). Consider the following statement from Balram in this regard: "Understand [. . .], it is not as if you come to Bangalore and find that everyone is moral and upright here. This city has its share of thugs and politicians. It's just that here, if a man wants to be good, he can be good. In Laxmangarh, he doesn't even have this choice" (262). Why does Balram make this statement? What are the factors that push Balram out of Laxmangarh? Does anything improve in the cities such as Bangalore or Delhi that are featured in the novel? Explain.

9   The official mission of SDG 11 (Sustainable Cities and Communities) is to "[m]ake cities and human settlements inclusive, safe, resilient, and sustainable" ("Goal 11"). Find examples in the novel of a lack of "inclusive, safe, resilient, and sustainable" cities or human settlements. Next, research the targets for SDG 11 and discuss which ones relate most clearly to the novel. For example, how does the novel promote the need to "upgrade slums" and "ensure access for all to adequate, safe and affordable housing and basic services" (Target 11.1) or to "reduce the adverse per capita environmental impact of cities, including by paying special attention to air quality and municipal and other waste management" (Target 11.6) ("Goal 11")? Does the novel question or critique any aspects of SDG 11, its targets, or their implementation in India?

10   The aim of SDG 16 is to "[p]romote peaceful and inclusive societies for sustainable development, provide access to justice for all and build effective, accountable and inclusive institutions at all levels" ("Goal 16"). In his paper "Democracy and Peacebuilding in the Framework of SDG 16+: Policy Recommendations from an Interregional and Multistakeholder Approach," Luis José Consuegra discusses the link between democracy and sustainable development, which, he states, is most evident within the SDG 16 framework (6). Consuegra observes that "SDG 16 reflects a commonly accepted understanding that democracy, peace and development are inherently intertwined, and that reducing violence, delivering justice and combating corruption are essential to achieving sustainable development" (16). Consuegra highlights the overlap between democracy and SDG 16 by sharing four characteristics of democratic institutions and systems, as outlined by the Foundation for Democracy and Sustainable Development (FDSD 2015): (1) "*inclusiveness:* all members of a political community have the right to participate and should have their voices heard"; (2) "*popular control:* decisions rest with the political community as a whole"; (3) "*considered judgement:* individual and collective decisions should be based on people being adequately informed and understanding the positions of others"; and

(4) *"transparency:* decision-making should be open and accountable" (6). In the chapter titled "The Fourth Morning" of *The White Tiger*, Balram describes the election season, the political deals between The Great Socialist and the Animals, the sold votes, and the fate of the poor rickshaw-puller who tried to exercise his right to vote. How does this narrative highlight the need for SDG 16, especially the need to "[e]nsure responsive, inclusive, participatory and representative decision-making at all levels" (Target 16.7) and to "[p]romote the rule of law at the national and international levels and ensure equal access to justice for all" (Target 16.3) ("Goal 16")? Considering the poverty, lack of opportunity, and overall lawlessness in Balram's community, how does *The White Tiger* highlight the linkage that Consuegra discusses between democracy and sustainable development, or, perhaps more accurately phrased, between dysfunctional democratic institutions and systems and the absence of (sustainable) development?

11 One of the focus areas of SDG 16 is to "[s]ubstantially reduce corruption and bribery in all their forms" (Target 16.5) ("Goal 16"). In his paper "Democracy and Peacebuilding in the Framework of SDG 16+: Policy Recommendations from an Interregional and Multistakeholder Approach," Luis José Consuegra emphasizes the need for engagement of all stakeholders to achieve SDG 16: "As with the rest of the agenda, while governments have a leading role to play, the achievement of SDG 16 requires a whole-of-society approach" that brings together civil society organizations (CSOs), the private sector, local governments, parliamentarians, and academia as critical stakeholders (7). What are the different forms of corruption and bribery shown in *The White Tiger*, both at individual and institutional levels? How does *The White Tiger* illustrate the need for a "whole-of-society approach" to achieve SDG 16, especially in combating corruption? Discuss what a "whole-of-society approach" would entail in the context of *The White Tiger* to reduce or eradicate corruption.

12 Balram can be considered lucky since he has a job, running water, and a roof over his head. In his writings, Balram describes the scores of people living on the streets and slums of Delhi, who are not as fortunate. What are the challenges faced by street and slum dwellers? What hazards do they face? What hazards do they pose to the health and well-being of the city at large? Which SDGs are highlighted through these scenarios and how can these SDGs and their targets help alleviate these issues?

13 Adiga paints an uncomfortably realistic picture of Indians living on two ends of a spectrum—the powerless poor and the powerful rich—omitting the vast middle class. In an interview, he explains his motivation for writing *The White Tiger* and defends his negative depiction of India:

> If a poorer person is present in cinema or books, in as much as they are present at all, they appear as stock, clichéd characters—weaklings you can be sympathetic to. That is a sentimentalised, condescending portrait of the poor. It makes them lesser figures. The actual people you talk to and interact with are just as human as you are. They don't tend to be nicer people; denying that in novels denies them a fundamental aspect of their humanity, which is the right to make evil choices. The two privileges accorded to the middle class in Indian literature that are denied to the poor tend to be a sense of humour and the capacity for vice. It was important that Balram, though he is a poor man, has both those privileges—that he could be funny and he would have the capacity to do something disturbing." (Kidd)

Adiga explains further, "I want readers, and especially the middle-class readers here in India, to realise that unless the poor are given the infrastructure to achieve their dreams—schools, better hospitals, a responsible police system—they will have few options other than crime or radical politics to achieve their goals. I don't know if a novel can change anything, but I at least want to stir debate, to get people talking and thinking" (Kidd). Has Adiga succeeded in telling the story of millions of disenfranchised Indians or has he inadvertently treated India (and by extension, other developing countries) in the same condescending manner that he set out to avoid for his protagonist? Has Adiga created a dystopian novel or a realistic portrait? Discuss the possible positive and negative impacts of this novel on people's perception of modern India and its efforts in implementing the UNSDGs.

14 Divide the class into five groups and assign one of the SDGs from Part 3 (8, 9, 10, 11, or 16) to each group. Each group will then prepare arguments for a debate in which they maintain that their assigned SDG is the most relevant or central to Adiga's *The White Tiger*. (The instructor of the course will decide on the format and length of the debate and facilitate a follow-up discussion with the class upon conclusion of the debate.)

15 How does Adiga's *The White Tiger* illuminate and reinforce the principles underpinning the UN SDGs and/or the concept of sustainable development? How does the novel question or critique any inherent presuppositions, biases, shortcomings, flaws, or gaps in the UN SDG framework or in the notion of sustainable development? Explain with textual examples whether the novel promotes or critiques sustainable development generally and the UN SDGs specifically.

V   Beyond Prosperity—Connections to SDGs on Planet, People, and Partnerships

Beyond SDGs 8, 9, 10, 11, and 16, what additional SDGs are addressed by Aravind Adiga in *The White Tiger*? Complete the table below with your ideas. Then compare and contrast your ideas with a classmate.

SDGs:	*Does Adiga's* The White Tiger *connect with additional SDGs? If so, which ones and how?*
SDG 1 No Poverty	
SDG 2 Zero Hunger	
SDG 3 Good Health and Well Being	
SDG 4 Quality Education	
SDG 5 Gender Equality	
SDG 6 Clean Water and Sanitation	
SDG 7 Affordable and Clean Energy	
SDG 12 Responsible Consumption and Production	
SDG 13 Climate Action	
SDG 14 Life below Water	
SDG 15 Life on Land	
SDG 17 Partnerships for the Goals	

VI   From Global to Local: On a Personal Level

1   How do you relate personally to Adiga's *The White Tiger*? Explain in detail how your own life experiences or personal beliefs intersect with the main ideas and themes of the featured work in this chapter.

2   How does Adiga's novel relate to your local environment? Explain the global-local connection between Adiga's *The White Tiger* and your home or current residence. What place-based considerations permit or prevent the application of the text to your geographical location?

3   As noted previously, Adiga won the 2008 Man Booker Prize for Fiction for *The White Tiger*. On its website, The Booker Prize states its motivation for giving this annual award: "We are driven by a simple belief—great fiction not only brings joy to millions, it has the power to change the way we think about the world we live in" ("The Booker Prize"). How has *The White Tiger* changed the way you think about the world in general and India in particular? What type of response did Adiga's novel elicit in you? Are you moved to action? Have your viewpoints or attitudes changes? Explain.

VII   Assignments

1   Research

1   Shashi Tharoor, in a debate at The Oxford Union Society in 2015, highlighted the adverse economic impact of colonization on India and the exploitative nature of the colonial rule that left India's economy in shambles. "This house believes Britain owes reparations to her former colonies," he argued ("Dr Shashi Tharoor MP - Britain Does Owe Reparations"). On a similar note, Aditya Mukherjee, author and Professor of Contemporary Indian History at Jawaharlal Nehru University (JNU) in New Delhi, in his article "Empire: How Colonial India Made Modern Britain," writes:

> India was the largest economy of the world for the entire thousand years of the first millennium, accounting for close to 30% of the world's GDP. Till as late as the beginning of the 18th century, India was still the largest economy with about 25% of the world's GDP, greater than that of entire western Europe put together and more than eight times that of the UK. The decline started soon after and, by 1950, at the end of nearly 200 years of colonial rule (during which apologists of colonialism like Tirthankar Roy claim 'colonial India experienced positive economic growth') India's share had been reduced to a mere 4.2%, less than two-thirds that of Britain. (75)

Examine Tharoor's and Mukherjee's commentaries on British policies toward its colonies in the context of the UN SDGs. Describe the policies that can be seen as a direct contradiction of the SDGs, focusing primarily on the prosperity-related SDGs treated in Part 3 of this textbook. Research the impact of these policies on the colonies as well as the colonizers. What lessons can be learned from this history that highlight the importance of establishing SDGs, especially in developing countries? (The instructor of the course will determine the mode of presentation and delivery—oral presentation, written report, timeline project, etc.—for this research assignment.)

2   The Indian Government has put several policies (called "schemes") into place to address issues being faced by the country. In "Government Schemes," The India Brand Equity

Foundation (IBEF) outlines 28 Indian policies, of which these 7 relate directly to the prosperity SDGs examined in this chapter:

- Self-reliant India campaign (*Atmanirbhar Bharat Abhiyaan*)
- Food security welfare scheme (*Garib Kalyan Yojana*)
- Financial inclusion program (*Jan Dhan Yojana*)
- Housing for all (*Pradhan Mantri Awaas Yojana*)
- Micro Units Development and Refinance Agency (*Mudra Yojana*)
- Skill India (*Pradhan Mantri Kaushal Vikas Yojana)*
- Smart Cities Mission (*Smart Cities Yojana*) ("Government Schemes")

Research three "government schemes" from the list above that reflect India's attempt to address the Prosperity SDGs: 8, 9, 10, 11, and/or 16. Individually or in groups, explain how each chosen scheme targets the related SDG(s). Find out the effectiveness of the chosen schemes based on published statistics and credible news sources. Comment on whether these schemes are a success or failure and why. Your report should summarize the objectives of the schemes, their level of effectiveness based on statistics, and the reasons for their success or failure. Finally, in the context of *The White Tiger*, explain whether these schemes could have benefited the characters, and if so, how. (The instructor of the course will determine the mode of presentation and delivery—oral presentation, written report, etc.—for this research assignment.)

2   Create

1   Adiga's novel, *The White Tiger*, was adapted into a film in 2021 of the same name. Upon watching the film, work in groups to select five "film stills" that visually portray concern with the five "Prosperity" goals treated in this chapter, namely, SDGs 8, 9, 10, 11, and 16. Explain the relationship between each chosen images and the relevant SDG. (The instructor of the course will determine the mode of presentation and delivery—photo essay, oral presentation, report on India's progress in meeting each goal, etc.—for this creative assignment.)

2   In groups, create a skit in which one student interviews Aravind Adiga (played by a second student) about the novel *The White Tiger*. The performance of the interview should include questions and answers about the relevance of SDGs 8, 9, 10, 11, and 16 to the novel as well as other topics of interest to the group. For groups of more than two, students could be assigned the role of additional interviewer(s), characters from the novel, the director (Ramin Bahrani) of the film, or actors from the film. (The instructor of the course will determine the mode of presentation and delivery—role play, video project, and interview script—for this creative assignment.)

3   Write

1   Write an essay in which you outline and explain the two most relevant SDGs to Adiga's novel as well as the novel's attitude toward the two selected SDGs. In the concluding paragraph of your essay, discuss which SDG is the most applicable to *The White Tiger* and why. Discuss whether the novel promotes the need for these two SDGs or questions their usefulness or applicability to the context of India. (The instructor of the course will determine the appropriate length for this writing assignment.)

2   Mahatma Gandhi outlined seven social sins to be avoided:

- "Politics without Principles"
- "Wealth without Work"
- "Pleasure without Conscience"

- "Knowledge without Character"
- "Commerce without Morality"
- "Science without Humanity"
- "Worship without Sacrifice" (Gandhi, *Young India* 360)

In "The '7 Social Sins' as a Warning and Way onto a Path Toward Equality and Liberation," Warren Blumenfeld explains that the origin of the seven social sins was a sermon given by an Anglican priest at Westminster Abbey in England in 1925, who called them the "7 Deadly Social Evils" (1). Gandhi published his list as seven social sins a few months later, in his weekly newspaper *Young India*. Gandhi wanted this list to serve as a guide to people living in civil society; as Blumenfeld explains: "Unlike the Catholic Church's list, which was meant as a compact between Christians and their God, Gandhi's intent in promoting the list focused on the conduct of the individual within society" (1). Write an essay on the relevance of Gandhi's list of seven social sins to Adiga's novel and to one or more of the featured SDGs in Part 3 on prosperity: 8, 9, 10, 11, and 16. Using examples from *The White Tiger*, explain the relevance of two or more social sins and how one or more SDG(s) can guide individuals, communities, and countries to "peace and prosperity for people and the planet, now and into the future," which is the overall objective of the sustainable development initiative of the United Nations ("The 17 Goals"). (The instructor of the course will determine the appropriate length for this writing assignment.)

Works Cited

Adiga, Aravind. *The White Tiger: A Novel.* e-book ed., Free Press, 2008. Kindle.
"Aravind Adiga Interview." *bookbrowse.com*, 2008, www.bookbrowse.com/author_interviews/full/index.cfm/author_number/1552/aravind-adiga.
Blumenfeld, Warren J. "The '7 Social Sins' as Warning and Way onto Path toward Equality and Liberation." *Academia.edu*, 19 July 2020, www.academia.edu/43665271/The_7_Social_Sins_as_Warning_and_Way_onto_Path_toward_Equality_and_Liberation.
"Brihadaranyaka Upanishad." *vyasaonline.com*, www.vyasaonline.com/brihadaranyaka-upanishad/.
Chadda, Rakesh K., and Koushik Sinha Deb. "Indian Family Systems, Collectivistic Society and Psychotherapy." *Indian Journal of Psychiatry*, vol. 55, Suppl 2, Jan 2013, S299–309. doi:10.4103/0019–5545.105555.
Consuegra, Luis José. "Democracy and Peacebuilding in the Framework of SDG 16+." *International IDEA*, 23 March 2020, www.idea.int/sites/default/files/publications/democracy-and-peacebuilding-in-the-framework-of-sdg-16-policy-recommendations.pdf.
Deshpande, Ashwini. "Affirmative Action in India and the United States." *World Bank Group Open Knowledge Repository*, World Bank Group, 2005, openknowledge.worldbank.org/handle/10986/9038.
Donahue, Deirdre. "Roundup: Debut Novels." *USA Today*, Gannett Satellite Information Network, 23 Apr. 2008, https://www.usatoday.com/story/life/books/2013/06/28/roundup-debut-novels/2468679/.
"Dr Shashi Tharoor MP - Britain Does Owe Reparations." *YouTube*, uploaded by Oxford Union, 14 Jul. 2015, www.youtube.com/watch?v=f7CW7S0zxv4.
Gandhi, M.K. "The Voice of Truth." *The Voice of Truth: Complete Book Online | The Selected Works of Mahatma Gandhi*, www.mkgandhi.org/voiceoftruth/voiceoftruth.htm.
———. "Young India." *Freedomnotes.com*, freedomnotes.com/Documents/MahatmaGandhi/Young%20India%201925-10-22.pdf.
"Goal 8 Department of Economic and Social Affairs." *United Nations*, sdgs.un.org/goals/goal8.
"Goal 9 Department of Economic and Social Affairs." *United Nations*, sdgs.un.org/goals/goal9.
"Goal 10 Department of Economic and Social Affairs." *United Nations*, sdgs.un.org/goals/goal10.
"Goal 11 Department of Economic and Social Affairs." *United Nations*, sdgs.un.org/goals/goal11.

"Goal 16 Department of Economic and Social Affairs." *United Nations*, sdgs.un.org/goals/goal16.

"Government Schemes in India | IBEF." *India Brand Equity Foundation*, Dec. 21, www.ibef.org/economy/government-schemes.

Higgins, Charlotte. "Out of the Darkness: Adiga's White Tiger Rides to Booker Victory against the Odds." *The Guardian*, 14 Oct. 2008, www.theguardian.com/books/2008/oct/14/booker-prize-adiga-white-tiger.

Holt, Diane. "Exploring Youth Entrepreneurship." *United Nations Department of Economic and Social Affairs*, Aug. 2020, https://sdgs.un.org/publications/exploring-youth-entrepreneurship-24572. Accessed 7 July 2023.

Jaysawal, Neelmani and Saha, Sudeshna. "Urbanization in India: An Impact Assessment." *International Journal of Applied Sociology*, vol. 4, no. 2, 2014, pp. 60–65. doi:10.5923/j.ijas.20140402.04.

Jeffries, Stuart. "Roars of Anger." *The Guardian*, 15 Oct. 2008, www.theguardian.com/books/2008/oct/16/booker-prize.

Kidd, James. "Archive: Interview with Aravind Adiga." *Asia Literary Review*, 2008, www.asialiteraryreview.com/archive-interview-aravind-adiga.

Mandal, B P. "Mandal Commission Report." *National Commission for Backward Classes*, 31 Dec. 1980, www.ncbc.nic.in/Writereaddata/Mandal%20Commission%20Report%20of%20the%201st%20Part%20English635228715105764974.pdf.

Mukherjee, Aditya. "Empire: How Colonial India Made Modern Britain." *Economic and Political Weekly*, vol. 45, no. 50, 2010, pp. 73–82, www.jstor.org/stable/25764217. Accessed 22 Sep. 2022.

"Mundaka Upanishad with Shankara's Commentary." *Wisdom Library*, 16 Feb. 2018, www.wisdomlib.org/hinduism/book/mundaka-upanishad-shankara-bhashya/d/doc145127.html.

"Pradhan Mantri Adarsh Gram Yojana (PMAGY)", *Government of India | Ministry of Social Justice and Empowerment*, pmagy.gov.in/aboutPMAGY.

"Religion and Living Arrangements Around the World" Pew Research Center, Dec. 12, 2019, www.pewresearch.org/religion/wp-content/uploads/sites/7/2019/12/PF_12.12.19_religious.households.FULL_.pdf.

"The Booker Prize." *The Booker Prizes*, thebookerprizes.com/the-booker-prize.

"The 17 Goals | Sustainable Development." *United Nations Department of Economic and Social Affairs Sustainable Development, United Nations*, sdgs.un.org/goals.

Tripathi, Ritu, and Uday Vijayan. "Collectivism: An Indian Perspective." *Indian Institute of Management Bangalore*, 2 June 2020, www.iimb.ac.in/turn_turn/collectivism-indian-perspective.php.

10 Ivan Sanjinés, Nicolás Ipamo, and Alejandro Noza's *Cry of the Forest*

Sustainable Development and the Indigenous Communities of Bolivia

Vicki Galloway

I   Text

Title	*Cry of the Forest*
Genre	Feature film
Directors	A collective production funded by indigenous community organizations and educational centers of Bolivia and led by indigenous filmmakers Iván Sanjinés, General Coordinator of the Consejo Latinoamericano de Cine y Comunicación de los Pueblos Indígenas (CLACPI) and director of the Centro de Formación y Realización Cinematográfica (CEFREC), Nicolas Ipamo, director of the Coordinadora Audiovisual Indígena Originaria de Bolivia (CAIB), and Alejandro Noza of the Aboriginal Indigenous National Plan for Audiovisual Communication.
Year	2008
Country	Bolivia

Considered Bolivia's first indigenous feature film, *Cry of the Forest* is a story told by and for the native peoples of the region of Beni, at the southern reaches of the Amazon Basin, in the years leading up to Bolivia's 1996 Forest Law. The film's actors are not professionals, but rather the inhabitants, or *comunarios,* of the indigenous villages. The perspectives, events, processes, challenges, and daily life interactions in the film are thus as authentic as their storytellers and allow an intimate view of indigenous understandings of forest sustainability, of territory as spiritual as well as material, and of timeless community and relationship with nature.

The film unravels the physical and emotional journey of Mercedes, a Moxeño woman whose village of Bella Selva (*Beautiful Forest*), is corrupted, desecrated, and finally burned to the ground by invasive loggers. After several days of walking alone, Mercedes arrives at the Guarayo community of Nueva Esperanza (*New Hope*), where she is warmly welcomed and quickly integrated due to her knowledge of midwifery and healing plants. The years pass and Mercedes is still an enigma to her fellow villagers, as she is unable to revisit the trauma of Bella Selva's destruction. It is not until the same logging company arrives at her adopted community and tempts its villagers with false promises of economic gain that Mercedes finally has the courage to speak out and tell her story, a story that gives powerful voice to the women of the community and ushers new ways of leadership.

Trigger Warning: The original Spanish title of the film is *Grito de la selva*. While translated as "cry," a *grito* is rather a sharp, piercing sound, such as one caused by fear or pain. Based on real events, the film includes some scenes of violence (assault, arson, and attempted rape) that,

DOI: 10.4324/9781003388869-14

in addition to depicting the threats to indigenous communities of the Amazon, serve as powerful metaphor to juxtapose the views of forest as *commodity* versus forest as *community*.

Cry of the Forest (with English subtitles) is available for purchase in DVD or screening license format from Third World Newsreel at https://www.twn.org.

II   Context

A landlocked country in the center of South America, Bolivia boasts the third largest portion of the Amazon rainforest (after Brazil and Peru) and one of the highest levels of biodiversity and endemism of animal and plant species in the world (Figure 10.1). Scientists believe that the richness of the Amazon rainforest creates about one-quarter of Earth's oxygen.

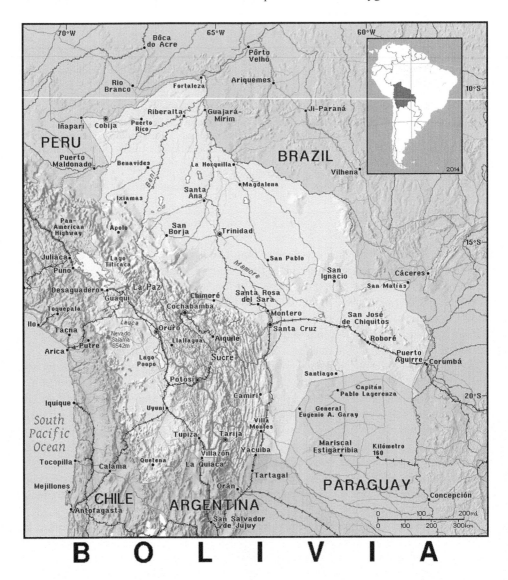

Figure 10.1 Map of Bolivia showing the Beni River and Amazon Basin. U.S. Central Intelligence Agency. CIA World Factbook, 2004. Public Domain.

Bolivia's biodiversity extends to human populations as well, with 62% of the country self-identifying as indigenous and belonging to 37 ethnic groups of some 36 languages. Over 80% of these indigenous groups reside in the Amazon region where for centuries they have enjoyed a dignified existence in an intimate relationship with their natural environment that sustains a lasting ecological balance. Today's Amazonian identities are built on the cultural legacy of their indigenous ancestors.

Bolivia's Beni region is the setting of the film *Cry of the Forest*. Although abundant in natural resources, the poverty level of its inhabitants is high, mainly as a result of exploitation. Once thought to be the site of the mythical El Dorado, this lowland region has experienced centuries of extraction and developmental neglect through irresponsible timber harvesting, commercial agriculture, and unsustainable cattle-ranching practices. The spiraling environmental destruction and resulting community fragmentation have imperiled the health and cultural longevity of the region's indigenous peoples.

In the 1990s, major pan-indigenous movements and protests known as the "March for Territory and Dignity" united Bolivia's diverse ethnic groups to seek justice in land tenure and to decry mismanagement of their forests. Their efforts incited a national stakeholder dialogue that incorporated indigenous concepts of "territory" and led to the passage of Bolivia's 1996 Forest Law galvanizing far-reaching reforms in management of silviculture and award of timber concessions and indigenous land titles. By the mid-2000s, Bolivia had emerged as a world leader in sustainable tropical forestry and had the most certified sustainable acreage of any country in the world (Dockry and Langston 2).

In 2009, a new constitution declared Bolivia a "plurinational state" and recognized the *Pachamama,* an indigenous concept of "Mother Earth," as the center of all life (*Political Constitution*). Reflecting the country's indigenous belief system of s*umak kawsay* (harmonious living or sustainable development), the Constitution established a legal relationship between humans and nature as interconnected, interdependent, and complementary "in an undivided community of all living things." Subsequently in 2012, a new law called the "Framework Law of Mother Earth and Integral Development for Living Well" (*La Ley Marco de la Madre Tierra y Desarrollo Integral para Vivir Bien*) established new rights for Nature, including the right to life, regeneration, biodiversity, water, balance, restoration, and freedom from genetic alteration ("Framework").

Viewers of *Cry of the Forest* will find the following resource very helpful for understanding the film's historical context both before and after the March for Territory and Dignity and for insight into the indigenous view of sustainable development:

Dockry, Michael J., and Nancy Langston. "Indigenous Protest and the Roots of Sustainable Forestry in Bolivia." *Environmental History*, vol. 24, no. 1, 2019, pp. 52–77.

This article is based on government-funded research and is in the public domain.

III   Interpretation

1   The film's story alternates between a past in Bella Selva ("Beautiful Forest") and a present in Nueva Esperanza ("New Hope") that blur into each other until the background of Mercedes, the protagonist, is finally revealed at the end. While Bella Selva is a real community, Nueva Esperanza is fictitious. How do the village names reflect the messages each conveys in the film? Why do you think the filmmakers decided to construct their narrative through Mercedes' memories? How does this approach reinforce the film's message? Why does Mercedes resist divulging her past to her adopted community of Nueva Esperanza? Discuss with a partner the ways in which the opening graveyard scene may be considered symbolic.

2   Throughout the film the villagers address each other as "sister" and "brother." Why? Cite scenes from the film that illustrate the indigenous perspective of *community* as reflected in views of the following:

- Family
- Work
- Territory
- Land "ownership"
- Social organization
- Past and future
- Nature
- Health and sickness
- Education

How and by whom are these values deliberately maintained? How is justice meted to those who forget (Valentín) or betray (Milton) the values of the collective? Cite scenes in which the filmmakers depict Milton as antithetical to the community's values. What do you think Milton represents? How is he shamed by others for his behavior? How does his final punishment fit both his crimes and the community's values?

3   How is the Marita Lumber Company portrayed in the film? Describe how Don Ruben, the company boss, demonstrates his power and influence throughout the film. What promises did the company make to the indigenous communities? What were the overriding factors in the decision to allow the loggers to harvest the forest? What oppositions were voiced? Discuss the gradual impact of the logging company's invasion on the village economy, natural environment, society, and culture, citing specific scenes to illustrate. What is the significance of the rape scene in this context?

4   On welcoming Mercedes to Nueva Esperanza, Leoncio, and Matilda offer her *chicha*, an alcoholic beverage made from fermented corn (Figure 10.2). In another scene, the loggers offer Mercedes' brother Valentín several shots of aguardiente, also an alcoholic (but much stronger) beverage (Figure 10.3).

What is the difference between these two offerings in terms of both attitude and intent? While both scenes depict interactions with "outsiders," what messages do the filmmakers seek to convey in their contrast? Discuss how the perspectives captured in each of these scenes are expanded upon throughout the film. How does the scene of Milton's drunken spousal abuse reinforce the filmmakers' message of invasion and intrusion on community values and structure (0:50:24–0:51:02)?

Figure 10.2 Film still from *Cry of the Forest*. The community's offering: "Have some chichi" (00:06:19).

Figure 10.3 Film still from *Cry of the Forest*. The loggers' offering: "Peasants only drink at parties. White men drink whenever they want" (00:37:36).

5   Describe in detail the various roles of men and women of the indigenous community as depicted in the film. Consider the following questions: In what areas do women exert leadership? In what areas are men expected to exert leadership? How do these roles intersect in decision making? What shift in roles is depicted at the end of the film and for what reasons? In small groups describe and compare the male–female dynamic and power balance of three town meetings from *Cry of the Forest* in Bella Selva in 1990 (00:33:33–00:36:35) and Nueva Esperanza in 1996 (00:57:12–01:00:34) and (01:28:02–01:30:35). Pay attention to details, such as how comunarios are seated; who speaks, when and about what; what tensions are present and how they are resolved; who holds more influence or sway? What took place between these landmark years to foment change? What do you think is the filmmakers' message in the final assembly scene? Give examples of how and why this is a story told primarily by and through women. Discuss whether you agree or disagree with this statement: In the film, while men are often the short-term decision makers, women are portrayed as the long-term change makers.

6   Work with a partner to identify the following quotations from the film and explain their context and significance. Do any of these reflect perspectives that are somewhat different from those of your home culture?

- "It was so happy…Would you like someone to cut off your finger?" (00:13:43–00:13:56)
- "Dreams come and go so you shouldn't believe them" (00:24:50)
- "She knew these things, and that's why we know" (00:13:06)
- "Do you know how to make a blower? Do you know how to weave?" (00:13:45)
- "The women aren't here to just sit quietly" (00:34:26)
- "The forest has an owner. You didn't ask permission, did you? (00:45:10)
- "Folks in the communities are easy sway" (00:53:40)
- "My party … They owe me some favors" (00:54:31–00:54:38)
- "How can you not have an ID card? How are you a citizen?" (01:11:35)
- "Don't believe what that woman says … Why is she always alone?" (01:16:42)
- "You are hereby declared in possession of your land" (01:30:08).
- "We have to join the march" (00:49:27)
- "These people never want our advancement" (01:15:20)
- "I take care of my own business" (00:53:15)
- "We've become scattered" (00:11:30)

7   In small groups, discuss the clash of perspectives in each of the following pairs of scenes. Then choose two scenes of your own to compare.

Group 1: Compare Figures 10.4 and 10.5

Figure 10.4 Film still from *Cry of the Forest.* "We have everything we need here" (00:33:12).

Figure 10.5 Film still from *Cry of the Forest.* "We are all guarayos and weaving we learn about everything" (00:17:20).

Group 2: Compare Figures 10.6 and 10.7

Figure 10.6 Film still from *Cry of the Forest.* "We are going to build a road" (00:31:30).

Figure 10.7 Film still from *Cry of the Forest.* "There's plenty of good wood" (00:55:44).

Group 3: Compare Figures 10.8 and 10.9

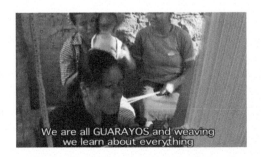

Figure 10.8 Film still from *Cry of the Forest.* "The trees were bleeding" (00:13:06).

Figure 10.9 Film still from *Cry of the Forest.* "I'm not like anyone else" (00:50:26).

Group 4: Compare Figures 10.10 and 10.11

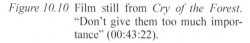

Figure 10.10 Film still from *Cry of the Forest.* "Don't give them too much importance" (00:43:22).

Figure 10.11 Film still from *Cry of the Forest.* "We have to march" (00:30:24).

8   Through radio broadcasts and conversations in flashbacks to Bella Selva in 1990 we hear that an indigenous march is planned to protest treatment of the forest and to address indigenous rights. What details can you find out about this march from the film itself? How was it conducted? What were its goals and demands? What was it protesting? From what you see in the film, how might the indigenous view of community have facilitated the effectiveness of the protest? How does *Cry of the Forest* contrast the land-grabbing strategies of Marita Lumber Company in 1990 (Bella Selva) and 1996 (Nueva Esperanza)? What political and legal acts do you suspect necessitated the company's change of approach?

9   Throughout *Cry of the Forest* the inseparability of nature and culture is emphasized, especially in the perception and use of forest medicine as ancestral knowledge. What do the terms "ethnomedicine" and "ethnobotany" mean and how are they conveyed in the film? Cite scenes that depict the indigenous view of sickness, medicine, and healing. Where does knowledge of healing come from and how is it transmitted? How does the film convey the fragility of this knowledge bank? How does the village healer portend community well-being through dreams? In the final scenes of *Cry of the Forest*, how does the new position awarded to Mercedes communicate the fragility of the world's cultural and natural heritage and the status of the healer? Bolivia's Constitution guarantees a health system that is "unitary" and includes "traditional medicine of the nations and the rural native indigenous peoples" (*Political Constitution* Sect. II, Art. 35. II). Vandebroek and colleagues note that while non-indigenous Bolivian doctors believe Western medicine is superior and should replace traditional medicine, there is a distrust of modern medicine in indigenous communities that stems from financial, psychological, physical, and cultural barriers. Can you explain this from your viewing of the film? While there exists no catalog of Bolivia's flora, it is estimated that 25% of Western-world pharmaceuticals are derived from Amazonian plants and animals. Why is indigenous ancestral knowledge of forest flora and fauna a valuable resource, not only to indigenous communities, but to the world?

10 *Cry of the Forest* is an example of indigenous "*cine propio*," cinema produced by and for local communities on their "own" topics and issues to "represent their identities, fortify their cultures, and claim the autonomy of their own ways of knowing" and to "make perceptible the co-presence of visible and invisible forms and forces" (Himpele 356). While a work of fiction, *Cry of the Forest* is based on real events and on the lives of the its actors

the *comunarios*, who are the production team's first engagement, who express their opinions about the dialogue, the music, and even about the course of the story. The Cinematography Education and Production Center (CEFREC) has trained indigenous communities through participatory production of over 300 such films, documentaries, and state-of-the-art digital projects. Its founder and coordinator, Ivan Sanjinés, prefers to be referred to as a "social communicator" and explains that the word "producer" is an inaccurate title for indigenous filmmakers since, strictly speaking, they as individuals do not produce culture but rather *communicate* culture (Himpele 357). As indigenous filmmaker Marcelina Cardenas puts it: "We have another manner of directing. We cannot demand that our 'brothers and sisters' follow a script. We give them ideas, they give us some input, and we incorporate these ideas" (Himpele 358). How was this film carried out with limited resources? In your opinion, why would the *comunarios* have wanted to be involved in this film project? Would this story have been improved by the use of professional actors rather than community members? How would the story have been different in that case? In chronicling the making of the film and how the community developed their dialogue, social anthropologist Gabriela Zamorano Villarreal notes how the filmed scenes reflect a lived reality: One day, as the villagers were packing up after filming an assembly scene, the mayor stood up to solemnly address the *comunarios*:

> As many of you have heard, there is again that tractor wandering around. We've told them they couldn't use our road to bring in their machines, we don't want them here. I ask the support of you all so we can go together, tonight or early tomorrow, to talk to that company owner for once! (Zamorano Villarreal 137–138).

Considering Zamorano Villarreal's description, discuss the potential impacts, both *local and global*, of indigenous cinema that authentically engages community. Share your view of the success of *Cry of the Forest* in achieving those objectives. Himpele contends that film credits themselves are "significant instruments in asserting self-determination for indigenous directors" (Himpele, p. 357). Watch the final credits of the film (1:32:43–1:34:32). What images roll alongside the credits and how do they support the message of *Cry of the Forest*?

IV   Prosperity-Focused Applications to SDGs 8, 9, 10, 11, 12, and 16

1   What does "prosperity" mean to you? According to your definition, is the indigenous community of Nueva Esperanza "prosperous?" Do you think the villagers would consider themselves prosperous? Why or why not? While we may tend to view prosperity mostly in economic terms (wealth, affluence, and material success), Merriam-Webster defines prosperity as a condition of flourishing or thriving. In what ways might the community of Nueva Esperanza be seen as "thriving"? In what ways does the film send the message that profit-focused decisions alone do not create prosperity? For the UN SDGs, prosperity means ensuring that "*all human* beings can enjoy fulfilling lives and that economic, social and technological *progress* occurs in *harmony with nature*" ("Transforming Our World"). As you reflect on that definition, discuss the meanings you typically associate with the following common expressions and compare and contrast their applicability to indigenous perspectives portrayed in *Cry of the Forest*: "harnessing nature," "the price of progress," "private property," "the disease of poverty," "make a killing," "back to nature," and "blind greed."

2   Just as all human beings do not share the same views of prosperity or of progress, soci-
ologist Geoff Holloway contends that people and cultures differ in what it means to live
"harmoniously" with nature, and contrasts *anthropocentrism* or shallow ecology, and *ecocentrism* or deep ecology, noting that environmentalists and conservationists may be either
of the two (3). The former values non-human life forms through the lens of their utility
for human well-being, self-interest, and profits; the latter views humankind as embedded
as one being in a living system of beings, a *part of* nature rather than *apart from* nature.
Which of these two perspectives seems to be reflected in the SDG definition of prosperity? How is each reflected in *Cry of the Forest*? Which is reflected in the ceremony of the
"challa" mentioned in the film (00:14:23–00:15:03)? Research this ceremony as it relates
to other rituals of Bolivian Carnaval: What is its purpose? How is it enacted? What does
it prohibit?

3   Discuss what issues *Cry of the Forest* reflects in terms of indigenous communities' focus
on "decent employment and a safe and secure working environment" ("Transforming Our
World" Target 8.8). Agriculture and forestry are the lifeline for multitudes of small indigenous villages throughout the Amazon, where economies are land-dependent and productive
enterprise is linked to secure territory entitlement. As we see in *Cry of the Forest*, however,
indigenous land tenure prior to 1996 was non-existent and exploitative practices reigned,
snagging communities in the precarious employment of irresponsible logging companies.
How is such precarious employment depicted in the film? What were the consequences in
Bella Selva of decisions made for short-term economic fixes and low-quality unsustainable
jobs? As one community leader of the day put it, "In those times, truthfully, the business-
men were given our natural resources [...] but not a cent returned to us [...] it did not even
generate work for us" (Dockry and Langston 70). Chronicling the progression of Bolivia's
indigenous communities toward "decoupling economic growth from environmental degradation" ("Transforming Our World" Target 8.4), Dockry and Langston describe as a matter
of life and death the historic 650-mile March for Territory and Dignity in 1990 that led, ultimately, to the passage of the 1996 Forestry Law granting indigenous collectives exclusive
rights to manage their forests for timber: "The marchers endured hardships because they
tied their demands to the survival of their cultures through control of their territories" (53)
How did this epic march begin, according to the film? How were marchers recruited? In the
film, which *comunarios* of Bella Selva were planning to participate? Why was this a march
for "dignity" as well as territory?

4   From your understanding of the film, of what does "territory" consist in the indigenous
worldview? What relationships does it connote? According to Dominga, the *curandera* of
Bella Selva, who owns the forest? In their article "Indigenous Protest and the Roots of
Sustainable Forestry in Bolivia," Dockry and Langston remind us that in the indigenous
worldview "territory" goes far beyond demarcation, jurisdiction, and ownership. It is habitat; socioeconomic space; biodiversity of animals and plants, rocks and rivers, and their
spiritual relationship; it is culture, tradition and ancestors, education, and identity (62–66).
In what ways does the film convey the "spiritual relationship" that is the indigenous sense
of territory? How does the film imply the interdependence between indigenous peoples'
economic development and their cultural values?

5   Prior to 1990, Bolivia's indigenous communities were banned from habitation or use of territory declared as "national park" and were excluded from all park-related decision making.
Pressure from united indigenous groups, however, prompted the government to designate
national parks as "collective indigenous territories" (*Tierras Comunitarias de Origen* or

TCOs) to be inhabited, used, harvested, and managed by indigenous communities according to their "own logic and rationale" (Dockry and Langston 65). In your experience, what is the purpose of a national park? What are national parks created to protect and from whom? What would happen without these protected areas? Do Bolivia's TCOs reflect a view of sustainability that is different from the view you associate with national parks? Dockry and Langston note that the biodiversity of Bolivian lowlands is actually due in part to past human land use: "The Bolivian tropical rainforest is not a 'pristine' landscape; rather, it is a cultural landscape resulting from generations of active Indigenous land management and use" (54). In your view, what are the sustainability benefits of indigenous communities living within national parks and harvesting timber within these territories according to their own "logic and rationale"? How does this view contrast with the predominant Western view of national parks as pristine wilderness to be protected from human "invasion" through regulated visits? What advantages does indigenous park habitation have for economic development through tourism?

6   According to the Servicio Nacional de Areas Protegidas (SERNAP), Bolivia has 22 national parks, which cover 16% of the country, offering huge potential to operate sustainable *ecotourism* and *ethnotourism* programs, initiatives recommended in SDGs 8 ("Transforming Our World" Target 8.9) and 12 ("Transforming Our World" Target 12b). How do these types of tourism differ from mass tourism in their goals and purported impact? While we may automatically associate ecotourism with sustainability, Malin Høyme, a specialist in Development Management, contends that such programs, if not built and maintained through direct communication and involvement with the local indigenous peoples, may leave communities untouched in terms of economic improvement or, at worst, may "fetishize or orientalize" indigenous groups as separate from "our so-called sophisticated style of living" (24–25). Can you give examples of what it means to "fetishize" a culture and how we might do this subconsciously as tourists? Høyme suggests, alternatively, that community-based ecotourism (CBE), as a form of social entrepreneurship controlled by the local people who inhabit the natural attraction, promotes sustainability in addition to supplementing the income of agriculture-based communities. Aside from its economic benefits, how might CBE help to foster intercultural learning as well as aid indigenous communities in the preservation of biodiversity, cultural heritage and traditional knowledge, and collective identity? What curbs and cautions might you suggest putting on such a program? How would you react as a tourist, for example, to the prohibition of all picture-taking inside the community? If you were to visit the community of Nueva Esperanza in a CBE program, what would you like to experience and learn about the culture? How would such a program help you?

For several years, the CIDOB (Confederation of Indigenous Peoples of Bolivia) has led a resistance movement against the government's plan to build a highway through the Isiboro Sécure National Park (TIPNIS) in the Beni region, territory that is considered sacred to its Moxeño inhabitants. The park is currently accessible only by boat and the government claims the road is necessary to provide basic services and health and education facilities. The protestors claim the road will trigger destruction of biodiversity, deforestation, illegal logging, and the settlement of coca farmers. Who should win this battle in your view? In small groups, weigh the pros and cons of the proposed highway, citing scenes from *Cry of the Forest,* as relevant.

7   How does *Cry of the Forest* respond to SDG 9's call for domestic technology development ("Transforming Our World" Target 9b) and "increased access to information and communications technology in developing countries" ("Transforming Our World" Target 9c)? A landlocked country with dispersed population, Bolivia has had challenges in rolling out

connectivity to remote regions; however, according to Kemp, internet permeability is at over 50% and cellphone use is common even in rural areas, where smartphone apps are used for social organization, environment monitoring, forest mapping, and recording and sharing ancestral knowledge of forest medicine. Yet, stubborn images of Bolivia as the "backwaters" of the world persist in North Atlantic media consumers' imaginations, according to Nell Hayes, who contends that there is often an "aura of unexpectedness" that accompanies discussions about indigenous peoples' engagement with technology, as if their experiences have been culturally isolated from global consumer capitalism and generally antithetical to technology. Do you agree with Nell Hayes regarding "low-tech" stereotypes of Bolivia and its peoples? Where do such views come from? Do you think we tend to equate technology use with "development"? According to filmmaker and principal collaborator Ivan Sanjinés, the mission of *Cry of the Forest* as a participatory project directly targets these stereotypes as part of a long-term *process* to train indigenous people from all regions of Bolivia in audiovisual technology and communicative reach in order to strengthen community defense, foment intercultural dialogue, and counteract messages in the mass media that devalue indigenous peoples and are incompatible with their realities (Himpele). In what ways do you think mass media tend to devalue certain peoples? As part of this horizontal and participatory communication tradition, radio is by far the primary medium in indigenous communities (Srinivasan and Ramos-Martín 289). In contrast to mass media, how is radio broadcasting employed in *Cry of the Forest?* To what specific event is the broadcasting aimed? How did it contribute to educating and building solidarity across diverse indigenous groups throughout the country? Bolivia has, in fact, developed an international reputation for innovation in grassroots radio programming integrating open-mic participation of ordinary people, rural viewpoints in reporting, and "radio chain" networking and mobilization as a tool of activism, cultural preservation, and democratic decision making. In expanding outlets for indigenous programming, filmmaker Sanjinés expects to demand television broadcast timeslots, noting that while Bolivian law requires 40% of television programming to be national, the vast majority is imported fare or advertising financed and tied to business interests in mining, commercial agriculture, and political parties (Himpele). Do you think the law should require that this percentage of programming be of indigenous voice and direction?

8   How do you explain the meaning of the quotation in Figure 10.12? SDG 10 focuses on inequality as a major obstacle to development and targets the promotion of legislation and policies that eliminate discriminatory practices ("Transforming Our World" Target 10.3). It is estimated that 60% of the Bolivian population is indigenous; yet, what factors have contributed to their marginalization? Cite specific examples from *Cry of the Forest* of perceptions and attitudes of non-indigenous and indigenous people toward one another. What obstacles were faced by indigenous communities in negotiating agreements and lodging complaints through legal channels? Why? How did marginalized indigenous communities such as Nueva Esperanza empower *themselves* to achieve political status and economic inclusion through non-violent strategies ("Transforming Our World" Target 10.2)? How does this approach reflect the concept of "community" as communicated in the film? In 1996, Bolivia's Forestry Law, a primary outcome of the March for Territory and Dignity, initiated a dialogue that led to a new national Constitution in 2009 and a reframing of national identity according to indigenous values. Read the Preamble and Article 30 of Bolivia's Constitution (*Political Constitution*) to learn how strongly indigenous mobilization against inequality impacted Bolivian law. Summarize the key ideas and espoused values of the Preamble and discuss how they pertain to sustainable "prosperity." How are these principles

Figure 10.12 Film still from *Cry of the Forest*. "The indigenous people of the Amazon also exist" (00:44:19).

reflected in *Cry of the Forest?* Article 31 guarantees indigenous communities the right to maintain a lifestyle that is isolated and out of contact with greater society. In your opinion, does this constitutional right align with the UN Sustainable Development Goals? In Bolivia's previous constitutions of 1994 and 1995, the country is described as "multiethnic" and "pluricultural," whereas the latest version in 2009 uses the word "plurinational." Discuss important distinctions in these words. In safeguarding indigenous cultural identity, Bolivia's constitution not only recognizes the 36 languages spoken by indigenous communities but declares all of them, along with Spanish, *official* languages of the country, moreover guaranteeing respect for "all cosmovisions" and authorizing the legality and equal status of community systems of justice. Could any of these provisions to preserve indigenous cultures be considered controversial or pose obstacles to national governance? What is the community's system of justice in the film's Nueva Esperanza community? How does it appear to work with "outsiders"? How are "insiders" punished for serious crimes against the community? In the case of Milton's frequent violations of community mores, how is *shaming* employed as the preferred corrective measure? How might his final punishment be seen as the maximum measure?

9   The Constitution's Preamble mentions the right to "a good life" (in Spanish *buen vivir*) as a principle to guide state action. What does a "good life" mean to you? Use of this term in the Constitution derives from the Quechua *sumac kawsay* which does not really convey the same sense as the English translation "good life." Why do some words and expressions not translate well into other languages? Find out what Bolivia's indigenous communities mean by the following words and how their meanings in cultural context differ from those inferred in the English translation:

- *sumac kawsay* ("good life")
- *minka* [or *minga* or *mita*] ("community service")
- *Pachamama* ("Mother Nature")

- *ayni* ("cooperation")
- *ayllu* ("community")
- *chachawarmi* ("equal rights")

10 While Bolivia's constitution stipulates that men and women are equal before the law, the indigenous tradition of *chachawarmi,* literally a synthesis of man (*chacha*) and woman (*warmi*) reflects the indigenous cosmovision of duality and reciprocity (as in day/night, hot/cold, summer/winter) so that what is often translated as "equal rights" has a meaning more in tune with a non-hierarchical *complementarity*, a unity of energy opposites that derives from the natural world. Can you give examples of this complementarity in nature? *Chachawarmi* thus explicitly values femininity on equal terms with masculinity and celebrates distinct but equally valued activities. How does this concept of "gender equality" differ from your own? Rather than the Western notion of separate gendered public and private spheres, *chachawarmi* connotes gender duality in all spheres (Rousseau 18). Moreover, the notion of wholeness being composed of equal opposites carries over to the view that men or women are not complete adults until they take on partners. To what extent is *chachawarmi* reflected in *Cry of the Forest*? What seems to violate it? How do the filmmakers show the clash between individualist and communitarian notions of gender? Consider the ideas presented in Figure 10.13 in this regard.

Figure 10.13 Film still from *Cry of the Forest*. "Why is she always alone?" (01:16:47).

Kate MacLean cautions that whereas ideas of gender equality associated with Western discourse are predicated on individual rights, indigenous women view their struggle as focused more on rights to voice in decision making for protection of community and its cosmovision. What then might a so-called "feminist movement" look like in the indigenous world? Caroline Dunn, writing for the NGO The Borgen Project, notes that while only a few decades ago Bolivia's women held a mere 4% of municipal assembly posts, Bolivia's Consitution of 2009 mandated a 50% proportion of female candidates in all national and sub-national elections and since 2014 Bolivia has consistently ranked second in the world for women's representation parliament (Inter-Parliamentary Union 7). However, representation by *indigenous* women lags far behind. How do the filmmakers of *Cry of the Forest* send a message about the need for indigenous women's engagement in political, economic, and cultural spaces? In 2013, Bolivia established a "Department of Depatriarchalization" and passed the "Comprehensive Law to Guarantee Women a Life Free From Violence" (Law 348), the first of its kind in the world, which broadened protection of women against various forms of violence and established the eradication of violence against women as a priority of the State (Avilés Irahola). In your opinion, how and to what extent can such legislation actually change patriarchal attitudes? Indigenous women refer to eradicating domestic violence as "decolonizing." Why? Why do many indigenous women believe that "decolonizing" means retrieving the values of *chachawarmi*?

11   In 2011, Bolivia further enshrined indigenous cosmovision into national policy through the *Ley de Derechos de la Madre Tierra* or "Law of Mother Earth," the first national legislation in the world to bestow rights to the *Pachamama* ("Framework"). How does this law define and describe Mother Earth? What does it mean to give nature the rights of human citizens? Discuss the implications of such a law and imagine ways in which this concept might be challenging to enforce in practice. A direct result of the indigenous movement initiated by the 1990 March for Territory and Dignity, Bolivia's constitution and Mother Earth laws respond directly to one of the targets of SDG 11, that of protecting and safeguarding the world's cultural and natural heritage ("Transforming Our World" Target 11.4). The World Wildlife Fund (WWF) notes that in Bolivia, indigenous communities now play a crucial role in the timber sector and wood supply chain and occupy a strategic and representative role in increasing the legality and sustainability of forest management. From your understanding of the film, how would indigenous communities define *sustainability*? What is the attitude toward waste and efficient use of natural resources that you encountered in the film *Cry of the Forest* and how is it taught in the community

Figure 10.14 Film still from *Cry of the Forest* (00:03:58).

("Transforming Our World" 12.2)? How does the Indigenous view of Mother Earth differ from that of your culture? Wandersee and Schussler warn of a growing phenomenon in Western societies that they call "plant blindness," the "misguided, anthropocentric ranking of plants as inferior to animals, unworthy of human consideration" (82). Monica Gagliano, in "Seeing Green," contends that our tendency to overlook plants as a passive, insensitive, non-threatening backdrop is part of a cultural worldview that must be reconsidered for our sustainable development (Gagliano 20). Do you agree? Do you see reasons for plant blindness in Western society? To what extent are you plant blind? Consider which scenes from *Cry of the Forest* you viewed as violent or disturbing. Did any of them make you turn your head away? How many of the scenes you cited were scenes of *nature* in which humans were not present? Would you consider the scene in Figure 10.14 equally violent? Why or why not?

How might your view differ from that of Mercedes or Dominga, the *curandera* of Bella Selva? Gagliano maintains that we have much to learn from how plants inter-act: as a model of coherence, the plant world demonstrates how competition and coop-eration can co-exist (27). Do you believe both cooperation and competition are essential to sustainability?

12 It is estimated that Bolivia's borders contain more than 14,000 higher plant species, a wealth vulnerable to extractive industries and deforesting practices. Also vulnerable is the trove of knowledge about the healing properties of plants and animals held by indigenous com-munity shamans and healers who, as seen in *Cry of the Forest*, guide the community in preventive procedures and, as Hance notes, have highly developed systems for diagnosing illness. Seventy percent of plants known to have anticancer properties exist only in the Ama-zon, one of the most biodiverse regions of the world. However, only a small percentage of Amazonian plant life has been tested for possible use in "modern" medicine. Why do you think this is so? What problems might be involved in entering a community to learn how nature is applied to healing, then exporting, patenting, manufacturing, and selling a product derived from that learning? In what ways is this similar to the practices of the lumber com-pany in *Cry of the Forest*? In each case, what has been stolen? In *Cry of the Forest*, we see the medicinal use of forest plant life by experienced healers and also learn of the threats: not only the loss of biodiversity through irresponsible logging but also the loss of traditional knowledge of the curative qualities and healing procedures for using nature's medicines. Bolivia's Constitution considers this ancestral knowledge and science "intellectual prop-erty" whose collective ownership is protected in use, promotion, and development. Yet, this knowledge is of great value to researchers exploring solutions and remedies to today's ills, and Bolivia has been a constant target of bioprospecting as well as biopiracy. Discuss the type of legal framework that might allow for the fair sharing of traditional knowledge about forest flora and fauna while abiding by the indigenous communities' rights under the Constitution to "collective ownership of the intellectual property in their knowledge, sci-ences and learning, as well as to its evaluation, use, promotion and development" (*Political Constitution* Sect. IV, Art. 30.11).

13 According to the filmmaker Iván Sanjinés, a primary aim of *Cry of the Forest* is that of pro-moting understanding and awareness of what it means to have a lifestyle in harmony with nature, the very essence of sustainable development ("Transforming Our World" Target 12.8): "We want to take the opportunity of the space and moment we are living in order to reach deeper and create spaces for communication [...] integrating social sectors, training

leaders […] to contribute to the construction of a new society […] a communitarian, supportive and reciprocal one as opposed to […] endlessly taking things away without solidarity, without thinking of human development. I mean, there is a different philosophy…" (Leyva Martínez). While *Cry of the Forest* is a denunciation of real events, the film seeks a reflection not only from indigenous communities but from "society in general," including Western middle-class urban sectors. Discuss how the message and aim of this film might transfer across different audiences and what parts of the message may or may not resonate with college audiences where Sanjinés has presented the film? How would you recommend efforts such as *Cry of the Forest* best capture the attention of young urban audiences outside of the indigenous communities to change minds or move toward action? According to filmmaker Sanjinés: "People have the idea that indigenous peoples are untouched, in an idyllic world, that they are all good and taking care of the environment and smiling all day" (Himpele 357). Did a similar thought come to your mind at any moment while watching *Cry of the Forest*? Discuss any assumptions or judgments you found yourself making about the *comunarios* and the indigenous communities represented in the film. What are the risks that *Cry of the Forest* could prompt homogenized or spatially bounded understandings in Western audiences that could cast the *sumac kawsay* values message as an artifact of isolated ancestral territories rather than dynamic, resilient, and mobilized communities? How might this be avoided or even counteracted?

14 Bolivia's extensive legal framework protecting indigenous lands and identity was the result of decision making involving multiple stakeholders and constituted a giant step forward in advancing the conditions of SDG 16 toward inclusive, non-discriminatory policies and the reduction of violence, crime, and corruption in the trafficking of biodiversity and desertification of forest. Bolivia's constitution, with expressed sensitivity to the threat of cultural extinction, espouses indigenous nationhood; honors cultural self-identification, communitarist values, and communitarian democracy; promises intercultural, intracultural, and multilanguage education and respect for traditional medicine; and specifically authorizes and protects indigenous rights to self-determination, to collective ownership of land and territories, to administration of community systems of governance, and to the exercise of consultative involvement in all legislative or administrative measures "that may be foreseen to affect them" (*Political Constitution* Sect. IV, Art. 30.15). Phillip Horn contends, however, that these rights and protections seem to stop at the rural border, as indigenous migrants displaced by violence, environmental destruction, and familial fragmentation, such as those of Bella Selva in *Cry of the Forest*, flee to the city only to encounter little support for building community and exercising traditional practices. Horn's study of indigenous urban settlers contends that failure to perceive indigenous rights as belonging to urban as well as rural indigenous peoples reflects a static, essentialized, and spatially bounded understanding of indigeneity. Do you agree? What would an urban articulation of the rights of the "indigenous native peasant" look like? Aside from the collective land tenure that has not been allowed by city authorities, what other specific demands might urban indigenous communities have in areas such as public health, housing, education, occupational training, tourism programs, cultural programs, decision making, and governance? How would collective land ownership contribute to helping urban indigenous communities realize some of these demands? In your view, what are the challenges of incorporating indigenous communitarian democracy within procedures of city-level governance? Do you believe that city-dwelling indigenous settlers should acculturate or assimilate into the mainstream urban context? What is the difference between assimilation and acculturation?

15 In groups, discuss how *Cry of the Forest* reinforces and/or questions the principles and perspectives underlying the UN SDG framework and the notion of sustainable development it
conveys. Consider the following and integrate details from the film into your discussion:

• Does *Cry of the Forest* allow us a more textured sense of the meaning of "development?"
  What do you typically associate with the word "development?" Did any aspect of the film
  cause you to question pat labels of "developed" and "developing" countries? What does
  the term "developed country" signal in terms of work to be done? Did the film in any
  way expand or deepen your understanding of sustainability? Berik and Gaddis propose
  a host of positive and negative consequences of consumption, which they combine in a
  dashboard of pluses and minuses called the "Genuine Progress Indicator" (GPI). Find the
  GPI graphic online and discuss with your group any features of "well-being" it depicts
  that may not typically be part of our mental framework for "developed."

• Does *Cry of the Forest* help us understand the interconnectedness of all spheres of sustainable development—environmental, social, economic, and cultural? How does the film
  reflect a values system in which the economic cannot be separated from the social, the
  spiritual, the cultural, and/or the environmental in the indigenous worldview? In what
  ways do the SDGs for Prosperity convey this interdependence? Do the SDGs reflect a bias
  toward any of the spheres, in your opinion?

• How does *Cry of the Forest* reflect the view of UNESCO that "cultural diversity is the
  driving force of sustainable development" (Matsuura)? Per Vortman contends that culture
  is so vital that it must be sustainability's *fourth pillar*, absolutely fundamental to the existence of society and to social progress: "Culture brings to society fundamental qualities
  that are just as important as the ecological, social and economic perspective. The very
  concept of sustainability must include a cultural dimension to ensure that the cultural
  qualities are understood to be absolutely fundamental to the existence of society and to
  social progress." Cite excerpts from the Prosperity SDGs that make reference to cultural
  identity. Do the SDGs give sufficient stature to cultural sustainability and the importance
  of preserving and respecting cultural identities and values as part of the development
  process?

• Does the study of *Cry of the Forest* provide an *emic* or insider perspective on the importance of the meeting of "differently cultured minds" in the process of sustainable development? Chelsea Jones in "Sin Cultura No Hay Desarrollo Sostenible" ("Without Culture
  There Is No Sustainable Development") highlights the cultural *specificity* of sustainable
  development in noting that culture is an essential part of conflict and the resolution of
  conflict, the context, values, subjectivity, attitudes, and abilities that should generate the
  process of development. In your view, do SDGs 8, 11, and 16 allow for "inclusive" development in a way that sufficiently addresses the inclusion of marginalized as well as mainstream cultural voices? How do the SDGs target consistent and structured involvement of
  different cultural stakeholders as a marker of the sustainable development process?

V   Beyond Prosperity—Connections to SDGs on
Planet, People, and Partnerships

Beyond SDGs 8, 9, 10, 11, and 16, what additional SDGs are addressed by the collective indigenous production *Cry of the Forest*? Complete the table below with your ideas. Then compare
and contrast your ideas with a classmate.

SDGs:	*Does* Cry of the Forest *connect with additional SDGs? If so, which ones and how?*

SDG 1 No Poverty

SDG 2 Zero Hunger

SDG 3 Good Health and Well Being

SDG 4 Quality Education

SDG 5 Gender Equality

SDG 8 Decent Work and Economic Growth

SDG 9 Industry, Innovation, and Infrastructure

SDG 10 Reduced Inequalities

SDG 11 Sustainable Cities and Communities

SDG 12 Responsible Consumption and Production

SDG 16 Peace, Justice, and Strong Institutions

SDG 17 Partnerships for the Goals

VI   From Global to Local: On a Personal Level

1 How do you relate personally to the indigenous collaboration *Cry of the Forest*? Explain in detail how your own life experiences or personal beliefs intersect with the film's main ideas and themes.
2 How does *Cry of the Forest* relate to your local environment? Explain the global-local connection between *Cry of the Forest* and where you live. What place-based considerations permit or prevent the application of this filmic text to your geographical location?
3 What type of response did *Cry of the Forest* elicit in you? Are you moved to action? Explain why or why not. Have your viewpoints or attitudes changed? Explain.

VII   Assignments

1   Research

1 Throughout *Cry of the Forest* the themes of UN SDG 16 are echoed: the desire for peace, justice, and protection of rights under law as they clash with realities of exploitation, corruption, bribery, illegal trafficking, and violence. The film shows us how radically opposing views of "nature as wealth" are contrasted: nature as monetized *commodity* to be grabbed for disinterested profit vs. nature as a living, breathing *community* into which human life is

embedded and on which physical and spiritual well-being depends. As the film illustrates, in the indigenous world, to speak of environmental destruction is to speak of cultural destruction—the displacement and fragmentation of kinships, communities, and languages; the loss of biodiversity and the ancestral knowledge surrounding its healing properties; the extinction of biodiversity; the contamination of soil and water of ancestral lands; the corruption of values and rituals and the loss of sacred spaces and spiritual totems. Individually or in groups, select from the topics below to expand your knowledge of the issues and struggles of indigenous communities for sustainable development. Each topic includes a suggested "springboard" reading, referenced in the "Works Cited" section, that may be used to begin your investigation.

- **Deforesting the Amazon**. In addition to the unregulated logging activities witnessed in *Cry of the Forest,* what are the causes of deforestation in the Amazon? What are the consequences, local and global, of rainforest depletion? What measures are being taken to curb this destruction?

    Springboard reading: Butler, Rhett A., "Deforestation in the Amazon."
- **Self Determination and Indigenous Rights.** Chronicle the change-making *process* triggered by the March for Territory and Dignity that ultimately led to constitutional enshrinement of the indigenous imaginary. While SDG 8.4 charges the so-called "developed" world with leading the way to decouple economic growth from environmental degradation, how did Bolivia assume this leadership role? Passage of Bolivia's 1996 Forestry Law awarding collective land tenure was unusual in that it happened under a distinctly free-market capitalist government and was the result of over four years of discussion among multiple stakeholders. What groups were involved in this discussion and how does such a process respond to SDG 16.7 and its call for "participatory and representative decision-making" and to SDG 12.4 and its promotion of multi-stakeholder partnerships and "bottoms-up inclusive processes" ("Transforming Our World")?

    Springboard reading: Dockry, Michael J., and Nancy Langston. "Indigenous Protest and the Roots of Sustainable Forestry in Bolivia."
- **Bioprospecting, Biopiracy, and Biopatenting the Amazon.** In *Cry of the Forest,* we see the medicinal use of forest plants such as totai palm, cinchona, and macororo (castor plant) by experienced healers and also learn of the threats: not only the loss of biodiversity through irresponsible logging but also the loss of traditional knowledge of the curative qualities and healing procedures for using nature's medicines. Indeed, around 25% of all drugs in Western modern medicine are derived from rainforest plants; yet, less than 5% of Amazon plant species have been studied for their potential medicinal benefits ("Bioprospecting"). Bolivia's Constitution considers this ancestral knowledge and science "intellectual property" whose collective ownership is protected in use, promotion, and development. Yet, this knowledge is of great value to researchers exploring solutions and remedies to today's ills and Bolivia has been a constant target of bioprospecting as well as biopiracy. As Roger Carvajal explains: "Foreign scientists visit our indigenous communities in an effort to gain their ancestral learnings on plants and herbs [...] They later sell medicines and other products made from stolen species." How does the patenting and sale of indigenous knowledge impact indigenous communities? Individually or in groups, investigate the issues of bioprospecting, biopiracy, and biopatenting in the Amazon region. What are the challenges in preventing the theft of indigenous ancestral knowledge of nature's medicines? What regulations or ethical guidelines are/should be in place? How can this important knowledge be shared fairly and who should be compensated for its use? What legal frameworks are in

place nationally and internationally to regulate the theft of intellectual property as well as afford its compensated sharing in Bolivia? What role do the Nagoya Protocol and the Convention on Biological Diversity (CBD) play in this regard?

> **Springboard reading:** Takeshita, Chikako. "Bioprospecting and Its Discontents:Indigenous Resistances as Legitimate Politics."

- **Intercultural and Holistic Healthcare.** As seen in *Cry of the Forest*, Bolivia's rural indigenous peoples award high value and status to the community healer, who is seen to employ not only ancestral knowledge but unique spiritual connections and oracular powers. Investigate how traditional and modern biomedical systems are integrated in Bolivia, where the Constitution describes a "unitary" health system that includes "traditional medicine of the nations and rural native indigenous peoples" (*Political Constitution*). What is "intercultural healthcare"? On what premises is it based? How does it meet the indigenous right to "dignity"? How effective have intercultural healthcare networking initiatives been in Bolivia? What differences between indigenous and Western practices and belief systems do they expose? What are the sources of mistrust between traditional healers and biomedical staff? How is the necessary culture of collaboration created?

> **Springboard reading:** Torri, Maria Costanza, and Daniel Hollenberg. "Indigenous Traditional Medicine and Intercultural Healthcare in Bolivia: A Case Study from the Potosi Region."

- **Community Justice.** Bolivia's Constitution of 2009 grants indigenous systems of justice the same status as that of the State. What does this mean in practice? How does this fulfill Bolivia's mandate to become a "plurinational" society? How is such justice carried out in *Cry of the Forest* and by whom is it decreed? Investigate how communitarian systems of justice or "customary law" mesh with the formal legal systems of State law that is oriented toward individual rights. What limitations are put on the jurisdiction of community justice? What are some significant differences between community and State systems of justice in terms of philosophy, goal or intention, codification or standardization, types of punishment, flexibility, and predictability?

> **Springboard reading**: Hammond, John L. "Indigenous Community Justice in the Bolivian Constitution of 2009."

- **Gender Equality and Women's Movement.** How do Bolivia's indigenous and non-indigenist women's movements differ? What issues do they have in common? What has each accomplished? How do non-indigenous feminists view *chachawarmi*? Why do indigenous women see the "institutionalized culture" of the feminist movement as pitting women against men? Why is the debate over the origin of patriarchy significant to the mission of indigenous women activists? How have indigenous women achieved collective agency in Bolivia? What is the Bartolina movement and what is its mission?

> **Springboard reading**: Burman, Anders, "*Chachawarmi*: Silence and Rival Voices on Decolonisation and Gender Politics in Andean Bolivia."
>
> (The instructor of the course will determine the length, format, number of required sources, and other guidelines for conducting and presenting this research assignment.)

2　*Cry of the Forest* illustrates the value of radio broadcast in building the solidarity and activism of Bolivia's indigenous peoples in a grand movement toward dignity, self-determination, and territorial rights. Individually or in groups, research and compare this phenomenon with the motives, methods, and outcomes of indigenous mobilizations in one other country of Latin America, such as Guatemala, Ecuador, or Mexico. In the case of Mexico, the Zapatista movement, led by women, was the world's first application of the Internet by an indigenous community to build solidarity, momentum, and international recognition of the sustainable development issues of marginalized peoples. (The instructor of the course will determine the length, format, number of required sources, and other guidelines for conducting and presenting this research assignment.)

2 *Write*

1 **A cultural dimension.** Following Per Vortman's contention that the concept of sustainability must include a cultural dimension, develop a proposal for the preservation of diverse cultural values, identities, and dialogues as the 18th SDG. Keeping in mind the messages of *Cry of the Forest*, what might be some of the "targets" of Goal 18? What might be markers of progress? (The instructor of the course will determine the length, format, and other guidelines for this writing assignment.)

2 **An impact assessment.** As illustrated in Figure 10.15, at the intersection of four dimensions of sustainable development we might imagine a connective "dialogic center" where stakeholders' minds meet to share clashing perspectives and seek mutually acceptable resolution to identified problems. Such was the dialogue that took place in the development of Bolivia's 1996 Forestry Law and is the process urged throughout the SDGs. Sustainable Impact Assessment (SIA) is an approach for exploring through the voices of stakeholders the combined impacts of decisions and actions on each of four dimensions of sustainable development. Develop an impact assessment for the meeting of Marita Lumber and the community of Nueva Esperanza that analyzes the issues connected to the company's proposed timber harvest. As you seek a sustainable solution to meet the needs of both parties,

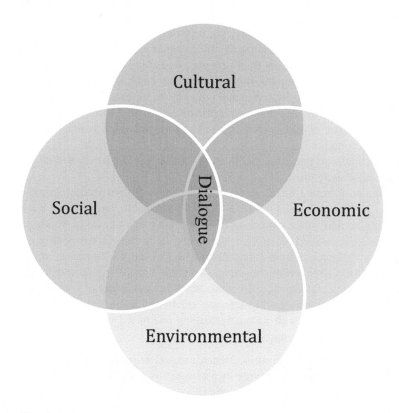

Figure 10.15 The dialogic center of four interdependent dimension of sustainable development.

aim to consider all impact areas, as suggested by the Organization for Economic Cooperation and Development (OECD 4–6): long-term as well as short term; indirect as well as direct; global and national as well as local; and all four dimensions, including cultural. Who are the additional stakeholders, including different generations, and what questions will they ask? What related problems need to be addressed? Alternatively, develop an SIA for a "wicked problem" in your school or campus community. (The instructor of the course will determine the length, format, and other guidelines for this writing assignment.)

3   Create

1   Choose from the following performative projects and highlight relevant SDGs as appropriate.

- **Help Nueva Esperanza develop a Community Based Ecotourism (CBE) program.** Imagining the community of Nueva Esperanza as a potential venue, work in a team to guide and engage the class as *comunarios* in discussion of issues to consider from a tourist perspective before setting up a sustainability-oriented CBE program. Begin by anticipating and recognizing some of the villagers' concerns and hesitations as you compile the benefits of such a community venture. Be realistic in discussing tourist needs in areas such as housing, food, transport, and essential facilities; include activities and types of learning that match *comunarios'* knowledge and skills. Anticipate the types of training the community will need; suggest tourist rules and prohibitions (such as no cameras). Calculate manageable size of tourist group and include room for brainstorming about community use of program profit and even for suggesting specific community members of Nueva Esperanza who might be in charge of specific areas of operation. To enhance your understanding of what is involved in designing and operating a CBE program, read about one indigenous community's experience in Peredo and Wurzelmann's "Indigenous Tourism and Social Entrepreneurship in the Bolivian Amazon: Lessons from San Miguel del Bala" and visit the San Miguel del Bala Ecolodge website.
- **Make your own *cine propio*.** Himpele describes *cine propio* as produced by and for local communities on their own topics and issues to "represent their identities, fortify their cultures" and "make perceptible the co-presence of visible and invisible forms and forces" (356). In a team, develop a short skit or film on a such a theme that you have identified in your own community.
  (The instructor of the course will determine the length, format, and other guidelines for this creative assignment.)

2   The Bolivian Forestry Research Institute (Instituto Boliviano de Investigación Forestal) sponsors a "Future Forest Challenge" to build leadership, amplify the voice for a sustainable lifestyle, and foster entrepreneurial leadership in indigenous youth. Proposals from young indigenous entrepreneurs for sustainable forest-based businesses have included such projects as the production of furniture and bricks from the residue of sustainable logging activities; the conversion of everyday waste into functioning robots; the development of an online trading platform for forest products; the translation of Facebook into Aymara to reconnect youth with ancestral roots; the creation of high fashion inspired by traditional Moxeno design. Work with a team to develop one of the following "Future Forest" challenges, highlighting relevant SDGs as appropriate.

- **Sustainable entrepreneurship.** Sketch out and propose a place-based product, procedure, or service arising from your own community context and compatible with your own culture that will promote a sustainable lifestyle.

- **Promoting a perspective**. Target your campus or a local park as your venue for a poster or signage campaign against "plant blindness." You may choose to focus on drawing attention and education about specific features of an overlooked plant world, but your campaign should be designed to help visitors and passers-by "see" nature as it is perceived in the indigenous worldview as more than fresh air and a scenic view. Do not forget to include a memorable slogan in your campaign.

(The instructor of the course will determine the format, presentation mode, length, and other guidelines for this creative project.)

Works Cited

Avilés Irahola, Dennis. "Decolonial Feminism and Buen Vivir." *Radical Ecological Democracy*, 13 Apr. 2022, https://radicalecologicaldemocracy.org/decolonial-feminism-and-buen-vivir/. Accessed 28 Mar. 2023.

"Bioprospecting South American Flora as a Source of Bioactive Compounds with Pharmacological and Biotechnological Potential." *Frontiers*, Apr. 2023, https://www.frontiersin.org/research-topics/30892/bioprospecting-south-american-flora-as-a-source-of-bioactive-compounds-with-pharmacological-and-biotechnological-potential.

Burman, Anders. "*Chachawarmi*: Silence and Rival Voices on Decolonisation and Gender Politics in Andean Bolivia." *Journal of Latin American Studies*, vol. 43, no. 1, 2011, pp. 65–91. https://doi.org/10.1017/s0022216x10001793.

Butler, Rhett A. "Deforestation in the Amazon." *Mongabay*, 22 Nov. 2021, https://rainforests.mongabay.com/amazon/amazon_destruction.html. Accessed 28 Mar. 2023.

Dockry, Michael J., and Nancy Langston. "Indigenous Protest and the Roots of Sustainable Forestry in Bolivia." *Environmental History*, vol. 24, no. 1, 2019, pp. 52–77, https://doi.org/10.1093/envhis/emy090.

Dunn, Caroline. "Gender Disparity and Women's Rights in Bolivia." *The Borgen Project*, https://borgenproject.org/womens-rights-in-bolivia/. Accessed 28 Mar. 2023.

"Framework Law of Mother Earth and Integral Development to Live Well, October 15, 2012." *Document-Cloud*, https://www.documentcloud.org/documents/7220617-Framework-Law-of-Mother-Earth-and-Integral (Google-translated versión of original found at S.R.L./LexiVox, DeveNet. "Bolivia: Ley Marco De La Madre Tierra y Desarrollo Integral Para Vivir Bien, 15 De Octubre De 2012." *Bolivia: Ley Marco De La Madre Tierra y Desarrollo Integral Para Vivir Bien*, 15 De Octubre De 2012, https://www.lexivox.org/norms/BO-L-N300.xhtml?+dcmi_identifier=BO-L-N300&format=xhtm.) Accessed 28 Mar. 2023.

Gagliano, Monica. "Seeing Green: The Re-Discovery of Plants and Nature's Wisdom." *The Green Thread: Dialogues with the Vegetal World*, edited by Patricia Vieira et al., Lexington Books, Lanham, 2016, pp. 19–35.

Hammond, John L. "Indigenous Community Justice in the Bolivian Constitution of 2009." *Human Rights Quarterly*, vol. 33, no. 3, 2011, pp. 649–681, https://doi.org/10.1353/hrq.2011.0030.

Hance, Jeremy. "Losing Nature's Medicine Cabinet." *Mongabay Environmental News*, 27 Nov. 2017, http://news.mongabay.com/2010/10/losing-natures-medicine-cabinet. Accessed 28 Mar. 2023.

Haynes, Nell. "Indigenous Women's Engagements with Technology: From Anomaly to Autonomy." *Platypus*, May 2018, https://blog.castac.org/2018/05/autonomy/. Accessed 28 Mar. 2023.

Himpele, Jeff. "Packaging Indigenous Media: An Interview with Ivan Sanjinés and Jesús Tapia." *American Anthropologist*, vol. 106, no. 2, 2004, pp. 354–363, https://doi.org/10.1525/aa.2004.106.2.354.

Holloway, Geoff. *Ecocentrism - Researchgate*. Apr. 2016, https://www.researchgate.net/profile/Geoff-Holloway/publication/332138102_Ecocentrism/links/5ca2bb6e299bf1116956b324/Ecocentrism.pdf?origin=publication_detail.

Horn, Philipp. "Diverse Articulations of Urban Indigeneity among Lowland Indigenous Groups in Santa Cruz, Bolivia." *Bulletin of Latin American Research*, vol. 41, no. 1, 2021, pp. 37–52, https://doi.org/10.1111/blar.13284.

Høyme, Malin. "Ecotourism in Bolivia: An Ethnographical Study of Ecotourism Impacts in Madidi National Park." *Academia.edu*, 9 Apr. 2018, https://www.academia.edu/36367982/Ecotourism_in_Bolivia_An_ethnographical_study_of_ecotourism_impacts_in_Madidi_National_Park.

Instituto Boliviano de Investigacion Forestal, https://ibifbolivia.org.bo/. Accessed 28 Mar. 2023.

Inter-Parliamentary Union. "Women in Parliament in 2020: The Year in Review." *International Knowledge Network of Women in Politics*, 2021, https://www.iknowpolitics.org/sites/default/files/2020-women_in_parliament_en.pdf.

Jones, Chelsea. "Cultura Para El Desarrollo Sostenible." *UNESCO*, 30 Sept. 2019, https://es.unesco.org/themes/cultura-desarrollo-sostenible. Accessed 28 Mar. 2023.

Kemp, Simon. "Digital 2022: Bolivia - DataReportal – Global Digital Insights." *DataReportal*, DataReportal – Global Digital Insights, 15 Feb. 2022, https://datareportal.com/reports/digital-2022-bolivia. Accessed 28 Mar. 2023.

Leyva Martínez, Yaima. "Iván Sanjinés: Toward the New Indigenous Perspectives." *La Fundación Del Nuevo Cine Latinoamericano*, http://cinelatinoamericano.org/texto.aspx?cod=2829. Accessed 28 Mar. 2023.

Maclean, Kate. "*Chachawarmi*: Rhetorics and Lived Realities." *Bulletin of Latin American Research*, vol. 33, no. 1, 2013, pp. 76–90, https://doi.org/10.1111/blar.12071.

Matsuura, Koïchiro. "Message from Mr Koïchiro Matsuura, Director-General of UNESCO." *UNESCO*, World Day for Cultural Diversity for Dialogue and Development, May 2009, https://en.unesco.org/links. Accessed 28 Mar. 2023.

OECD. "Guidance on Sustainability Impact Assessment." *OECD ILibrary*, Organization for Economic Cooperation and Development, 5 Jul. 2010, https://www.oecd-ilibrary.org/environment/guidance-on-sustainability-impact-assessment_9789264086913-en.

Peredo, Bernardo, and Samuel Wurzelmann. "Indigenous Tourism and Social Entrepreneurship in the Bolivian Amazon: Lessons from San Miguel Del Bala." *International Indigenous Policy Journal*, vol. 6, no. 4, 2015, pp. 88–98, https://doi.org/10.18584/iipj.2015.6.4.5.

Pittman, Thea. "Sumak Kawsay and the Sustainable Development Agenda: Critical Debates and Creative Responses from a Latin American Indigenous Perspective." *UK Research and Innovation*, https://gtr.ukri.org/projects?ref=AH%2FR004242%2F1. Accessed 28 Mar. 2023.

Political Constitution of the Plurinational State of Bolivia 2009. Oxford UP, Comparative Constitutions Project: Max Planck Institute, www.constituteproject.org/constitution/Bolivia_2009.pdf. Accessed 28 Mar. 2023.

Rousseau, Stéphanie. "Indigenous and Feminist Movements at the Constituent Assembly in Bolivia: Locating the Representation of Indigenous Women." *Latin American Research Review*, vol. 46, no. 2, 2011, pp. 5–28, https://doi.org/10.1353/lar.2011.0020.

Sanjines, Ivan, et al., directors. *Cry of the Forest (Grito De La Selva)*. Centro De Formación y Realización Cinematográfica (CEFREC), Bolivia, 2008.

Srinivasan, Ramesh, and Juan Ramos-Martín. "Double Codes: Community Radio in Bolivia." *The Information Society*, vol. 34, no. 5, 2018, pp. 289–301, https://doi.org/10.1080/01972243.2018.1497742.

Takeshita, Chikako. "Bioprospecting and Its Discontents: Indigenous Resistances as Legitimate Politics." *Alternatives: Global, Local, Political*, vol. 26, no. 3, 2001, pp. 259–282, https://doi.org/10.1177/030437540102600302.

Torri, Maria Costanza, and Daniel Hollenberg. "Indigenous Traditional Medicine and Intercultural Healthcare in Bolivia: A Case Study from the Potosi Region." *Journal of Community Health Nursing*, vol. 30, no. 4, 2013, pp. 216–229, https://doi.org/10.1080/07370016.2013.838495.

"Transforming Our World: The 2030 Agenda for Sustainable Development." *United Nations Department of Economic and Social Affairs*, https://sdgs.un.org/2030agenda. Accessed 28 Mar. 2023.

Vandebroek, Ina et al. "Use of Medicinal Plants and Pharmaceuticals by Indigenous Communities in the Bolivian Andes and Amazon." *Bulletin of the World Health Organization*, World Health Organization, 1 Apr. 2004, https://www.scielosp.org/article/bwho/2004.v82n4/243-250/.

Vortman, Per. "'Promoting a Sustainable Nordic Region through Strong Cultural Partnerships.'" *Nordic Culture Point*, 16 Feb. 2023, https://www.nordiskkulturkontakt.org/en/. Accessed 28 Mar. 2023.

Wandersee, James H., and Elisabeth E. Schussler. "Preventing Plant Blindness." *The American Biology Teacher*, vol. 61, no. 2, 1999, pp. 82–86, https://doi.org/10.2307/4450624.

Zamorano Villarreal, Gabriela. *Indigenous Media and Political Imaginaries in Contemporary Bolivia.* U of Nebraska P, 2017.

11 Hao Jingfang's "Folding Beijing"

Unequal Time and Space in a Dystopian City

Lu Liu

I Text

Title	"Folding Beijing"
Genre	Science fiction short story
Author	Born in 1984, Hao Jingfang graduated from Tsinghua University in the People's Republic of China with a B.S. and M.S. in physics and a Ph.D. in economics. She is currently working in the China Development Research Foundation think tank, where she organizes research and non-profit projects concerning China's urbanization, rural education, and the impact of artificial intelligence. In her spare time, Hao writes both science fiction and nonfiction. Recognized by the prestigious Hugo Award as the 2016 Best Novelette, "Folding Beijing" brought her both domestic and international reputation as the first Chinese female writer to win this award. In 2020, Hao's sci-fi novel *Vagabonds* was translated by Ken Liu and published by Saga Press.
Year	2012
Country	China

In the sci-fi story "Folding Beijing," the overcrowded city has been technologically transformed into three segregated zones. Half of Beijing is assigned to the upper class as the First Space, and 5 million residents can enjoy 24 hours, abundant natural and social resources, and a carefully constructed pastoral landscape. When the day of the First Space ends, the earth flips to the Second Space, where 25 million people of the middle class, including white collars and university students, are allocated 16 hours from 6 a.m. to 10 p.m. Sharply at 10 p.m., the change takes place once again, putting the Second Space into sleep and waking up 50 million of the lower-class people residing in their cocoons in the Third Space. These peddlers, janitors, and waste workers toil at night in intensive-labor occupations. The protagonist Lao Dao, a waste worker from the Third Space, breaks out of the boundary to the Second and First Spaces in order to raise money for his adopted daughter Tangtang's education. His mission is to deliver a love message from Qin Tian, a graduate student from the Second Space, to his sweetheart Yi Yan in the First Space. During his 48-hour journey, Lao Dao, for the first time, explores the two other zones and gradually realizes the hidden disparities in the folding city.

Published initially on Tsinghua University's online forum in 2012, "Folding Beijing" was reprinted in China's leading literary journal *Fiction Monthly* the next year and was translated to English by Ken Liu in 2015. It is available online at *Uncanny Magazine*'s website (https://www.uncannymagazine.com/article/folding-beijing-2/) and collected into *Invisible Planets* with other Chinese sci-fi short stories. Although "Folding Beijing" has been characterized as both a short story and a novella, this chapter will treat it as an anthologized short story.

DOI: 10.4324/9781003388869-15

II Context

Set in the context of China's explosive economic growth and urbanization, "Folding Beijing" critically reflects on China's structural inequalities and discrimination against urban working classes, which are often overshadowed by the spectacular GDP, skyscrapers, and an expanding and vocal middle class. In a short article written after winning the Hugo Award, Hao summarizes "Folding Beijing" as a literary precursor to "a history of inequality," a subject that has long interested Hao since she was an undergraduate student:

> I've been troubled by inequality for a long time. When I majored in physics as an undergraduate, I once stared at the distribution curve for American household income that showed profound inequality, and tried to fit the data against black–body distribution or Maxwell–Boltzmann distribution. I wanted to know how such a curve came about, and whether it implied some kind of universality: something as natural as particle energy distribution functions, so natural it led to despair. (Hao, "I Want to Write a History of Inequality")

Deeply informed by Hao's expertise in both physics and economics, "Folding Beijing" amalgamates "scientific fantasy" (the literal translation of sci-fi in Chinese) and sharp social critiques. The result is a quasi-social experiment, albeit fictionally, that provides one of many possibilities to project the future if the roots of inequality continue to grow unchecked. "Folding Beijing" thus attempts a "vivid…yet not the most important" answer to the two overarching questions: "Why do we have inequality in the world? And why is it so hard to eliminate?" (Hao, "I Want to Write a History of Inequality").

On the other hand, the rich, realistic details from the story, from haggling at a wet market to bureaucracy in government organs, are indebted to Hao's observation of everyday life. The origin of the story, she recounts elsewhere, is "an image":

> One morning, I was shopping at a street market just like the one described at the start of the story: Crowded, chaotic, dirty, lively, full of cheap goods piled up everywhere. Everyone was devoted to the task of bargaining. I thought then that Beijing was a city divided into multiple groups who did not interact at all in daily life. They had completely different lifestyles, habits, and socializing spaces—in fact, they rarely even met. (Stanish)

The paradoxical cohabitation of strangers within the same space lies at the kernel of the story's dramatic setting.

III Interpretation

1 In "Folding Beijing," people live in segregated chronotopes with uneven access to space and time. What are the rationales and standards of spatial and temporal divisions? How does temporality modify our understanding of segregation or apartheid, which is often spatially based? Is this speculative element of uneven time relevant to the real world? Identify where the two motifs of time and space repeatedly appear in the story and what facets or dimensions are accentuated. How does the distribution of time and space structure inequality in labor, income, education, natural resources, urban landscape, infrastructure, technology, mobility, and representation? Which aspect(s) of the inequality surprise you the most and why?

2 Who has successfully transgressed administrative and spatial boundaries in the story? Compare their different routes, motives, and means. What does the division symbolize, and what

are possible interpretations of these transgressions? The story ends with Lao Dao returning to the Third Space after his 48-hour adventure, where the formerly mesmerized zone starts to wake up as if nothing happened. Do you think the ending is conservative or fatalistic? Despite the seeming tranquility, what changes does Lao Dao's trip bring?

3   Rationality and irrationality drive forward the plot of "Folding Beijing," where many characters straddle between a moral or affective situation, on the one hand, and an economic or utilitarian position, on the other. Examine the motives, actions, and struggles of Lao Dao, Peng Li, Yi Yan, and Lao Ge. How are their actions and choices underlined at once by calculation, quantification, sensibility, and interpersonal connections? What is your interpretation of their prevalent dilemma?

4   Identify and analyze the metaphors and imagery that suggest people in the Third Space, such as Lao Dao, are dehumanized. Does dehumanization only occur in this zone? Are non-animate beings anthropomorphized or even personalized? How do you make sense of the blurred boundary between humans and nonhumans in the story? What are the relationships between people, machines, and infrastructure?

5   "Folding Beijing" briefly mentions a fourth group of people in addition to people living in the three zones: truck drivers moving on the Seventh Ring Road outside the municipal boundary of the three zones that encompass six ring roads:

> The break in the highway was just outside the Seventh Ring Road, while all the ground rotation occurred within the Sixth Ring Road. The distance was perfect for taking in the whole city, like gazing at an island in the sea.
>
> In the early dawn, the city folded and collapsed. The skyscrapers bowed submissively like the humblest servants until their heads touched their feet; then they broke again, folded again, and twisted their necks and arms, stuffing them into the gaps. The compacted blocks that used to be the skyscrapers shuffled and assembled into dense, gigantic Rubik's Cubes that fell into a deep slumber.
>
> The ground then began to turn. Square by square, pieces of the earth flipped 180 degrees around an axis, revealing the buildings on the other side. The buildings unfolded and stood up, awakening like a herd of beasts under the gray-blue sky. The island that was the city settled in the orange sunlight, spread open, and stood still as misty gray clouds roiled around it.
>
> The truck drivers, tired and hungry, admired the endless cycle of urban renewal.
> (Hao, "Folding Beijing" 229–230)

How is the group of truck drivers depicted? Perform a close reading analysis of the above passage. Why is this group important? Compare them with Lao Dao, who, as the second generation of Beijing's migrant workers, is the city's permanent resident by birth, yet has since then been confined in the Third Space. What are the similarities and differences between the two groups? How are they differently disenfranchised, victimized, and/or empowered?

6   The high official vetoes Wu Wen's proposal for an automated waste management system, not out of consideration for the livelihood in the Third Space but to maintain social stability derived from restraining the unemployment rate. Lao Dao's job seems to be out of pity from the First Space. His labor, not contributing to social productivity and economic development, has become "surplus labor" in late capitalism. Ironically, Marxist theory states that surplus value over the value of wage workers' labor constitutes profit in capitalism. What is your interpretation of the transition from creating surplus value to becoming surplus labor? Is the labor of people like Lao Dao exchangeable and disposable in a world of mechanization and technological innovation?

7   Alienation is people's sense of estrangement from the world they live in. Marxism understands alienation in terms of labor and its product in the form of the commodity in the capitalist society, that is, the laborer sells their labor for a wage and loses ownership of the product. Where do we see the two senses of alienation, from one's environment and from one's labor, in "Folding Beijing"? In Lao Dao's case, his job is to process the waste from the other two Spaces' consumption instead of producing any commodity. Does waste processing create value? You may wish to refer to Jin Liu's chapter in this same Part for points of comparison.

8   On top of Hao Jingfang's description of the three Spaces, continue to conceptualize the folding city's infrastructural mechanism and operations. What industries, institutions, and government organs do they have? What does everyday life look like? How are material, economic, and social relations maintained within and across the Spaces? What kind of technology does it require? Consider a specific scenario such as online shopping, food deliveries, or K-12 education and discuss the nuts and bolts of how this would work in this imaginative sci-fi world.

9   Is "Folding Beijing" utopian or dystopian? Do utopia and dystopia always conflict with each other? How do they co-exist in the story? Is their co-existence inevitable in the self-betterment of human society? Watch Hao Jingfang's acceptance speech for the Hugo Award on YouTube, where she refused to cast "Folding Beijing" as simply bleak or dystopian: "I also gave a scenario of a possible future. All humans have to face the problem of automation, technological development, unemployment, inequality and other issues. In my story I give one of the solutions—a quite dark one. Obviously, it's not the optimal one. However, it's also not the worst one" ("2016 Hugo Awards—Best Novelette," 3:53–4:46). How does "Folding Beijing" engage with both utopian and dystopian genres?

10 Among the Chinese readership, "Folding Beijing" is sometimes critiqued as neither science fictional enough nor literary enough. What does the reception say about the reader's assumptions of science fiction and literature? Find examples and analyze what specifically about the texts may have induced such evaluations, for instance, the subject matter, narrative structure, voice, tone, imagery, and language style. What is your reading response and assessment? What effects does such a hybrid "neither-nor" style create? Why do you think Hao Jingfang wrote a sci-fi story in this way? Recently, Chinese sci-fi writers and scholars started exploring the concept of "science fictional realism," stressing the complicated relationship between sci-fi writings, the development of science and technology, and the social commentary and critique that sci-fi affords (Song xiii–xv, Healey 6). Where do you find elements of science fictional realism in "Folding Beijing"? How does the new analytical perspective broaden your understanding of science fiction in general?

IV   Prosperity-Focused Applications to SDGs 8, 9, 10, 11, and 16

1   SDG 8 promotes "sustained, inclusive and sustainable economic growth, full and productive employment and decent work for all" ("SDG Goal 8"). How do the tensions between economic growth, productive employment, and decent work unfold in "Folding Beijing"? What does "full and productive employment" entail? In the Third Space, everyone has their job, and sustaining a high employment rate is set as the top priority. What is sacrificed if the employment rate is the sole indicator?

2   The second target of SDG 8 is to "achieve higher levels of economic productivity through diversification, technological upgrading and innovation, including through a focus on high-value added and labour-intensive sectors" ("SDG Goal 8"). How does "Folding Beijing" engage with this target? What roles do science and technology play in sustained, inclusive,

and sustainable economic growth? When do science and technology solve problems and when do they threaten sustainable development in the story?

With these questions in mind, re-read Lao Ge's explanation to Lao Dao regarding the challenge of automation:

> This kind of automation is absolutely necessary if you want to grow your economy—that was how we caught up to Europe and America, remember? Scaling! The problem is, now that you've gotten the people off the land and out of the factories, what are you going to do with them? In Europe they went with the path of forcefully reducing everyone's working hours and thus increasing employment opportunities. But this saps the vitality of the economy, you understand?

In contrast, Beijing adopts a different approach:

> The best way is to reduce the time a certain portion of the population spends living, and then find ways to keep them busy. Do you get it? Right, shove them into the night. There's another advantage to this approach: the effects of inflation almost can't be felt at the bottom of the social pyramid. Those who can get loans and afford the interest spend all the money you print. The GDP goes up, but the cost of basic necessities does not. And most people won't even be aware of it. (Hao, "Folding Beijing" 256)

In small groups, expand the conversation between Wu Wen and the senior official on the potential impacts of automatic waste processing. Then, insert a third voice of Lao Dao, speaking from the perspective of waste workers.

3   SDG 8.5 aims to achieve "equal pay for work of equal value" and eliminate gender, age, and disability discrimination. Once a construction worker in the folding city, Lao Dao's father was fortunate enough to be one of the few "strong, skillful, discerning, organized, diligent, and unafraid of the stench or difficult environment" candidates for permanent residents (Hao, "Folding Beijing" 231). What was Lao Dao's father rewarded for his labor? Why was Lao Dao's father so eager to settle in Beijing? Do you think he received equal pay for work of equal value?

4   The mission of SDG 9 is to "build resilient infrastructure, promote inclusive and sustainable industrialization and foster innovation" ("SDG Goal 9"). Scholars of infrastructural criticism argue that infrastructure embodies the ideological roots of socio-economic production. What infrastructure does "Folding Beijing" depict, and how is infrastructure represented? How does infrastructure reflect and reinforce inequality?

5   SDG 10 focuses on "reducing inequality within and among countries" ("SDG Goal 10"). In an interview, Hao Jingfang talked about what inspired her writing: "In today's society, although people might live in the same city, their lives are very different, and they have little connection to one another. I wanted to show this in the story in a more direct way—the idea that people live together but can't see one another. I want people to realize that there are so many invisible people in their lives. And also that their decisions, no matter how harmless or small they may seem, might have a huge and irreversible impact on other people's lives" (Hernández and Kan). In "Folding Beijing," not only are people in the Third Space isolated from truths about the other two Spaces, but the banquet celebrating 50 years of the folding city also makes the Third Space and its people invisible in the visualization of Beijing's technologized infrastructure, built and maintained by construction workers, waste workers, and blue collars—laborers like Lao Dao and his father.

At the banquet, when Lao Dao searches for traces of the city's construction in vain, he cannot help but reminisces about his father's repetitive storytelling and an old photo of his father laying bricks. What is made invisible here, and for what purposes? Why is visibility so significant in addressing inequality? Does "Folding Beijing" propose any solution to the invisibility of inequality?

6 How does "Folding Beijing" dramatize the following targets of SDG 10? What is the effect of addressing inequality through the sci-fi genre?

- Social, economic, and political inclusion (10.2)
- Balanced distribution of opportunity and resources (10.3)
- Equality-promoting policy-making (10.4)
- Representation and voice for under-developed areas (10.6)
- Orderly, safe, regular, and responsible migration and mobility of people (10.7)

7 What is structural inequality? Analyze the structural inequality and systemic violence in "Folding Beijing" by examining (1) the intersectionality of gender, age, class, and rural–urban divide and (2) the intersectionality of environmental, social, political, and economic sustainability.

8 With a focus on "making cities and human settlements inclusive, safe, resilient, and sustainable," SDG 11's first target is to improve housing conditions and upgrade slums ("SDG Goal 11"). As a by-product of the city, slums have been expanding at a pace superseding urbanization since the 1970s (Davis). Do you see slums in "Folding Beijing"? How are future slums projected in the story deviant from our common conceptualization? Are there similar "new slums" in today's urban spaces?

9 SDG 11 emphasizes "participatory, integrated and sustainable settlement planning and management" in its third target ("SDG Goal 11"). How do you evaluate the planning of the folding city, where key phrases such as "green economy" and "recycling economy" resonate at both the First-Space banquet and the Third-Space waste-processing station? Instead of reducing inequalities, why do these eco-friendly modes of the economy seem to be accomplices of central planning? If the two slogans are not mere lip service, deep irony is that the green economy and recycling economy may perpetuate inequalities and border on a pet project of people in the First and Second Spaces. Why? How does "Folding Beijing" challenge our techno-optimism toward practices and policies such as recycling, green transportation, and the smart city?

10 SDG 11 also explicitly addresses urban waste management in its sixth target, which states the need "by 2030, [to] reduce the adverse per capita environmental impact of cities, including by paying special attention to air quality and municipal and other waste management" ("SDG Goal 11"). In "Folding Beijing," the setting of waste processing in the otherwise invisible Third Space reflects the reality that by the early 2010s, 11 legal landfills and over 500 illegal dumping sites had encircled Beijing to process waste produced by the metropolis continuously. These hidden sites, never shown on any map of Beijing, are aesthetically photographed, carefully marked on satellite images, and documented by filmmaker Wang Jiuliang, out of which came the documentary *Beijing Besieged by Waste* (2011). Check Jin Liu's chapter in this Part for more information on waste processing and recycling in contemporary China. In what ways is Beijing's waste management inspirational to the depiction of the Third Space in "Folding Beijing"? What are some consequences of disconnecting urban life from the refuse it produces? Search what happened to these dumping sites following the release of Wang Jiuliang's documentary: is it a good solution? Please explain.

11   China's official household registration system or *hukou* system differentiates rural and urban population by linking one's social welfare, housing, education, and even employment opportunity to a *hukou* location inherited from that of one's parents. The change of one's *hukou* location is possible but could be non-transparent, sometimes with great barriers and complex administrative procedures. How does "Folding Beijing" implicitly refer to and speculatively dramatize the hukou system? In light of SDG 16, which specifically targets at promoting legal identity for all and enforcing "non-discriminatory laws and policies for sustainable development" ("SDG Goal 16"), evaluate the social consequences of the *hukou* system in the story.

12   While the rural landscape is nowhere to be seen in "Folding Beijing" except for the pastoral, idealized, and artificial nature in the First Space, the boundary between the city and the countryside is never so clearcut in Chinese cities. In mega-cities such as Beijing and Shenzhen, many migrant workers live in what is called "urban villages," overcrowded shantytowns developed out of "informal urbanization" and hidden beneath the skyscrapers and neon lights (Poon). Working in menial jobs such as waiters, construction workers, and security guards and providing cheap labor for urban prosperity, these migrant workers are often denied basic welfare due to their lack of a city *hukou* and stigmatized as "rat people" living in "dirty, messy, low quality," and unsafe areas (Saint-Paul). Such biases against urban villages were reinforced in 2017, when a tragic fire in a Beijing urban village killed 19 migrant workers and led to the municipality's directive of "cleaning out low-end population." Almost overnight, the village was demolished and migrant workers were evicted (Goldkorn). As critiques of the movement were soon censored from the mass media, the phrase "folding Beijing" was strategically deployed as a substitute phrase for the abject conditions of the urban poor.
       What environmental, social, economic, and political issues related to the SDGs from Part 3 do China's urban villages and the "cleaning out low-end population" movement unveil? Read the articles by Poon and Goldkorn if necessary for more information. In what ways could urban villages serve as a source of inspiration for Hao Jingfang's depiction of the Third Space? What does the naming of "low-end" suggest about the municipality and the public impression of migrant workers? Do you find similar stereotypes in "Folding Beijing"?

13   Science fiction is said to be heterotopia *par excellence*. According to the philosopher Michel Foucault, "heterotopia," literally "other (*hetero-*) spaces," are spaces that represent, contest, and distort reality. Different from utopian perfection and dystopian darkness, heterotopias are spaces of "alternate ordering" that "organize a bit of the social world in a way different to that which surrounds them" and "mark them out as Other and allows them to be seen as an example of an alternative way of doing things" (Hetherington, qtd in Lacey 12). Through its imperfect representation, heterotopia embraces plurality and diversity and challenges the production of social reality as natural and inevitable. Foucault uses the metaphor of the mirror to characterize the differences between utopia and heterotopia:

> The mirror is, after all, a utopia, since it is a placeless place. In the mirror, I see myself there where I am not, in an unreal, virtual space that opens up behind the surface; I am over there, there where I am not, a sort of shadow that gives my own visibility to myself, that enables me to see myself there where I am absent: such is the utopia of the mirror. But it is also a heterotopia in so far as the mirror does exist in reality, where it exerts a sort of counteraction on the position that I occupy. From the standpoint of the mirror I discover my absence from the place where I am since I see myself over there. Starting from this gaze that is, as it were, directed toward me, from the ground of this virtual space that is on the other side of the glass, I come back toward myself; I begin again to direct my eyes toward myself and to reconstitute myself there where I am. The mirror functions as

a heterotopia in this respect: it makes this place that I occupy at the moment when I look at myself in the glass at once absolutely real, connected with all the space that surrounds it, and absolutely unreal, since in order to be perceived it has to pass through this virtual point which is over there. (Foucault 24)

In other words, utopia/dystopia concerns what science fiction depicts, while heterotopia concerns the relations between the sci-fi text and the world surrounding it. How does "Folding Beijing" engage with the social, economic, and political reality of contemporary Chinese society? What changes does heterotopia bring?

14 Divide the class into five groups and assign one of the SDGs from Part 3 (8, 9, 10, 11, or 16) to each group. Each group will then prepare arguments for a debate in which they maintain that their assigned SDG is the most relevant or central to Hao Jingfang's "Folding Beijing." (The instructor of the course will decide on the format and length of the debate and facilitate a follow-up discussion with the class upon conclusion of the debate.)

15 Does Hao Jingfang's "Folding Beijing" only reinforce and illuminate the principles underpinning the UN SDGs and the concept of sustainable development, or does it question any inherent presuppositions, biases, shortcomings, flaws, or gaps in the UN SDG framework or the in the notion of sustainable development? Explain with details from the story.

V   Beyond Prosperity—Connections to SDGs on Planet, People, and Partnerships

Beyond SDGs 8, 9, 10, 11, and 16, what additional SDGs are addressed by Hao Jingfang in "Folding Beijing"? Complete the table below with your ideas. Then compare and contrast your ideas with a classmate.

SDGs:	Does "Folding Beijing" connect with additional SDGs? If so, which ones and how?
SDG 1 No Poverty	
SDG 2 Zero Hunger	
SDG 3 Good Health and Well Being	
SDG 4 Quality Education	
SDG 5 Gender Equality	
SDG 6 Clean Water and Sanitation	
SDG 7 Affordable and Clean Energy	
SDG 12 Responsible Consumption and Production	
SDG 13 Climate Action	
SDG 14 Life Below Water	
SDG 15 Life on Land	
SDG 17 Partnerships for the Goals	

VI   From Global to Local: On a Personal Level

1   How do you relate personally to Hao Jingfang's "Folding Beijing"? Explain in detail how your own life experiences or personal beliefs intersect with the main ideas and themes of the featured work in this chapter.
2   How does Hao Jingfang's "Folding Beijing" relate to your local environment? Explain the global-local connection between Hao Jingfang's "Folding Beijing" and your home or current residence. What place-based considerations permit or prevent the application of the text to your geographical location?
3   When asked about the impact of science fiction on real life, Hao answered that she hoped her work can "inspire people to imagine different futures, whether those futures are good or bad, bright or dark" (Gewirtz). What effect did "Folding Beijing" have on you as a reader? Did the sci-fi story motivate you to imagine different futures and did the imagination move you to action? If so, how? If not, why not? Have your viewpoints or attitudes changed? Explain.

VII   Assignments

1   Research

1   The spatial layout of the fictional Beijing is grounded on the city's multiple reconfigurations in history. Beijing as palimpsest consists of overlaying designs encompassing the symmetrical and harmonious diagram inherited from the Yuan (1271–1368), Ming (1368–1644), and Qing (1636–1911) dynasties, and the modernizing expansion and transformation that started in the Republican Era (1911–1949) and continued after the founding of the People's Republic of China (1949–present). Individually or in groups, choose one of the following stages in the modern history of Beijing's urban planning, research their guiding principles, controversies, and legacies with the help of the keywords, and evaluate the consequent urban transformation according to SDGs 8, 9, 10, 11, and 16.

   * Liang-Chen proposal in the early 1950s
   * Demolishment of *siheyuan* or courtyard and *hutong* under the market economy in the 1990s
   * Displacement of migrant workers and demolishment for Beijing Olympics in 2008
   * Xiong'an New Area under Xi Jinping

   (The instructor of the course will determine the mode of presentation and delivery—oral presentation, written report, short video documentary, digital timeline project, etc.—for this research assignment.)
2   Written in 2012, "Folding Beijing" presents a scenario of the future city transformed by technologized material infrastructure. The decade after its publication witnessed the explosive growth of digital infrastructure in China. Promoted by the state and aided by big tech companies, 5G technology, machine learning, big data, blockchain, and AI have collectively restructured China's urban everyday life and management. These newly emerged "smart cities" represent the latest trend of China's urbanization. Individually or in groups, investigate one aspect of digital infrastructure in Beijing and evaluate its impacts on SDGs 8, 9, 10, 11, and 16. (The instructor of the course will determine the mode of presentation and delivery— oral presentation, written report, short video documentary, digital timeline project, etc.—for this research assignment.)

2 Write

1   Write an essay that analyzes the co-existence of utopia (where everything is good), dystopia (where everything is bad), and heterotopia (an alternative space that mirrors, engages with, and predicts the future path of social reality) in "Folding Beijing." Pay attention to the text's literary and sci-fi elements. Integrate class discussions into your analytical writing. (The instructor of the course will determine the length and format of this writing assignment.)

2   Write a sequel to "Folding Beijing." Consider possible ramifications and unintended consequences of Lao Dao's illegal border-crossing trip, then focus on one to two aspects of what may or may not change to both the personal lives of characters in the story and/or the management of the city. Integrate class discussions into your creative writing. (The instructor of the course will determine the length and format of this writing assignment.)

3 Create

1   In small groups, students will creatively fold a city of their choice, taking into consideration and integrating the following aspects in their urban design:

- Number of zones
- Allocation of time, space, residents, and social and natural resources.
- Sustainability challenges that the city is currently facing and hopes to solve through the folding mechanism
- Connections to SDGs 8, 9, 10, 11, and 16
- Inter-zone communication and mobility
- Science and technology needed to maintain the folding city
- Specific landmarks

Each group will visualize or present their folding city to the class. (The instructor of the course will determine the appropriate length, format, and mode of delivery for this creative assignment.)

2   "Folding Beijing" draws attention to the invisibility of some people, spaces, occupations, discriminations, and environmental and social hazards related to SDGs 8, 9, 10, 11, and 16. Individually or in small groups, design a literary, artistic, or visualizing project addressing what is otherwise half-hidden or disconnected from where you live. In addition to "Folding Beijing," projects in Handshake 302, repurposed art space in a Shenzhen urban village, also provide a case in point ("Handshake 302"). (The instructor of the course will determine the appropriate length, format, and mode of delivery for this creative assignment.)

Works Cited

"2016 Hugo Awards - Best Novelette." *YouTube*, uploaded by Charles Tan, 20 Aug. 2016, https://www.youtube.com/watch?v=SKNuFDRnmEI. Accessed 12 Sep. 2022.

Davis, Mike. *Planet of Slums*. Verso, 2006.

Foucault, Michel. "Of Other Spaces." *Diacritics*, vol. 16, no. 1, 1986, pp. 22–27.

Gewirtz, Julian. "Uneven and Combined Development: Hao Jingfang on Building the Future." *Logic*, no. 7, 1 May 2019, https://logicmag.io/china/hao-jingfang-on-building-the-future/. Accessed 5 Dec. 2022.

Goldkorn, Jeremy. "The Week of Low-end Population." The China Project, 1 Dec. 2017, https://thechinaproject.com/2017/12/01/the-week-of-low-end-population/. Accessed 12 Sep. 2022.

"Handshake 302." Shenzhen Noted, https://shenzhennoted.com/czc-special-forces/. Accessed 12 Sep. 2022.

Hao, Jingfang. "Folding Beijing." *Invisible Planets: Contemporary Chinese Science Fiction in Translation*, edited and translated by Ken Liu, Tor Books, 2016, 219–262.

———. "I Want to Write a History of Inequality." Translated by Ken Liu, *Uncanny Magazine*, 6 Dec. 2016, https://www.uncannymagazine.com/article/want-write-history-inequality/. Accessed 12 Sep. 2022.

Healey, Cara. "Estranging Realism in Chinese Science Fiction: Hybridity and Environmentalism in Chen Qiufan's 'The Waste Tide.'" *Modern Chinese Literature and Culture*, vol. 29, no. 2, 2017, pp. 1–33.

Hernández, Javier C., and Karoline Kan. "Author's Vision of a Future Beijing Looks to China's Present." *New York Times*, 29 Nov. 2016, https://www.nytimes.com/2016/11/29/world/asia/china-hao-jingfang-science-fiction.html. Accessed 12 Sep. 2022.

Lacey, Lauren J. "Heterotopian Possibilities in Science Fictions by Stephen Baxter, Terry Pratchett, Samuel Delany and Ursula K. Le Guin." *Environments in Science Fiction: Essays on Alternate Spaces*, edited by Susan M. Bernando, McFarland & Company, 2014, pp. 10–27.

Poon, Linda. "Inside the Architecture of Shenzhen's Urban Villages." *Bloomberg*, 31 May 2016, https://www.bloomberg.com/news/articles/2016-05-31/inside-the-architecture-and-design-of-shenzhen-s-urban-villages. Accessed 12 Sep. 2022.

Saint-Paul, Patrick. *The Rat People: A Journey through Beijing's Forbidden Underground*. Translated by David Homel, Arsenal Pulp Press, 2020.

"SDG Goal 8." *United Nations Department of Economic and Social Affairs Sustainable Development*, 2022, https://sdgs.un.org/goals/goal8. Accessed 12 Sep. 2022.

"SDG Goal 9." *United Nations Department of Economic and Social Affairs Sustainable Development*, 2022, https://sdgs.un.org/goals/goal9. Accessed 12 Sep. 2022.

"SDG Goal 10." *United Nations Department of Economic and Social Affairs Sustainable Development*, 2022, https://sdgs.un.org/goals/goal10. Accessed 12 Sep. 2022.

"SDG Goal 11." *United Nations Department of Economic and Social Affairs Sustainable Development*, 2022, https://sdgs.un.org/goals/goal11. Accessed 12 Sep. 2022.

"SDG Goal 16." *United Nations Department of Economic and Social Affairs Sustainable Development*, 2022, https://sdgs.un.org/goals/goal16. Accessed 5 Dec. 2022.

Song, Mingwei. "Introduction: Does Science Fiction Dream of a Chinese New Wave?" *The Reincarnated Giant: An Anthology of Twenty-First-Century Chinese Science Fiction*, edited by Mingwei Song and Theodore Huters, Columbia University Press, 2018, pp. xi–xxi.

Stanish, Deborah. "Interview: Hao Jingfang." Translated by Ken Liu, *Uncanny Magazine*, 6 Dec. 2016, https://www.uncannymagazine.com/article/interview-hao-jingfang/. Accessed 12 Sep. 2022.

12 Wang Jiuliang's *Plastic China*

Unveiling the Façade of Prosperity

Jin Liu

I   Text

Title	*Plastic China*
Genre	Documentary film
Director	Born in 1976, Wang Jiuliang studied photography at the Communication University of China and works as an independent filmmaker and photographer in Beijing. He is one of the most acclaimed directors in Chinese ecocinema. He has made two powerful documentary films so far: *Beijing Besieged by Waste* (*Laji weicheng*, 2011) and *Plastic China* (*Suliao wangguo*, 2016). His latest short "Seagulls" (*Hai'ou*, 2021), a UN-sponsored project, documents the struggles that seagulls face as a result of deteriorated ocean ecology and pollution.
Year	2016
Country	China

The documentary film *Plastic China* is set in a small town in the coastal eastern Shandong Province in contemporary China. Over 50,000 workers toil in the town's 5,000 household-level plastic recycling factories. It follows two families who spend their lives sorting and recycling plastic waste from the United States, Europe, and Asia.

Peng's family, of the Yi ethnic minority group, migrated thousands of miles from a poor village in Sichuan Province in Southwest China in order to make a living. Their eldest daughter, 11-year-old Yijie, works alongside her illiterate parents in the recycling facility while yearning to go back to their hometown and to attend school. Their boss, Kun, is a high-school-educated young peasant native to the town. Under the enticing allure of money, he works as hard as his employees, aspiring to buy a new car and secure a better life for his family and a better education for his four-year-old son, Qiqi. In the end, Peng still cannot afford to buy train tickets for Yijie to return home. For Kun, although he eventually buys a new red sedan with the help of a loan, his health condition is deteriorated and his hometown is heavily polluted and thus inhabitable.

Through the experience of these two families, this poignant film explores issues of economic development and environmental pollution, unsustainable communities, social and regional inequality, women's education, and global capitalism and consumerism.

This documentary film, mainly in Mandarin and with English subtitles, is available to watch on streaming sites such as Amazon Prime Video, YouTube, the Roku Channel, and Kanopy. The 82-minute film version should be distinguished from the director's media version with the same title, *Plastic China*, which is a 26-minute video exposing the global trash business that can be accessed for free on YouTube via the link: https://youtu.be/rKEbGYTbLdg.

DOI: 10.4324/9781003388869-16

II   Context

China has been undergoing rapid economic growth and dramatic social transformation since the reform years, exemplifying the slogan popularized during the 1980s by the late Chinese leader Deng Xiaoping: "Development is the only indisputable truth." However, after more than three decades of economic reform, a growing environmental crisis, characterized by smog, polluted water, and contaminated produce, has become a new priority for the state and its citizens.

As a pioneering artist working with trash, Wang acutely observes how fast-paced industrialization, urban development, and consumer capitalism have resulted in the accelerated production of waste and the expansion of dumpsites. He investigated garbage disposal in the Beijing area from 2008 to 2011 and subsequently produced his first documentary *Beijing Besieged by Waste,* as well as a series of photographs with the same name. He traveled 15,000 kilometers (9,300 miles) on his motorbike and visited 460 legal and illegal landfill sites. He used Google Earth to locate these sites, which formed a huge circle around the capital city on the map. From this graphic display of evidence, Wang drew the alarming conclusion that Beijing was besieged by trash.

With a continued focus on trash, Wang's second film project, *Plastic China,* explores how imported foreign plastic waste has transformed numerous small towns in China into "plastic kingdoms." According to the director, the film was inspired by his first visit to the United States in 2011. During Wang's time as a visiting scholar at the University of California, Berkeley, he visited a large waste recycling factory in Oakland, California. Toward the end of the visit, the manager told him that after the initial sorting, the recyclables such as paper and plastic items would be shipped to China for the final treatment. He was astonished to hear this, and started to wonder: Why China? How would this plastic waste be processed after it arrived? In the year after he returned to China (from May 2011 to May 2012), Wang started to do research on this project and investigated many locations. After the initial investigation, he learned that China is the world's largest importer of plastic waste. In other words, China is not only the factory of the world, but its trash yard as well. The purpose of his film was to present what he witnessed and discovered and to highlight issues related to the environmental crisis, education, and economic inequality (For the artist's statement on why he made this film, see https://sites.gatech.edu/gmfchinaevents/artist-statement-plastic-china/).

It took Wang six years (2011–2016) to complete his second film. However, *Plastic China* was immediately banned in China when it came out at the end of 2016. In January 2017, Wang's Yixi talk (the Chinese equivalent of a TED Talk) about his latest project on environmental woes became an instant Internet sensation, but the video link, which was widely circulated on WeChat and other social media, disappeared after four days. Environmental protection is a very sensitive topic in public discourse in China, and unofficial and independent media productions that take the initiative to expose environmental issues are strictly monitored by the state. Produced outside the state studio system and its ideological censorship, Wang's work on the environmental crisis contributes to the broader Chinese independent and underground film movement, which has been one of the major developments in Chinese cinema.

As an informative and alarming portrait of brutal reality and rosy illusion set in a world of trash, *Plastic China* exposes the dark underbelly of China's economic prosperity and criticizes the consumerism, capitalism, and global waste plastic recycling business. It won many awards including the Special Jury Award at the 2016 International Documentary Film Festival Amsterdam (IDFA) and the prize for Best Film on Sustainable Development at the 2017 Millennium International Documentary Film Festival in Belgium and was nominated for Best Documentary at the 2017 Golden Horse Film Festival in Taiwan.

III   Interpretation

1   Right after the film's title appears on the screen, *Plastic China* depicts how foreign plastic trash is transported by container ships and trucks to a small town in Shandong. In Figure 12.1, a COSCO England container from Hong Kong arrives at Qingdao port. Figures 12.2 and 12.3, respectively, show the first and second appearances of the female protagonist, Yijie. How and to what end is the importation of trash cinematically presented on the screen? Please describe the contrast between the cinematic presentation of the plastic trash and the human subjects. What does this spatial imbalance signify?

2   In one scene, the natural landscape of ripe wheat coexists with the background's manufactured landscape, composed of a long stretch of high piles of trash (Figure 12.4). In the next shot, the standing mountains of trash reflect themselves upon the rippling river, forming another manufactured landscape (Figure 12.5). If you perceive these pictures as art, what symbolic motifs can you discern, especially relating to the plants and water? Please compare these images to other artistic representations of trash in various works treated in this textbook such as Fabrice Monteiro's *The Prophecy*, Fernando Contreras Castro's *Única Looking at the Sea*, or Agnès Varda's *The Gleaners and I* as well as other trash-themed films such as *Wall-E*.

Figure 12.1 Film still from *Plastic China* (0:02:08).

Figure 12.2 Film still from *Plastic China* (0:02:42).

Figure 12.3 Film still from *Plastic China* (0:06:26).

Figure 12.4 Film still from *Plastic China* (0:20:56).

Figure 12.5 Film still from *Plastic China* (0:21:03).

3   In terms of cinematography, the film makes extensive use of low-angle shots, shooting from the ground or slightly below the human subject. Wang mentioned in an interview that this was to show respect to the subject that he was filming (Liu, "Interview"). This angle portrays to the viewers the intimacy and the bond that Wang created with the two families. It also gives a stark reminder of the situation that these two families are in—living on the ground with trash. The human subjects are often dwarfed by the imposing environment and the enormous piles of trash. What other effects—both aesthetically and thematically—do

these low-angle shots have? Do you know any other films that utilize low-angle shots? If so, are their aesthetic and thematic effects similar or different? Finally, try to take some pictures from a low angle and share them with your classmates.

4   In the film, Yijie has a strong desire to go to school. At the same time, she yearns to return to her hometown in Sichuan. Discuss how these two things are interchangeable and why they are so closely related. (Note that part of the reason may be related to the *hukou* residence registration system in China. Due to her status as a migrant child, Yijie had been unable to attend school for free in Shandong, and she is only allowed to go to school in her village in Sichuan.) Yijie was finally able to attend her local elementary school in Sichuan in fall 2014. By spring 2017, she had advanced to the third grade, but she dropped out in fall 2017 to work as a migrant again. Later in the film, she discusses getting old enough to get a job to help send her brothers to school. How effective is schooling for migrant children and particularly for peasant girls? What is the difference between Yijie and Kun's son? How do other countries deal with similar problems?

5   In the Yi minority, only men sing. Peng is good at singing, but Peng's wife never sings. She seldom utters a word and is always quiet. Even when she was giving birth, she was seen biting her hair and did not utter a groan of pain (See Figures 12.6 and 12.7). How do you interpret her silence during such a painful ordeal? What does the silence of Peng's wife and other women imply for Yijie's future?

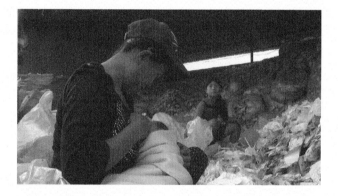

Figure 12.6 Film still from *Plastic China* (0:36:06).

Figure 12.7 Film still from *Plastic China* (0:33:12).

6   As a migrant child, Yijie mainly speaks in accented Mandarin instead of her native tongue, the Yi ethnic minority language. Her very first utterance in the film is a voice-over in accented Mandarin: "I don't like it here. I like Sichuan better. All my friends are there. My uncle and grandma are in Sichuan. My uncle misses me, and I miss him too." Only when she calls her grandma over the phone do we hear Yijie speak in her native Yi language, which enables her to return to her linguistic home marked by her mother tongue. If a language indicates one's identity, how does Yijie's use of language relate to her sense of belonging or her sense of community in Shandong versus Sichuan. Do you have any personal experience with language and in-group/out-group identity to share with the class?

7   In the same phone scene, we can hear piano music playing in the background. According to Tyler Strickland (2017), a Los Angeles-based composer who scored most of the post-production music, "When approaching the music for *Plastic China*, an important perspective to highlight that of was Yijie's. It was a sensitive balance between dreaminess and sadness. With Yijie, there is a strong mix of emotions that stem from her curious awareness of the extent to how bad those living conditions are, her dreams for the future, and her sadness of being away from home." Please discuss the use of music to convey both "dreaminess and sadness" in the video clip from 0:16:43 to 0:18:52. What other emotions are conveyed to you in this scene?

8   When Yijie and her father and brother are sitting outside the station after they cannot afford the train tickets to return home (see Figures 12.8 and 12.9), a Yi ethnic minority song is heard on the nondiegetic soundtrack in the video clip from 1:10:39 to 1:11:02. The song "The Passion for the Torch in July" is about a major festival for the Yi people that features a torch parade, a bonfire dance, and other celebrations. How does the song enhance Yijie's disappointment and homesickness in this film?

Figure 12.8 Film still from *Plastic China* (1:10:39).

Figure 12.9 Film still from *Plastic China* (1:10:46).

9   As a child, Yijie enjoys playing. When she comes back from the auto show, she puts on a mimic auto "show" of her own with the scavenged car stickers and Western doll princesses as car models. She also makes a "computer" out of a Japanese cupboard. If play suggests dabbling in the unrealistic part of the imagination, how do you interpret her playing with the residues of the modern world and the excesses of consumeristic society?

10 Working a menial job at the bottom rung of the global plastic processing business chain, Kun can hardly be considered a beneficiary of China's economic development. In the auto show, Kun is ecstatic to sit in a luxurious Cadillac SRX, which he cannot afford at all at that time. Shot from outside of the car, he seems buried by the window reflection of colorful banners and advertisements (0:58:13). By the end of the film, when Kun finally buys the new car, the dim light of the winter evening conceals the glamor of the new car, and his face is blurred by the mist on the windshield (1:07:32). What do these two shots suggest about Kun's aspirations?

IV   Prosperity-Focused Applications to SDGs 8, 9, 10, 11, and 16

1   SDG 8 promotes "sustained, inclusive and sustainable economic growth, full and productive employment and decent work for all." In the specific sub-goals 8.6, 8.7, and 8.8, it aims to "substantially reduce the proportion of youth not in employment, education or training" by 2020, "end child labour in all its forms" by 2025, and "protect labour rights and promote safe and secure working environments for all workers, including migrant workers, in particular women migrants, and those in precarious employment" ("Goal 8"). How does Wang address these concerns in the film? Consider the fact that, on one hand, China is making strides and has become the world's second largest economy, while, on the other hand, it is often the marginalized and under-privileged peasants, migrant workers, and their children who have been victimized, sacrificed, and disposed. Would SDG 8 be a daunting challenge to achieve in China, based on what you have learned from this film? What are possible or proposed solutions to these challenges?

2   For SDG 9 (Industry, Innovation, and Infrastructure), the 1992 Rio Declaration states, "business and industry must recognize environmental management as among the highest corporate priorities and as a key determinant for the success of sustainable development" (Sitarz). However, among the massive foreign garbage in this factory where Yijie and her family work, three close-up shots highlight: a dirty empty bag of Hill's® dog food, whose packaging is "100% recyclable;" a tape of Italy's F.lli Magro Company, which makes responsibly sourced paper; and a crushed can cover of the Flora® Spreads, which promotes sustainable, plant-based food. How do each of these companies and others practice "environmental management," a rather broad and vague term, to promote their products? Are there any versions of environmental management that serve as a form of performative activism? Explain.

3   The final products of the primitively processed plastics in Kun's factory will turn into tiny hard pellets. These become the raw materials for the manufacture of toys and other plastic products that will ultimately be exported to the West, restarting another cycle of production, consumption, and environmental destruction. Moreover, according to the EU's European Environmental Agency, of the 30 million tons of plastic waste generated in the EU in 2015, only 5 million tons was recycled in Europe, and nearly half of plastic packaging waste was exported outside Europe, mainly to China ("Reducing loss"). In addition, according to a study, "the positive emotions associated with recycling can overpower the negative emotions associated with wasting" (Guillot). How can we do a better job of showing the economic and environmental costs of recycling? When companies tout the benefits of recycling, how does this affect consumers' spending behavior? What instead should companies be focusing on?

4   Still related to SDG 9, "96 percent of the world's population lived within reach of a mobile-cellular signal in 2018," although not all can afford to use them ("SDG Goals 9"). How do you understand the scene by the end of the film in which Azi inserts a Netherlands Labara Mobile's SIM card that he found in the trash into their cellphone, and he immediately receives a message that reads: "welcome in [sic] China?"

5   In terms of industrialization, China is transitioning from a traditional agricultural society to a modern industrial country. The character Kun comes from a family of peasants, and his parents' maize field is shown in the film besides the yard where Yijie's mother gives birth (see Figure 12.10). How would you interpret his first utterance as a voice-over, "I make a living by recycling the plastics. It's not bad for a farmer" (see Figure 12.11)? How does the film depict Kun's close relationship with mechanical objects such as tricycles, machines with pulleys, cars, and computers? If soil is associated with farming, nature, and home, how do you interpret Kun's working posture of always standing, as in Figure 12.11, while Yijie's family often sits on the dirt ground while sorting waste? Finally, note that when describing his work in the plastics industry in the middle of the film, Kun says, "It's tiring, dirty, and not making much money. But to make a living, I have no choice. I'm just a farmer and don't have other skills. If I don't do this, how can I make money?" Compared with what he said at the beginning of the film, how does Kun's attitude change? Why does he still internalize his identity as a farmer?

Figure 12.10 Film still from *Plastic China* (0:33:03).

Figure 12.11 Film still from *Plastic China* (0:04:15).

6   Compared with Kun, Yijie is more nostalgic about her rural past. As she said in the film, "We have everything in my hometown. There are horses, goats, cows, chickens, ducks, pigs, and baby pigs. There are apples, oranges, and grapes. We pick our own grapes and eat them." However, according to the director, "there is nothing in her hometown, a very poor region" (Wang 2017). Why do they have different views? How does the film depict the stratification within the peasant class in terms of their attitudes toward industrialization?

7   Kun's fantasy with the modern industrial world is best represented by his strong desire to buy a new car. To acquire this machine, he is enticed to work hard like a machine. In other words, humans are dehumanized and mechanized as a cog in a system to make money. How does the film explore the relationship between human and machine? Please share some examples or personal experiences in which human beings are being maneuvered and controlled by machines, devices, or technology (including social media) in general.

8   For SDG 10 (Reduced Inequalities), how does the film address inequality among countries? Consider the fact that so-called global trash recycling is actually trash relocation, from the rich, developed countries to the poor, developing countries. Do people in the film have a much closer relationship with trash than we do in the West, where trash remains largely invisible? In Figure 12.12, Yijie is surrounded by labels from yogurt made by the German company Ehrmann, the French/Canadian company Lactel, the Italian company Stuffer, and the American company Kraft. What are other examples of locals re-using and re-consuming the "trash" from developed regions? How do you view the fluid boundary between "goods" and "trash"?

9   It is estimated that there were 292 million rural migrant workers in China in 2021, comprising more than one-third of the entire working population ("Migrant Workers"). People from the landlocked, rural villages migrated to the coastal, bigger cities for job opportunities, just as Peng and his family migrated from Sichuan to Shandong. Concerning social and regional inequality within China, how does the film address the inequality and discrimination that Peng and his family experience as migrant workers? What is the director's ethical responsibility when Kun slaps Peng—to stop the fight or to keep filming?

Figure 12.12 Film still from *Plastic China* (0:54:39).

10 How does Kun, himself a part of the lower class, reinforce class inequality? In one scene, he tells his son to study hard in order to attend college, buy cars and houses in the capital city, and live a life "like those wealthy people" in the future. For Kun, education is equivalent to social mobility and wealth. By encouraging his son to engage in consumerism, Kun unwittingly reinforces the cycle that is the root cause of his own dangerous work environment. What alternative values might he instill in his son that would promote a more equal society (Berthel)?

11 The mission of SDG 11 is to "make cities and human settlements inclusive, safe, resilient, and sustainable" ("Goal 11"). Discuss the ways in which the imported trash has degraded the natural landscape, ruined the local community, and made Kun's hometown inhabitable and unsustainable. Next, please use google maps to research the distance (in miles or kilometers) from Kun's hometown near Qingdao in Shandong to Yijie's hometown in Liangshan Yi autonomous prefecture in Sichuan. If home denotes security, stability, permanence, and attachment (Liu, "Dislocation and Displacement"), discuss the similarities between Kun and Yijie in their experience of dislocation and homelessness.

12 In Wang's first film, a dramatic landscape makeover unfolds onscreen in which a corn field, a vegetable shelter, an international school, and a factory are built right on the foundation of the previous dumpster sites. As the director narrates in the film, "We're creating an economic miracle aboveground, but at the same time, we're building a trash world underground." How do Wang's films expose the dark side of China's economic miracle and unveil the façade of prosperity? Discuss this contrast between under and above, hidden and visible. In a similar vein, Wang Jiuliang has noted in several interviews that the word "plastic" in the film title also means "fake, unreal," analogous to the term "plastic surgery." How do you understand the word "plastic" in the English title of the film? Discuss the various meanings suggested by the film.

13 The mission of SDG 16 is "to promote peaceful and inclusive societies for sustainable development, provide access to justice for all and build effective, accountable and inclusive institutions at all levels" ("SDG Goals 16"). How does the film demonstrate the need for SDG 16? What commentary does Wang Jiuliang's film make about the lack of inclusion, sustainable development, access, justice, accountability, etc.?

14 Divide the class into five groups and assign one of the SDGs from Part 3 (8, 9, 10, 11, or 16) to each group. Each group will then prepare arguments for a debate in which they maintain that their assigned SDG is the most relevant or central to Wang Jiuliang's *Plastic China*. (The instructor of the course will decide on the format and length of the debate and facilitate a follow-up discussion with the class upon conclusion of the debate.)

15 Does the featured text in this chapter only reinforce and illuminate the principles underpinning the UN SDGs and the concept of sustainable development, or does it question any inherent presuppositions, biases, shortcomings, flaws, or gaps in the UN SDG framework or the notion of sustainable development? Explain with details from the text.

V   Beyond Prosperity—Connections to SDGs on Planet, People, and Partnerships

Beyond SDGs 8, 9, 10, 11, and 16, what additional SDGs are addressed by Wang Jiuliang in *Plastic China*? Complete the table below with your ideas. Then compare and contrast your ideas with a classmate.

SDGs:	*Does Wang's* Plastic China *connect with additional SDGs? If so, which ones and how?*

SDG 1 No Poverty

SDG 2 Zero Hunger

SDG 3 Good Health and Well Being

SDG 4 Quality Education

SDG 5 Gender Equality

SDG 6 Clean Water and Sanitation

SDG 7 Affordable and Clean Energy

SDG 12 Responsible Consumption and Production

SDG 13 Climate Action

SDG 14 Life below Water

SDG 15 Life on Land

SDG 17 Partnerships for the Goals

VI   From Global to Local: On a Personal Level

1   How do you relate personally to the featured text in Chapter 12? Explain in detail how your own life experiences or personal beliefs intersect with the main ideas and themes of Jiuliang Wang's *Plastic China*.

2   How does the global humanities text featured in Chapter 12 relate to your local environment? Explain the global-local connection between Wang's *Plastic China* and your home or current residence. What place-based considerations permit or prevent the application of the text to your geographical location?

3   What type of response did Wang's *Plastic China* elicit in you? Are you moved to action? If so, explain. If not, why not. Have your viewpoints or attitudes changed? Explain.

VII   Assignments

1   Research

1   As an environmental activist, Wang's work has been described as "socially engaging." It concerns reality in contemporary China, and the final work, in turn, has an impact that can change that reality. His first film earned keen Chinese media coverage and the attention of government officials. The Beijing government soon reacted and dedicated 100 billion RMB (around 14,800 million USD) to deal with the problem. For his second film, despite being banned in January 2017, the Customs in China confiscated foreign waste with a value of 10 million USD in March, and the central government banned imports of plastic waste in July, which Wang believed was a reaction to his film.

In groups or individually, research the latest progress on the China ban, its impact on China and the Chinese people, the flow pattern of the international plastic waste trade, and global environmental sustainability. Consider also the responses, changes, and possible solutions from the United States and other countries. Please try to relate your research to SDGs 8, 9, 10, 11, and 16. (The instructor of the course will determine the mode of presentation and delivery—oral presentation, written report, short video documentary, digital timeline project, etc.—for this research assignment.)

2   In 2016, around the time when this film was completed, 151.6 million children aged 5 to 17 years were engaged in child labor globally. At the start of 2020, nearly 79 million children in child labor were engaged in hazardous work ("SDG Goals 16"). In the film, Yijie, the 11-year-old girl, provides free labor and works alongside with her parents to sort out plastics in the factory. She and her younger brother Yiduo also use plastic scraps as burning fuel, unaware of the danger of explosive PVC products. In groups or individually, research on the topic of child labor in China and try to identify the correlation between child labor and education, drop-out rate, and the rural-urban divide, as well as the related government policies to deal with the issue and protect children. (The instructor of the course will determine the mode of presentation and delivery—oral presentation, written report, short video documentary, digital timeline project, etc.—for this research assignment.)

2   Write

1   Please write a film review or a response essay in which you analyze the cinematic features of the film, discuss the main issues, and outline the most related SDGs. Make sure you integrate class discussions, academic perspectives, and your personal viewing experience. (The instructor of the course will determine the length and format of this writing assignment.)

2   In his 2011 book *Slow Violence: Environmentalism of the Poor*, Bob Nixon introduced the term of "slow violence." He defines it as an environmental violence that occurs gradually and incrementally. Because the destructive effects and consequences are delayed, it is very hard for the victims to track, identify, and pin down the sources or agents held accountable. Please write a reflection of how "slow violence" disproportionally impacts the community in this film. Besides including scenes in the film that showcase unsafe working conditions, you are also encouraged to integrate scenes from Wang's 26-minute YouTube version of *Plastic China*. (The instructor of the course will determine the length and format of this writing assignment.)

3   Create

1   In order to find out where his daily rubbish went, Wang Jiuliang followed the garbage truck around his neighborhood in Beijing and made his first film. Obsessed with the same question of the route traveled by plastic trash, he completed his second film. Have you ever wondered where your daily trash goes? In groups or individually, create a route of your trash's itinerary by visiting and interviewing your trash company. (The instructor of the course will determine the mode of presentation and delivery—mapping project, interview and written report, oral presentation, etc.—for this creative assignment.)

2   Have students bring in a variety of plastic items from their home, dormitory, or school recycling bins. Ask the students to come up with creative ways to reuse or repurpose the items instead of recycling them (Berthel). The Chinese artist Xu Bing transformed trash into many artworks. For example, his *Bronze Phoenix* was made from trash on a construction site in

Beijing (Xu). (The instructor of the course will determine the mode of presentation and delivery for this creative assignment.)

Works Cited

Berthel, Ken. "Teacher's Guide for *Plastic China*," 2019, https://misc.docuseek2.com/gej/guides/gj-022a_guide.pdf. Accessed 10 August 2022.

"Goal 8." *United Nations Department of Economic and Social Affairs Sustainable Development*, 2022, https://sdgs.un.org/goals/goal8. Accessed 10 August 2022.

"Goal 11." *United Nations Department of Economic and Social Affairs Sustainable Development*, 2022, https://sdgs.un.org/goals/goal11. Accessed 10 August 2022.

Guillot, Louise. "How Recycling Is Killing the Planet," *Politico*, 16 September 2020, https://www.politico.eu/article/recycling-killing-the-planet/. Accessed 10 August 2022.

Liu, Jin. "A Cinematic Presentation of Trash: An Interview with Wang Jiuliang," *Modern Chinese Literature and Culture Resource Center*, May 2020, https://u.osu.edu/mclc/online-series/jin-liu/. Accessed 10 August 2022.

———. "Dislocation and Displacement: An Analysis of Wang Jiuliang's *Plastic China*," *Journal of Chinese Cinema*, vol. 14, no. 3, 2020, pp. 181–198. DOI: 10.1080/17508061.2020.1834302.

"Migrant Workers and Their Children." China Labor Bulletin, 26 May 2022, https://clb.org.hk/content/migrant-workers-and-their-children. Accessed 10 August 2022.

Nixon, Rob. *Slow Violence: Environmentalism of the Poor*. Harvard UP, 2011.

Plastic China. Directed by Wang Jiuliang, CNEX, 2016.

"Reducing Loss of Resources from Waste Management is Key to Strengthening the Circular Economy in Europe." European Environmental Agency, 28 Oct. 2019, https://www.eea.europa.eu/publications/reducing-loss-of-resources-from/reducing-loss-of-resources-from. Accessed 10 August 2022.

"SDG Goals 9 Industry, Innovation and Infrastructure." *United Nations Statistics Division*, 2019, https://unstats.un.org/sdgs/report/2019/goal-09. Accessed 10 August 2022.

"SDG Goals 16 Peace, Justice, and Strong Institutions." *United Nations Statistics Division*, 2021, https://unstats.un.org/sdgs/report/2021/Goal-16/. Accessed 12 March 2023.

Sitarz, Daniel. ed. *Agenda 21: The Earth Summit Strategy to Save Our Planet*. EarthPress, 1993.

Strickland, Tyler. "Re: about Music You Composed for the Film 'Plastic China.'" Received by Jin Liu, 21 Dec. 2017.

Wang, Jiuliang. WeChat Voicecall Communication. Received by Jin Liu, 18 Sept. 2017.

Xu, Bing. "Bronze Phoenix." 2016, http://www.xubing.com/en/work/details/611?year=2016&type=year#611. Accessed 10 Aug. 2022.

Conclusion
Think Global, Act Local: Partnerships and Projects (SDG 17)

Kelly Comfort and Jennifer Hirsch

This concluding chapter has three main objectives: (1) to summarize SDG 17 (Partnerships for the Goals) and establish its importance as the culminating goal in the UN SDG framework; (2) to propose various end-of-course activities that involve re-engaging with the 12 global humanities texts treated in this book; and (3) to put forth a series of projects that can be done in partnership with campus- and community-based partners (organizations and/or artists, authors, or directors) to advance the UN SDGs through humanities-related efforts taking place in students' own backyards.

I   Summary of SDG 17: Partnerships for the Goals

SDG 17 on "Partnerships for the Goals" aims to "[s]trengthen the means of implementation and revitalize the Global Partnership for Sustainable Development" ("SDG Goals 17"). SDG 17 includes 19 targets, which are helpful to consider in five thematic categories as outlined below:

Financial and Trade Targets:

- 17.1 "Strengthen domestic resource mobilization [. . .] to improve domestic capacity for tax and other revenue collection"
- 17.2 "Developed countries to implement fully their official development assistance commitments [. . .] to developing countries"
- 17.3 "Mobilize additional financial resources for developing countries from multiple sources"
- 17.4 "Assist developing countries in attaining long-term debt sustainability through coordinated policies aimed at fostering debt financing, debt relief and debt restructuring"
- 17.5 "Adopt and implement investment promotion regimes for least developed countries"
- 17.10 "Promote a universal, rules-based, open, non-discriminatory and equitable multilateral trading system under the World Trade Organization"
- 17.11 "Significantly increase the exports of developing countries"
- 17.12 "Realize timely implementation of duty-free and quota-free market access on a lasting basis for all least developed countries"
- 17.13 "Enhance global macroeconomic stability, including through policy coordination and policy coherence"

Technology and Innovation Targets:

- 17.6 "Enhance North-South, South-South and triangular regional and international cooperation on and access to science, technology and innovation and enhance knowledge sharing"

DOI: 10.4324/9781003388869-17

- 17.7 "Promote the development, transfer, dissemination and diffusion of environmentally sound technologies to developing countries on favourable terms"
- 17.8 "Fully operationalize the technology bank and science, technology and innovation capacity-building mechanism for least developed countries [. . .] and enhance the use of enabling technology, in particular information and communications technology"

Capacity-Building Targets:

- 17.9 "Enhance international support for implementing effective and targeted capacity-building in developing countries to support national plans to implement all the Sustainable Development Goals"
- 17.18 "[E]nhance capacity-building support to developing countries [. . .] to increase significantly the availability of high-quality, timely and reliable data disaggregated by income, gender, age, race, ethnicity, migratory status, disability, geographic location and other characteristics relevant in national contexts"
- 17.19 "[B]uild on existing initiatives to develop measurements of progress on sustainable development that complement gross domestic product, and support statistical capacity-building in developing countries"

Policy Targets:

- 17.14 "Enhance policy coherence for sustainable development"
- 17.15 "Respect each country's policy space and leadership to establish and implement policies for poverty eradication and sustainable development"

Global Partnership Targets:

- 17.16 "Enhance the Global Partnership for Sustainable Development, complemented by multi-stakeholder partnerships that mobilize and share knowledge, expertise, technology and financial resources, to support the achievement of the Sustainable Development Goals in all countries, in particular developing countries"
- 17.17 "Encourage and promote effective public, public-private and civil society partnerships, building on the experience and resourcing strategies of partnerships." ("Goals 17: Targets and Indicators")

As this grouping suggests, nearly half of the targets involve economic policy, and the majority of targets are oriented toward developing countries.

For the sake of this textbook's concluding chapter, we are most interested in target 17.16, because it describes the ideal global partnership as multi-stakeholder, aimed at sharing expertise, knowledge, technology, and financial resources, oriented toward mobilization, and supporting the advancement of the UN SDGs everywhere, in both developing and developed countries. The UN publication, "Multi-Stakeholder Partnerships and Voluntary Commitments," explains that the "achievement of the 2030 Agenda for Sustainable Development and the Sustainable Development Goals" requires "all hands on deck" insofar as "different sectors and actors" such as "public, public-private and civil" sectors must work together "in an integrated manner by pooling financial resources, knowledge and expertise." In her book, *SDG 17 Partnerships for the Goals: Strengthening Implementation through Global Cooperation*, Monica Thiel explains further that SDG 17 "is an ambitious goal to first, integrate and implement the remaining 16 SDGs within partnerships and second, create public value that simultaneously extends to an interconnected world while encouraging innovation for sustaining the SDGs" (Thiel 1). In short, SDG 17 calls for "innovative and collaborative partnerships to provide effective implementation of all the other 16 SDGs" (Thiel 14). According to Thiel, global partnerships should constitute "a collaborative endeavor" with "mutually shared goals and relationships" (2, 8). In the context of the UN SDGs, partnerships should "focus on benefitting all and not just a few countries, regions, organisations or individuals" through "an inclusive and mutually beneficial approach for advancing economic, social, and environmental development" (Thiel 16–17).

II   Partnerships and Projects: Global Humanities Texts Revisited

In this section, we present five end-of-course discussion activities and projects that involve re-examining the 12 global humanities texts presented in this textbook in terms of SDG 17's emphasis on partnerships and on effectively implementing the other SDGs.

1 **Identify existing and new partnerships:** Reconsider the 12 global humanities texts featured in Chapters 1–12 in terms of the existing partnerships featured as well as the need for new partnerships to solve the problems depicted. Complete the table below either individually or in groups. Then, compare your table with another student or group and discuss the following questions: Which text provides the best example of a successful or effective existing partnership and why? Which work demonstrates the greatest need for a new partnership and why?

Global Humanities Text	**Existing Partnerships:** *What partnerships are featured in each text? How successful or unsuccessful is each partnership and why?*	**New Partnerships:** *What new partnerships might be helpful to solve the problems or address the issues featured in ea. text? How might they be helpful?*
Aya Hanabusa's *Holy Island* Barbara Dombrowski's *Tropic Ice* Fabrice Monteiro's *The Prophecy* Kip Andersen and Keegan Kuhn's *Cowspiracy* Fernando Contreras Castro's *Única Looking at the Sea* Agnès Varda's *The Gleaners and I* Agustina Bazterrica's *Tender is the Flesh* Kief Davidson and Pedro Kos's *Bending the Arc* Aravind Adiga's *The White Tiger* Ivan Sanjinés, Nicolás Ipamo and Alejandro Noza's *Cry of the Forest* Hao Jingfang's "Folding Beijing" Wang Jiuliang's *Plastic China*		

2 **Propose a new organizational structure for this textbook using a different SDG grouping model:** Although this textbook is divided into four parts on Planet (Part 1, Chapters 1–4), People (Part 2, Chapters 5–8), Prosperity (Part 3, Chapters 9–12), and Partnerships (Conclusion), there are many other possible groupings of the 17 UN SDGs. Work in groups to research other possible groupings. Choose one of those groupings or design your own

original grouping and use it to propose a different organizational structure for this textbook that includes all 17 SDGs and the same 12 global humanities texts. The final product for this assignment will be a new table of contents and an accompanying oral presentation that reflects on the advantages and disadvantages of the newly proposed textbook structure and SDG grouping framework.

3 **Explore ESD themes and design a curricular development project:** Education for Sustainable Development (ESD) has identified 26 themes related to the SDGs, classified as "Core Themes" (1–8) and "Other Themes" (9–26) as follows:

Core Themes:

1   Biodiversity
2   Climate Change
3   Disaster Risk Reduction
4   Health and Nutrition
5   Sustainable Consumption and Production
6   Traditional Knowledge
7   Youth
8   Higher Education

Other Themes:

9   Agriculture
10 Arts
11 Cities
12 Community Education
13 Curriculum Development
14 Diversity, Equality, and Justice
15 EcoTourism
16 Energy
17 Food and Hunger
18 Forests/Trees
19 Freshwater and/or Marine Ecosystems
20 Innovation, Infrastructure, and Technology
21 Jobs and Economic Growth
22 Plants and Animals
23 Secondary Education
24 Technical and Vocational Education and Training
25 Waste
26 Water

("Global RCE Network").

Part A: Discuss some or all of the following questions related to these themes, the SDGs, and this textbook:

- Which themes interest you the most and why?
- What do you think differentiates "core" themes from "other" themes?
- Which one or two themes best relate to each of the 12 global humanities texts treated in this textbook?
- Which themes are most relevant to this textbook overall and why?

- Which themes are not treated in this textbook? Why do you think they are not addressed?
- What other themes seem important to multiple SDGs that are not included in this list? Agree on one or two additional themes that you would suggest adding as either "core" or "other."

Part B: Work in groups on a "Curricular Development" project for "Youth," "Secondary Education," "Higher Education," "Community Education," or "Technical and Vocational Education and Training." Each group will design a course syllabus that relates to one (or more) additional ESD theme(s) as listed above. For this project, you should identify relevant UN SDGs, key readings, important subtopics, and appropriate discussion topics and graded assignments for your chosen target audience. (The instructor of the course will provide additional details and requirements about this curricular design project and its mode of delivery.)

4 **Develop a global partnership:** Partners In Health, the global health and social justice organization featured in Kief Davidson and Pedro Kos's *Bending the Arc*, offers an example of a successful "global partnership" as defined in target 17.16: "Enhance the Global Partnership for Sustainable Development, complemented by multi-stakeholder partnerships that mobilize and share knowledge, expertise, technology and financial resources, to support the achievement of the Sustainable Development Goals in all countries, in particular developing countries" ("Goals 17: Targets and Indicators"). Using Partners In Health as a model, imagine that two or more of the authors, filmmakers, or photographers from the other global humanities texts featured in this book were asked to work together to design a "global partnership" that would effectively address one of the common issues or themes treated across their works and nations. The potential groups are as follows:

Group 1 on Responsible Production and Consumption and/or Sustainable Waste Management: Fabrice Monteiro (*The Prophecy*), Fernando Contreras Castro (*Única Looking at the Sea*), and Wang Jiuliang (*Plastic China*)

Group 2 on Food Security and/or Food Sustainability: Kip Andersen and Keegan Kuhn (*Cowspiracy*), Agustina Bazterrica (*Tender is the Flesh*), and Agnès Varda (*The Gleaners and I*)

Group 3 on Decent Work and Economic Growth and/or Sustainable Cities and Communities: Aravind Adiga (*The White Tiger*) and Hao Jingfang ("Folding Beijing")

Group 4 on Environmental Sustainability, Sustainable Communities, and/or Traditional Knowledge: Aya Hanabusa (*Holy Island*), Barbara Dombrowski (*Tropic Ice*), and Ivan Sanjinés, Nicolás Ipamo and Alejandro Noza (*Cry of the Forest*)

For this global partnership design project, work in your own groups and be sure to include the following components:

- Name of the proposed partnership
- Problem(s) or issue(s) to be addressed by the partnership
- Stakeholders to be included
- Mission statement
- UN SDGs to be addressed
- ESD themes to be addressed
- Partnership model or organizational structure to be used
- Key actions to be proposed

(The instructor of the course will provide additional details and requirements about this global partner design project and its format and mode of delivery.)

5 **Analyze and assess critiques of the UN SDGs:** Some noteworthy critiques or shortcomings of the UN SDG framework are presented in the following publications:

- "Indigenous Knowledge and Implications for the Sustainable Development Agenda" by Giorgia Magni (2017)
- "Leaving No One Behind? Persistent Inequalities in the SDGs" by Inga T. Winkler and Margaret L. Satterthwaite (2017)
- "Politics of 'Leaving No One Behind': Contesting the 2030 Sustainable Development Goals Agenda" by Heloise Weber (2017)
- "The Sustainable Development Goals, Anthropocentrism and Neoliberalism" by Sam Adelman (2018), which is Chapter 2 in the book *Sustainable Development Goals*, edited by Duncan French and Louis J. Kotzé
- "The Sustainable Development Goals: An Existential Critique alongside Three New-Millennial Analytical Paradigms" by Louis J. Kotzé (2018), which is Chapter 3 in the book *Sustainable Development Goals*, edited by Duncan French and Louis J. Kotzé
- "Degrowth and the Sustainable Development Goals" by Ben Robra and Pasi Heikkurinen (2019)
- "Inequality, the SDGs, and the Human Rights Movement in the US and around the World" by Sarah E. Mendelssohn (2020)
- "Growing a Movement for Social Justice: An Examination of the Sustainable Development Goals" by Echoing Green (2021)

Select one of the aforementioned articles or book chapters to read and then complete the following tasks in oral or written form, according to guidelines from your instructor:

- Summarize the main critiques or shortcomings of the UN SDG framework as presented in the selected text.
- Explain whether you agree or disagree with each critique made in the selected text and why.
- Discuss which artist, author, or director treated in this textbook might agree most with the critique(s) outlined in the article or book chapter that you read. Include specific references to the corresponding global humanities text.
- Expand on one existing critique or develop one additional critique of the UN SDG framework, based on one of the global humanities texts in this textbook and/or your own knowledge or experience.

III   Partnerships and Projects: Local Applications

In this section, we present four end-of-course group projects for students to choose from, all of which involve exploring how the UN SDGs are playing out in the context of your own campus, local communities, or region and using the humanities to raise awareness of local SDG-related issues and work. Collaborate in small groups to work on one or more of these projects, according to guidelines from your instructor. All groups will share their final products with the class and answer questions about them.

1 **Write a sample book chapter using a local humanities text:** Choose a "humanities text" by a local artist, author, photographer, or filmmaker in your community. Write a sample book chapter for this textbook that features the chosen work. Decide whether the text should be featured in Unit 1, Unit 2, or Unit 3. Be sure to include all chapter sections as follows, using the textbook chapters as a model in terms of the length of and number of questions for each section:

I   Text
II   Context
III   Interpretation
IV   One of the following as relevant:
 • Planet-Focused Applications to SDGs 6, 7, 12, 13, 14, and 15
 • People-Focused Applications to SDGs 1, 2, 3, 4, and 5
 • Prosperity-Focused SDGS 8, 9, 10, 11, and 16

V   One of the following as relevant:
 • Beyond Planet—Connections to SDGs on People, Prosperity, and Partnerships
 • Beyond People—Connections to SDGs on Planet, Prosperity, and Partnerships
 • Beyond Prosperity—Connections to SDGs on Planet, People, and Partnerships

VI   From Global to Local: On a Personal Level
VII   Assignments
VIII Works Cited

2 **Explore a local sustainability challenge and create your own humanities text:** Identify a local sustainability challenge on your campus or in your current city or town of residence. Choose three SDGs that intersect with the identified sustainability challenge. Now, create your own "humanities text" to raise awareness and promote action about the challenge and the chosen SDGs. Your text can take the form of any genre, including but not limited to short story, poem, photograph, painting, performative art, documentary, short film, comic book, etc. In addition, write a one-to-two-page Overview Sheet about your text, briefly answering the following questions: (1) What is the sustainability challenge you chose and why did you choose it?; (2) What are the three SDGs that you identified as intersecting with the challenge and how do they intersect with it?; (3) What form did you choose and why?; and (4) How would you describe the content of the text and what ideas and/or actions do you hope it will activate in people who read or view it? Each group will share the final text with the class and answer questions about it. We offer two examples below.

Example 1:

 • **Local sustainability challenge**: Lack of access to higher education for undocumented students in your geographical area
 • **Three most relevant SDGs**: Quality Education (4), Reduced Inequalities (10), and Decent Work and Economic Growth (9)
 • **Humanities Text**: A short documentary film that features interviews with university admissions officers, policymakers, undocumented students (minus identifying information), teachers, etc. about the challenges and repercussions of this issue

Example 2:

 • **Local sustainability challenge**: Food waste at the main dining halls on campus combined with food insecurity for some students at your university
 • **Three most relevant SDGs**: No Poverty (1), Zero Hunger (2), and Responsible Consumption and Production (12)
 • **Humanities Text**: Two poems written from different perspectives: one poem, titled "Zero Waste," is told from the perspective of food that goes to waste and ends up in a campus dumpster; another poem, titled "Zero Hunger," is told from the perspective of a student who is hungry and does not have enough money to eat at the campus dining hall

3 **Explore a local educational effort that advances the SDGs:** The SDG target most directly relevant to higher education is 4.7, focused on education for sustainable development, which states:

> by 2030 ensure all learners acquire knowledge and skills needed to promote sustainable development, including among others through education for sustainable development and sustainable lifestyles, human rights, gender equality, promotion of a culture of peace and non-violence, global citizenship, and appreciation of cultural diversity and of culture's contribution to sustainable development. ("Goals 4: Targets and Indicators")

There is just one indicator for this target (4.7.1): "Extent to which (i) global citizenship education and (ii) education for sustainable development are mainstreamed in (*a*) national education policies; (*b*) curricula; (c) teacher education and (*d*) student assessment" ("Goals 4: Targets and Indicators").

Upon considering the information presented in this book's "Introduction" about education for sustainable development and global citizenship education, identify a local educational effort—such as a program, unit, or class at your university or college; a K-12 initiative in your community; or a training program in your region—that you think advances SDG 4.7 in an interesting way. In a format of your choosing, based on guidance from your instructor, develop a presentation about this educational effort that covers the following questions: (1) What is the local effort and why did you choose it?; (2) How does the effort advance SDG 4.7 and its desire to educate people of all ages to take action?; (3) How does the effort also advance (at least) two other SDGs?; and (4) How does the effort use the humanities to enhance its delivery and/or impact, or if it does not, how might it use the humanities?

4 **Develop a course lesson about a local partnership that advances the SDGs:** Identify a local partnership—bringing together two or more partners—on your campus or in your local community or region that is advancing the SDGs. (Examples of partnerships include RCE networks—, which are United Nations-affiliated regional sustainability education networks anchored in higher education that comprise government, education, nonprofit, community, and business partners—and regional government networks, such as the Southeast Sustainability Directors Network.) Now, develop an interactive course lesson to teach to high school or college students (your choice) as an SDG case study. See examples of a few SDG case study activities here: https://sls.gatech.edu/tool-category/Sustainable-Development-Goals-sdgs. Your lesson should do the following: (1) introduce the partnership and what it does; (2) explain how it advances (at least) two SDGs; (3) engage students in one or two interactive activities to learn about the partnership and its relationship to the SDGs; and (4) include at least one humanities text as part of the lesson.

Works Cited

Adelman, Sam. "The Sustainable Development Goals, Anthropocentrism and Neoliberalism." *Sustainable Development Goals*, edited by Duncan French and Louis J. Kotzé, Edward Elgar Publishing, 2018, pp. 15–40.

Giorgia Magni. "Indigenous Knowledge and Implications for the Sustainable Development Agenda." *Special Issue: Education for People, Prosperity, and Planet: Can We Meet the Sustainability Challenges?*, vol. 52, no. 4, 2017, pp. 437–444.

"Global RCE Network Education for Sustainable Development." Search Engine: Themes. https://www.rcenetwork.org/portal/cust-search?keys=themes&type=All&tid_1=All&field_country_listed_tid=All&tid=All&tid_3%5B%5D=613&tid_2%5B%5D=677. Accessed 07 Mar. 2023.

"Goals 4: Targets and Indicators." *United Nations Department of Economic and Social Affairs, Sustainable Development*, https://sdgs.un.org/goals/goal4. Accessed 7 Mar. 2023.

"Goals 17: Targets and Indicators." *United Nations Department of Economic and Social Affairs, Sustainable Development*, https://sdgs.un.org/goals/goal17. Accessed 7 Mar. 2023.

"Growing a Movement for Social Justice: An Examination of the Sustainable Development Goals." Echoing Green, 2021, https://echoinggreen.org/news/growing-a-movement-for-justice-an-examination-of-the-sustainable-development-goals/. Accessed 26 Apr. 2023.

Kotzé, Louis J. "The Sustainable Development Goals: An Existential Critique alongside Three New-Millennial Analytical Paradigms." *Sustainable Development Goals*, edited by Duncan French and Louis J. Kotzé, Edward Elgar Publishing, 2018, pp. 41–65.

Mendelssohn, Sarah E. "Inequality, the SDGs, and the Human Rights Movement in the US and around the World." Brookings, 2020, https://www.brookings.edu/blog/future-development/2020/06/12/inequality-the-sdgs-and-the-human-rights-movement-in-the-us-and-around-the-world/. Accessed 26 Apr. 2023.

"Multi-Stakeholder Partnerships and Voluntary Commitments." *United Nations Department of Economic and Social Affairs, Sustainable Development*, https://sdgs.un.org/topics/multi-stakeholder-partnerships-and-voluntary-commitments. Accessed 7 Mar. 2023.

Robra, Ben, and Pasi Heikkurinen. "Degrowth and the Sustainable Development Goals." *Decent Work and Economic Growth*, edited by W. Leal Filho et al., Spring Nature, 2019, pp. 1–10.

"SDG Goals 17 Partnerships for the Goals." *United Nations Statistics Division*, 2021, https://unstats.un.org/sdgs/report/2021/Goal-17/. Accessed 7 Mar. 2023.

Thiel, Monica. *SDG 17 Partnerships for the Goals: Strengthening Implementation through Global Cooperation*. Emerald Publishing, 2019.

Weber, Heloise, "Politics of 'Leaving No One Behind': Contesting the 2030 Sustainable Development Goals Agenda." *Globalizations*, vol. 14, no. 3, 2017, pp. 399–414.

Winkler, Inga T., and Margaret L. Satterthwaite, "Leaving No One Behind? Persistent Inequalities in the SDGs." *The International Journal of Human Rights*, vol. 21, no. 8, 2017, pp. 1073–1097.

Index

Note: *Italic* page numbers refer to figures and page numbers followed by "n" denote endnotes.

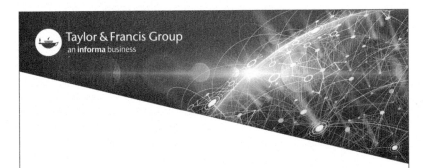